The
Filipino
Americans

**Other Titles in
The New Americans Series**
Ronald H. Bayor, Series Editor

The Filipino Americans

Barbara M. Posadas

THE NEW AMERICANS
Ronald H. Bayor, Series Editor

Greenwood Press
Westport, Connecticut • London

Library of Congress Cataloging-in-Publication Data

Posadas, Barbara Mercedes, 1945–
    The Filipino Americans / Barbara M. Posadas.
      p.   cm. — (The new Americans, ISSN 1092–6364)
    Includes bibliographical references and index.
    ISBN 0–313–29742–8 (alk. paper)
    1. Filipino Americans. I. Title. II. Series: New Americans
(Westport, Conn.)
    E184.F4P67 1999
    973'.049921—dc21   99–10140

British Library Cataloguing in Publication Data is available.

Library of Congress Catalog Card Number: 99–10140
ISBN: 0–313–29742–8
ISSN: 1092–6364

First published in 1999

Greenwood Press, 88 Post Road West, Westport, CT 06881
An imprint of Greenwood Publishing Group, Inc.
www.greenwood.com

Printed in the United States of America

The paper used in this book complies with the
Permanent Paper Standard issued by the National
Information Standards Organization (Z39.48–1984).

10 9 8 7 6 5 4 3 2 1

For

Alipio Gutierrez Posadas
(1901–1979)

and

Estelle Hazack Posadas
(1910–   )

My Parents
who endured much to stay together

Contents

Illustrations

Series Foreword

Oscar Handlin, a prominent historian, once wrote, "I thought to write a history of the immigrants in America. Then I discovered that the immigrants were American history." The United States has always been a nation of nations where people from every region of the world have come to begin a new life. Other countries such as Canada, Argentina, and Australia also have had substantial immigration, but the United States is still unique in the diversity of nationalities and the great numbers of migrating people who have come to its shores.

Who are these immigrants? Why did they decide to come? How well have they adjusted to this new land? What has been the reaction to them? These are some of the questions the books in this "New Americans" series seek to answer. There have been many studies about earlier waves of immigrants— e.g., the English, Irish, Germans, Jews, Italians, and Poles—but relatively little has been written about the newer groups—those arriving in the last thirty years, since the passage of a new immigration law in 1965. This series is designed to correct that situation and to introduce these groups to the rest of America.

Each book in the series discusses one of these groups, and each is written by an expert on those immigrants. The volumes cover the new migration from primarily Asia, Latin America, and the Caribbean, including: the Koreans, Cambodians, Filipinos, Vietnamese, South Asians such as Indians and Pakistanis, Chinese from both China and Taiwan, Haitians, Jamaicans, Cubans, Dominicans, Mexicans, Puerto Ricans (even though they are already

U.S. citizens), and Jews from the former Soviet Union. Although some of these people, such as Jews, have been in America since colonial times, this series concentrates on their recent migrations, and thereby offers its unique contribution.

These volumes are designed for high school and general readers who want to learn more about their new neighbors. Each author has provided information about the land of origin, its history and culture, the reasons for migrating, and the ethnic culture as it began to adjust to American life. Readers will find fascinating details on religion, politics, foods, festivals, gender roles, employment trends, and general community life. They will learn how Vietnamese immigrants differ from Cuban immigrants and, yet, how they are also alike in many ways. Each book is arranged to offer an in-depth look at the particular immigrant group but also to enable readers to compare one group with the other. The volumes also contain brief biographical profiles of notable individuals, tables noting each group's immigration, and a short bibliography of readily available books and articles for further reading. Most contain a glossary of foreign words and phrases.

Students and others who read these volumes will secure a better understanding of the age-old questions of "who is an American" and "how does the assimilation process work?" Similar to their nineteenth- and early twentieth-century forebears, many Americans today doubt the value of immigration and fear the influx of individuals who look and sound different from those who had come earlier. If comparable books had been written one hundred years ago they would have done much to help dispel readers' unwarranted fears of the newcomers. Nobody today would question, for example, the role of those of Irish or Italian ancestry as Americans; yet, this was a serious issue in our history and a source of great conflict. It is time to look at our recent arrivals, to understand their history and culture, their skills, their place in the United States, and their hopes and dreams as Americans.

The United States is a vastly different country than it was at the beginning of the twentieth century. The economy has shifted away from industrial jobs; the civil rights movement has changed minority-majority relations and, along with the women's movement, brought more people into the economic mainstream. Yet one aspect of American life remains strikingly similar—we are still the world's main immigrant receiving nation and as in every period of American history, we are still a nation of immigrants. It is essential that we attempt to learn about and understand this long-term process of migration and assimilation.

Ronald H. Bayor
Georgia Institute of Technology

Preface

In the year 2000, if the predictions of demographers hold true, Filipino Americans will be the largest Asian American group in the United States with a population of more than two million comprising mostly immigrants who came after 1965 and their children. Since 1960, when the Filipino American population totalled fewer than 200,000, record numbers of Filipinos have come to the United States, in large measure because of changes in U.S. immigration law dating generally from the post–World War II era and more specifically from passage of the Immigration Act of 1965.

Post-1965 immigration from the Philippines also derives from the connection established in 1898 when the United States acquired Spain's Southeast Asian colony and forestalled Philippine independence for nearly half a century. During the first half of the twentieth century, the United States instituted American-style government and English-language schooling in its colonial possession, and Filipino sojourners and immigrants became a noticeable, not always welcome presence in the United States. Although Philippine independence, finally accomplished in 1946, is itself more than fifty years old, strong ties, sometimes described as a "love-hate relationship," still link the two nations. Today, substantial emigration from the Philippines and continuing interaction among Filipinos on both sides of the Pacific has become an increasingly important tie between the two countries.

This book examines the twentieth-century history of Filipino Americans with a particular emphasis on those who have established themselves in the United States since 1965. Throughout, readers are reminded that Filipino

Americans, despite their designation as an "ethnic" group, are extraordinarily diverse in ways that this book hopes to make clear. Three parts define the volume's organization. Part I, "Before 1965," surveys the first two-thirds of the century in two chapters. Chapter 1 presents readers with necessary background on the Philippines, while Chapter 2 offers a broad sweep of pre-1965 Filipino American history. Part II, "Filipino Immigration after 1965," explores post-1965 Filipino immigration, the growth of the Filipino American population, and the creation of contemporary Filipino American ethnicity in four chapters. Chapter 3 details the impact of changes in U.S. immigration law on immigration from the Philippines. Chapter 4 examines the transplantation and transformation of Filipino values and customs in an American setting. Chapter 5 scrutinizes the nature of cultural and ethnic identity among Filipino Americans, while Chapter 6 focuses on their economic and political power. Part III, "Filipino Americans Entering the Twenty-First Century," assesses Filipino Americans in the 1990s with a view toward their prospects in the next century. Chapter 7 probes current issues of concern among Filipino Americans, while Chapter 8 examines recent legislation affecting Filipino immigrants and social welfare recipients. Finally, Chapter 9 probes the diverse identities that Filipino Americans claim in contemporary American life.

Acknowledgments

I am deeply grateful to those who have offered encouragement and have shared their knowledge with me—Fred and Dorothy Laigo Cordova of the Filipino American National Historical Society who have worked tirelessly to collect the primary sources of Filipino American history and to promote its study and who graciously permitted me to use photographs from the collection of the Filipino American National Historical Society in this book; other friends and fellow devotees of Filipino American history, especially Dr. Virgilio R. and Elena E. Pilapil, Albert S. Bacdayan, Marina E. Espina, the late Don Guimary, Antonio J. A. Pido, and fellow Chicagoans, Estrella Ravelo Alamar and the late Justo Alamar, Terry Alayu, and Fran Alayu Womack; Dr. Marian L. Smith, historian of the Immigration and Naturalization Service in Washington, D.C., who facilitated my use of newly opened archival materials; Alma Plancich of the Ethnic Heritage Council in Seattle, Washington, who opened her photograph files to me; Ed Bates, who permitted me to photograph his 1904 World's Fair playing cards; Catherine Ceniza Pet Choy, Plaridel E. Seneris, and Rodolfo S. Bernardo, who generously allowed me access to their own work; Purita Aquino Dimalanta, my aunt, who loaned me her family photographs; and Earl Shumaker and Ed Grosek of the Government Publications Department of the Northern Illinois University Library who helped me locate crucial documents. Others have expressed their confidence that I could and would complete this project even when my spirits sagged periodically during the long months of writing: my mother, Estelle H. Posadas; Phillip A. Lontoc, our dear friend who is one of

Chicago's last surviving Filipino old-timers; Robert McColley, C. H. George, Robert H. Wiebe, W. Bruce and Mary Lincoln, Susan Montague, and Nancy Wingfield. I wish to thank both the National Endowment for the Humanities and the Graduate School of Northern Illinois University for grants that supported the research for this book.

Finally, two historians have been there for me at every stage of my work on Filipino Americans. In the early 1980s, when my research was just beginning, I met Roger Daniels who has now been my mentor, strong supporter, and dear friend for almost two decades, even as he still waits for the book on Chicago's Filipino old-timers that I promised him too many years ago. During our more than twenty-five years together, Roland L. Guyotte, my husband, has made my research and writing on Filipino Americans possible in countless ways, always with love.

PART I

BEFORE 1965

1

The Philippines

American immigration from the Philippines has a special character, much like the "special relationship," the Philippines and the United States have had for more than one hundred years. That relationship has been military, economic, cultural, and demographic, but most notably political. From 1898 to 1946, the Philippine Islands were the only densely populated place outside the North American continent to be ruled as a colonial possession by the United States. And the society Americans encountered there and tried to transform was far from monolithic. Both themes, Philippine diversity and the encounter with the United States, help frame the origins of the Filipino Americans.

GEOGRAPHY

The Philippine Islands are an archipelago of more than 7,000 islands located southeast of China and northeast of modern-day Indonesia. Historically, the Philippines have been divided into three major regions. The first and northernmost is Luzon, the largest island, which includes the city of Manila and several Tagalog-speaking provinces; the central province of Pampanga; the northern Pangasinan and Ilocano-speaking provinces; and the Cordillera mountain range, which includes territories inhabited by the Ifugao, Kalinga, Igorot, and other mountain people who remained relatively immune to Spanish influence. South of Luzon are the Visayan Islands, the second major region, including Panay, Negros, Cebu, Bohol, Leyte, and

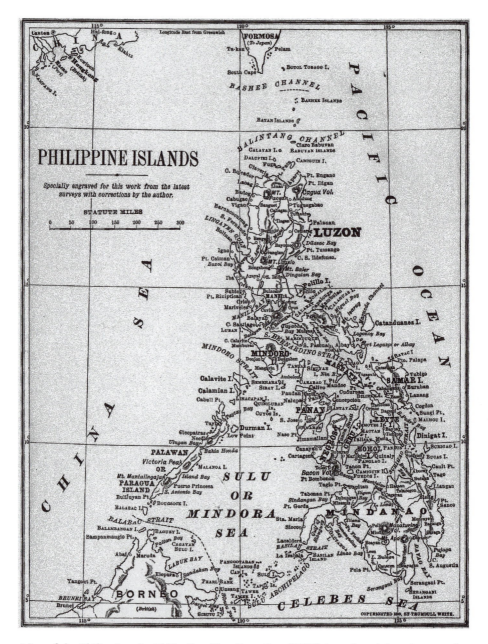

Map of the Philippines in 1898. *Our New Possessions* (1898) introduced Americans to the United States' new territorial acquisitions, including the Philippines. From Trumbull White, *Our New Possessions* (Richmond, VA: B. F. Johnson Publishing Co., 1898): 32.

Samar, whose inhabitants claim their own linguistic and cultural histories. The third region is the southernmost, containing the island of Mindanao and the Sulu archipelago, many of whose inhabitants retain the Muslim faith and local customs derived from it, even as they co-exist uneasily with more recent transplants from other Philippine regions.

The lowland coastal strips and central plains of Luzon have long been actively cultivated in rice, sugar, hemp, coconuts, and fruits. Under Western influence, tobacco and coffee crops were introduced. Well into the twentieth century, four out of five Filipinos have lived in rural areas, mostly as cultivators of small plots of land, but also as workers, in American times and under independence, on large plantations, notably the sugar centrals of the Visayas.

BEFORE 1898: MALAY, ISLAMIC, CHINESE, AND SPANISH ROOTS

The population of the Philippines has long been among the most cosmopolitan of Asia. Among the earliest settlers were dark-skinned Negritos, who are also called *Aetas*. Following them came much larger numbers of people of Malay stock. From the 1500s onward, Chinese have inhabited portions of the Islands, sometimes remaining as a separate recognizable group and sometimes intermarrying to create a distinct class of Chinese *mestizos* (mixed bloods). Though relatively few Spaniards stayed permanently in the Philippines, many Filipinos claim Spanish blood. Other Filipinos claim American ancestry. Filipinos have been among the most exogamous of Asians at home and when they have migrated overseas.

Another element of diversity has been language. Luzon claims several linguistic groups as do the Visayas and Mindanao. Some sources cite eighty-nine dialects spoken in the Philippines, though half a dozen native languages predominate. Spanish never became a unifying language, and while many Filipinos learned at least some English during the American period, language continued to divide the Islands. Filipinos themselves disagree over the extent to which *Pilipino*, the national language proclaimed in 1946 and based largely on the Tagalog language of Manila and much of Luzon, has unified the nation, with dissension most likely to come from Cebuano speakers in the Visayas and Ilocano speakers in northern Luzon.

Spain established its rule over the Philippines in the 1570s, two generations after Ferdinand Magellan "discovered" the Islands and died there in 1521 in a clash with Filipinos commanded by the chieftain Lapu-Lapu. The Spaniards found a decentralized society organized in *barangays*, primarily around kinship groups of from thirty to a hundred families. In these self-sufficient units, Filipinos traced their descent bilaterally, from both the father's and mother's side. Women held positions of respect and influence greater than in many societies. For example, in rural settings, the wife often served as the family treasurer.

The Spaniards' major accomplishment during their three centuries in the Philippines was the conversion of the vast majority of the population to Roman Catholicism, an achievement unique among Europeans in the Far East. In some instances this meant a conversion away from Islam, but in most, Catholicism replaced and blended with folk religious traditions. Five of six Filipinos enumerated by recent censuses belong to the Roman Catholic Church. Muslims, mostly concentrated on Mindanao and the Sulu Islands, account for about a twelfth of the population. Members of the Philippine Independent Church (Aglipayan), *Iglisia ni Kristo* (a Protestant Fundamentalist group), and various other Protestants make up less than ten percent of the total.

One of the most important social consequences of Roman Catholicism in the Philippines has been the emergence of *compadrinazgo*, or ritual co-parenthood. This tradition brought together the Catholic practice of god-parenthood with various pre-Hispanic regional customs to form a distinctive and wide-ranging aspect of Philippine culture. Godparents in the Philippines do not function solely as spiritual guides to their godchildren but also as important intra- and inter-class allies of the parents as well. The resulting ethic of reciprocity and patron-client relationships, based on the tie of fictive kinship, has, in turn, shaped the ways Filipinos conduct business and political activities.

While some Philippine communities had interacted with Chinese traders for several centuries, Spanish rule subordinated the Islands to a military and clerical rule devoted more to religious conversion, labor discipline, and taxation than to Spanish settlement or substantial economic development. Spain isolated the Philippines from its Asian neighbors and from other Europeans and confined international trade for two and a half centuries to an annual galleon which sailed from Manila to Acapulco. Limited to the galleon trade, Manila developed largely as a trade center. Mexican silver, Chinese silks, and other goods were exchanged. Chinese mercantile settlement in the Philippines has evoked periodic hostility, including a massacre in Manila in 1603, but also the emergence of an identifiable Chinese *mestizo* population, which includes many members of the Philippine economic and political elite in both Luzon and the Visayas.

Among the beneficiaries of eighteenth- and nineteenth-century economic development were a small but growing and ambitious urban middle class, some of whom had ties to the countryside. Increasingly cosmopolitan, members of this group came to resent their racial subordination by the Spaniards as *indios*. (For many years, in Spanish parlance, the word "*Filipino*" was reserved for Spaniards born in the Islands.) These local gentry became assertive as they sought a greater economic and political role in their homeland. In addition, in these years a trickle of students studied abroad in Spain and elsewhere in Europe and brought back elements of its Enlightenment, romanticism, and nationalism. Thus they provided the basis to justify local autonomy in the context of a fast-changing world.

By the mid-nineteenth century, Spain faced recurrent revolts among the peasantry and a growing agitation against repressive rule, especially that of the Spanish friars, who controlled many estates and participated actively in land disputes. Spanish refusal to grant equality to native-born clergy further promoted nationalist feelings which increasingly resulted in violence. These rebellions drew upon both what some Filipinos had learned from abroad and upon indigenous folk religious traditions in various Philippine regions.

Following a mutiny among Filipino troops in Cavite, south of Manila, where friar estates composed more than half of the rice and corn lands, many reformers were arrested and three native priests—Mariano Gomez, a full-blooded Filipino, José Burgos, a Spanish Creole, and Jacinto Zamora, a Chinese *mestizo*—were executed in February 1872. These disorders culminated in the 1890s with the emergence of a radical secret society, Andres Bonifacio's *Katipunan*, and the execution on December 30, 1896, of Dr. José M. Rizal, who soon became the national hero of the Philippines. Rizal, a fifth-generation Chinese *mestizo* from an important family in Calamba, south of Manila, was an ophthalmic surgeon, a poet, a novelist, and a social critic. He epitomized *ilustrado* aspirations toward individual achievement, national autonomy if not independence, and recognition. Rizal's novels, *Noli Me Tangere* and *El Filibusterismo*, became texts of social criticism for a generation and classics of Philippine literature.

The subsequent declaration of Philippine independence, on June 12, 1898, by Emilio Aguinaldo, a regional aristocrat, in Kawit, Cavite, proclaimed the first republic in Asia, but independence efforts faltered during the Spanish-American War, which happened simultaneously and entwined the United States and the Philippines.

THE AMERICAN COLONIAL PERIOD: 1898–1946

Rather than recognize and support the independence of the Philippines from Spain, Americans under President William McKinley decided to claim

José Rizal's execution by Spanish colonial authorities
in 1896 made him the Philippines' preeminent hero.
Courtesy of the Filipino American National
Historical Society, Seattle, Washington.

the Islands, ostensibly for the "tutelage" of Filipinos toward eventual self-
rule, but also for strategic and economic reasons. The bloody Philippine-
American War ensued in 1899, led initially by Aguinaldo and largely directed
by local elites who invoked the loyalties of patron-client relationships. The
war spread throughout the Islands and lasted for more than three years into
the next decade. Hundreds of thousands of Filipinos died, some under especially brutal conditions. The war joined with the spread of disease to create
an ecological catastrophe that damaged the Islands for years.

However violent its onset, American rule proved relatively mild in practice.
A policy of "attraction" aimed at ensuring the loyalty of prominent Filipinos,
especially in Manila, by promising an elected legislature and consultation in
colonial affairs. At the same time, the U.S. government sponsored roadbuild-

ing and public health programs that improved the lot of many Filipinos (May 1980).

Perhaps the Americans' most notable legacy was in education. Although the Spanish had established the University of Santo Tomas in Manila in 1626, a decade before English Puritans founded Harvard College in Massachusetts, Spain did little to promote intellectual development in the Islands. The Americans soon transformed the system, emphasizing primary schooling throughout the Philippines. Enrollment soared from 150,000 in 1900 to more than 1,000,000 in 1921, and public high schools grew from fewer than 500 students in 1903 to almost 75,000 in 1929.

For some, this aid was inspirational, as well as material. A group of American teachers, dubbed "Thomasites" after the ship that brought them to the Philippines in 1901, enthusiastically strove to spread democratic values, as well as basic literacy skills in English. They portrayed an American ideal of a career open to talent, hard work, and free of racial prejudice. The kindness of such individuals encouraged many Filipinos to migrate to America in a quest for adventure and further education.

But before long, most Americans lost interest in their imperial venture, and the administration of the Islands devolved upon a Filipino civil servant class, gently supervised by an American Governor General in the years before the U.S. Congress passed the Tydings-McDuffie Act of 1934, promising independence in ten years. Twenty years after the inauguration of American rule, Filipinos numbered more than 13,000 civil servants out of a total of fewer than 14,000. Some of these had been educated in the United States as *pensionados* (government-sponsored scholarship students).

Whatever the good intentions of colonial administrators, the downside of U.S. rule lay in its reaffirmation of a preexisting Filipino elite in its domination of the countryside. Struggles over land tenure in the provinces, that Americans tried to regularize, soon meant the dispossession of many peasants from their customary holdings, often by fraudulent means, reducing many to permanently indebted sharecropping on large *haciendas.*

By the 1930s, Filipinos in central Luzon, not especially hostile to the Americans, were ready to take up arms against their indigenous local and absentee landlords. Only the Japanese invasion and occupation of the Philippines between 1942 and 1945 forestalled a more violent confrontation.

THE PHILIPPINE REPUBLIC: 1946–1965

The inauguration of the Philippine Republic in 1946 brought independence, but did not solve the many problems of the new nation. An American-inspired system of political parties, a bicameral legislature, and quadrennial presidential elections did not replicate the polity of the United States. Grafted onto a society of great inequalities and a patron-client system alien to American ways, electoral politics in the Philippines led to violence, charges of vote-buying and ballot-box stuffing, and persistent party-switching among the elite, so that the same faces wound up on the winning side each time. The agrarian Huk rebellion of the Luzon countryside, originally provoked by the Japanese, now turned against the Philippine government. It dragged on for years and embedded the Philippines in the politics of the Cold War, as Filipino leaders relied on American counterinsurgency experts to put down the revolt of their countrymen.

Despite previous ties, the United States remained unwilling to provide substantial development aid to its former colony. Equally irritating to Filipino nationalists, Americans retained large military bases at Clark Field, in Pampanga, and at Subic Bay, south of Manila. Even though the Philippines stood relatively well compared to other Asian nations in 1960, it had not, for most, fulfilled its promise. By the mid-1990s, its economy had been far surpassed by such neighboring "Asian Tigers" as Thailand, Taiwan, South Korea, and even Indonesia.

POST-1965

The last third of the twentieth century posed political challenges to the Philippines in other ways as well. Two decades of rule by Ferdinand and Imelda Marcos, half under martial law declared in 1972, stifled Philippine democracy and further despoiled the Philippine economy. "Crony capitalists," the president's friends, were the beneficiaries of government largesse. Foreign debt ballooned, and the per capita gross national product fell eighteen percent between 1981 and 1986. The murder of opposition leader Benigno Aquino on the tarmac at Manila airport as he returned from exile in 1983 drew unfavorable worldwide attention to the nation's plight. Persistent rebellion in the northern Luzon countryside and in Mindanao drained resources from social programs and led elements of the armed forces to seek political power.

The celebrated "People Power" revolution of 1986 that drove the Marcoses from power in favor of a government presided over by the widowed Corazon Aquino gave a moral boost to the ideal of peaceful change, but disappointingly little improvement in the lives of the Philippine poor. By the decade's end, the Islands depended more than any other nation on the remittances of those members of its population that it had "exported," many of them to the Persian Gulf, Singapore, and Japan. Their labor, most often as maids, drivers, construction workers, and entertainers, was typically poorly paid, risky, and disruptive of family life.

Writing in 1987, the American journalist James Fallows portrayed "a damaged culture" symbolized by Manila's giant garbage dump, the "Smoky Mountain," inhabited by more than 15,000 homeless Filipinos (Fallows 1987). Even the relatively light-hearted traveler Pico Iyer saw and heard in Manila's downtown the worst of international influences: "In Ermita I felt as if I was living inside a Top 40 radio station" in "perhaps the world's largest slice of the American empire in its purest, impurest form," a "junk-neon flash of teen America" uninterested in anything more than the moment (Iyer 1988: 164, 168, 169).

The 1990s promised better. The economy revived under Aquino's elected successor, Fidel Ramos, who cleaned up the "Smoky Mountain" and staved off until the end of his term in the centennial year 1998 the financial crashes that befell Thailand, South Korea, and Indonesia. Persistent disparities between rich and poor, underemployment among the relatively well educated, the loss of jobs after the sudden closure of U.S. bases at Clark and Subic in 1991, and a series of ecological disasters—highlighted by the eruption of Mt. Pinatubo—all tested Filipinos. Yet, the country and its people remained sturdy. Non-governmental organizations strove to overcome the failures of government. Generosity from overseas Filipinos, especially in America, helped many.

The post-1965 emigrants to America, the subject of this book, were a product of these years. Lured by economic and professional opportunities, but largely educated in the Philippines and speaking a Philippine language rather than English at home, they remember their roots and try to pass on Philippine culture to their children born in the United States. They do their best, in a transnational setting, to sustain their historic cultures at home and abroad as the century comes to a close.

2

Filipinos in the United States before 1965

Immediately after American acquisition of the Philippines from Spain in 1898, Filipinos began arriving in the United States and Hawaii (then an American possession). Typically, Filipinos came either to earn American dollars or to obtain an American education. With varying degrees of success, some combined schooling and work on the mainland. Virtually all originally intended to return to the Philippines, but many temporary sojourners ultimately became lifelong immigrants, establishing families and communities far from home. The *Pinoys*, as Filipinos living in the United States before World War II called themselves, also came to be known as the "old-timers" decades later, thus distinguishing them from the Filipino immigrants who arrived after 1965.

FILIPINOS IN THE AMERICAS BEFORE 1898

Prior to 1898, an undetermined number of Filipinos, called *indios* during the Spanish colonial period, arrived in the Americas and settled in territory that would ultimately become the United States, as well as in Mexico. Between 1565 and 1815, four years after Mexico won independence from Spain, galleons travelled between Manila and Acapulco, manned by crews that included Philippine natives. Thus, Filipinos participated in voyages of discovery along the Pacific Coast. "Luzon indians" accompanied Pedro de Unamuno when he landed at Morro Bay on the California coast in 1587 (Pilapil 1996: 43). Three centuries later, in *Harper's Weekly* in 1883, Lafcadio

Louisiana's Manila Village, circa 1890s. Filipino fishermen, who brought their shrimp-drying techniques to the Louisiana bayous in the late 1800s, named their settlement Manila Village. Courtesy of the Filipino American National Historical Society, Seattle, Washington.

Hearn wrote of "Malay fishermen—Tagalas from the Philippine Islands" living in the bayous of Louisiana (Hearn 1883: 198).

Direct continuity between the *indios* on the galleons and the Filipinos in the bayous has never been proven, but the work of Marina E. Espina indicates that by 1898 a handful of Filipinos and their descendants were well established in the New Orleans area.

THE OLD-TIMERS' ERA: 1898–1945

The vast majority of Filipinos who left their homeland before the mid-1930s were set in motion by the integration of the Philippines into the capitalist world market as an agricultural export economy. The process, which began under late eighteenth-century Spanish rule, grew more intense under American sway. As the production of export crops, such as sugar, *abaca*, tobacco, and coffee, on large-scale plantations became increasingly important, both to colonial rulers and to Filipino elites, the growing of rice

Table 2.1
The Filipino Population in the United States and Hawaii,
1910–1940

Year	United States	Hawaii
1910	406	2,361
1920	5,603	21,031
1930	45,208	63,052
1940	45,876	52,569

Source: Harry H. L. Kitano and Roger Daniels, *Asian Americans: Emerging Minorities.* 2nd ed. (Englewood Cliffs, NJ: Prentice-Hall, 1995): 87.

by small-scale farmers declined, and "tenancy and landlessness" rose (Sharma 1984[a]: 343).

Displaced agricultural workers came first to Hawaii, where the Hawaiian Sugar Planters Association (HSPA) experimented with the importation of Filipino workers as early as 1906. At the turn of the century, Hawaiian sugar growers had depended heavily on Japanese labor. By 1910, a shift to Filipino labor had begun. Growers actively recruited Filipino contract workers, called *sakadas*, out of fear that their continuing access to cheap Japanese labor would be restricted by a government ban on their future entry. By 1915, Filipinos were 19 percent of sugar plantation employees; by 1922, 41 percent; and in 1932, 69.9 percent, by which time, Japanese workers in sugar had declined to 18.8 percent (Alcantara 1981[a]: 27–37; Sharma, 1984[b]: 581, 586).

Between 1909 and 1934, the HSPA imported 118,556 *sakadas* into Hawaii—103,513 men, 8,952 women, and 6,091 children—large numbers from the Ilocano-speaking provinces of northern Luzon. By 1935, 58,281 had returned to the Philippines (Sharma 1984[a]: 339–340; Sharma 1984[b]: 585). Still, despite poor wages, dreadful working conditions, and continuing agitation for improvement which led to the deportation of labor leader Pablo Manlapit in 1935, those *sakadas* who remained, along with their offspring, established thriving, ethnically based communities throughout Hawaii.

Prior to World War II, Filipinos in Hawaii consistently outnumbered those in the mainland United States, although by 1940, the gap was narrowing (Table 2.1). The large number of pre-1935 Hawaii-to-mainland transmigrants indicates the likely possibility that at least a third of the 45,876 Filipinos living in the United States in 1940 had worked first in Hawaii.

After they arrived in the mainland, many of these laborers most likely found seasonal jobs in agriculture in the Pacific Coast states and as so-called *alaskeros* in the canneries of Alaska, as did many others who came directly from the Philippines.

For the price of a ticket across the Pacific, a worker could journey to the United States free of any constraints imposed by immigration legislation. Unlike Chinese and Japanese laborers, already or soon to be excluded by anti-Asian immigration policies, Filipinos—whatever their economic class— might, as U.S. nationals, enter without restriction. Soon, Filipino workers became an attractive labor source for West Coast employers in agriculture, in salmon canning, and in service occupations.

By contrast with Hawaii, the first Filipinos to arrive in the mainland after the turn of the century were students, initially the sons of elite Filipinos. Just as American colonial administrators worked to establish a system of public education in the Philippines during the early decades of the century, so too did they emphasize education for a chosen few in the United States as essential to their aim of binding current and future Filipino leaders to the American colonial administration.

In 1900, before the end of the Philippine-American War, Philippine Commission member Dean C. Worcester suggested that Manila's elite *Club Internacional de Manila* sponsor a competitive examination to select several students for education in the United States. Before the year ended, the first three journeyed across the Pacific aboard a U.S. Army transport ship, en route to their destination, Ann Arbor, Michigan.

Their stories of the "ludicrous situations" and financial straits into which naive Filipinos might blunder in foreign territory were probably among the first youthful accounts to reach their homeland—the three watermelons they ordered at a San Francisco hotel, thinking that each would be an individual's portion—the dime rubber collars they wore to cut their laundry bills—the ill-fitting suit one bought on an installment plan ("The First Pensionados" 1932: 56). If such tales both entertained and instructed, the story of their ultimate success, credited to hard work and persistence in an unfamiliar land, seemingly set an example that others might follow.

Established in 1903, the *pensionado* program provided government scholarships to students supposedly chosen by merit from each Philippine province; in actuality, local prominence and connections played a major role in the selection process. In return for each year of education in the United States, *pensionados* were required to work for the government in the Philippines for the same length of time.

The initial and largest group, the 104 young men who departed the Philippines in 1903 spent their first school year (1903–1904) in close proximity, living with families while attending California schools. Perhaps most important to their future success, according to William Alexander Sutherland, who had them in his personal charge, they made a "record . . . of credit to themselves and to their race" (Sutherland 1953: 925).

In August 1904, the *pensionados* spent a month at the St. Louis World's Fair where they served three hours per day "as guides to visitors in the different Philippine buildings" (Republic of the Philippines, "Report of Wm. Alex. Sutherland . . . June 30, 1905," 1954: 796). During the World's Fair, public interest in the Philippines focused particularly on the Philippine Reservation where ethnological villages displayed the seeming barbarism and savageness of the "wild tribes," especially the Igorots' and Negritos' lack of clothing (Rydell 1984: 172). The *pensionados* counteracted both the impression and the argument. Indeed, the St. Louis World's Fair would be just one occasion when Filipino students found themselves upholding their people and their nation.

Pensionado stories became legend, fueling the migration of larger numbers of Filipino students during the next decades. The individual triumphs they achieved in the service of their homeland upon their return from America marked them, for Filipinos and Americans alike, as the leaders of a nation in the making. Their competence over the years seemed to offer a tangible realization of both the loftiest and the most self-interested goals of U.S. foreign policy on one hand and a concrete proof of the capability of the Filipino people on the other.

By the early 1920s, unlike the period immediately after the turn of the century, far fewer Filipino students enjoyed complete support, their numbers eclipsed by the many more who were self-supporting. Two examples can illustrate the differences between those who enjoyed either family or scholarship support and those who had to support themselves. Fully funded by his wealthy family, Carlos Quirino, later a prominent author, remembered his years at the University of Wisconsin in Madison where he earned a journalism degree "as a series of tennis games rather than classes." In contrast, his contemporary and friend, Agustin Rodolfo, lived "in the Animal Husbandry laboratory . . . [where he kept] his clothes, a Bunsen burner for heating soup and a toaster. At night he slept with a close friend in a bit of forest by the shore of Lake Mendota. When the weather forced them to seek shelter, they retired to the boathouse which they owned in common, or to the canoe kept there" (Posadas and Guyotte 1992: 97–98). Although Rudolfo, like Quirino, ultimately earned his degree and returned to establish a career as an educator in the Philippines, countless others did not achieve their original

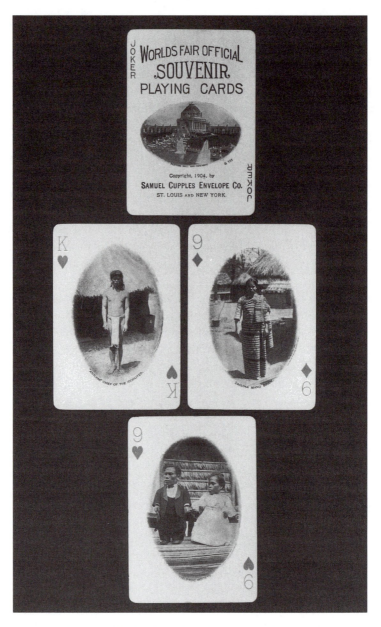

Souvenir playing cards distributed at the 1904 St. Louis World's Fair depicted Filipinos as uncivilized tribespeople. Courtesy of Edward L. Bates.

Attending school in the United States on government scholarships, the *pensionados'* presence at the 1904 St. Louis World's Fair counteracted notions of Filipinos as "savage." Photo originally taken in 1903. From William Alexander Sutherland, *Not By Might: The Epic of the Philippines* (Las Cruces, NM: Southwest Publishing Company, 1953): 30.

educational goals and instead became "unintentional immigrants" (Posadas and Guyotte 1990).

In urban locales, Filipinos who hoped to succeed as self-supporting students filled niches in local economies, typically as service workers in restaurants, hotels, and private clubs, and as personal servants. Occasionally, Filipinos found factory work, perhaps the largest number in the Detroit area working for the Ford Motor Company.

During the 1920s and the 1930s, as today, most Filipinos lived on the West Coast. Some came, as they did to the Midwest, to continue their educations; others, to make money. Some travelled, following jobs locally, while others moved in their youth among regions, not quite transient, but never quite permanent. Born in 1896 in La Union province and already nearing forty when he "rode steerage" to the United States, Julio Orille left school after the second grade. Arriving in California in 1934 and moving frequently before World War II, he worked in a county hospital in San Jose; dug a garden, picked strawberries and prunes, washed dishes, and picked "tomatoes, lettuce, squash and other vegetables," all in the Sacramento area; raised "cabbage, cauliflower, broccoli and sprouts" on a farm near Half Moon Bay;

At Chicago's Crane Junior College in 1926, Filipino Club members and students from other school organizations entertained at Rizal Day festivities. From *The Philippine Republic* (January–February 1927): 16.

picked tomatoes again near San Jose; and worked in a nursery in Redwood City and in a cafeteria in San Francisco. "I didn't write many letters home but I always sent money." During these years, he also "went to school a lot"—"to improve my English" (Vallangca 1977: 136–138).

Those who did successfully complete their educations sometimes found their entry into their chosen profession barred by discrimination. Having worked as a janitor while he earned his civil engineering degree, one Filipino proudly displayed his diploma on the wall of his apartment where his children could see it, but continued to work as a janitor.

Pervasive social and economic hostility against Filipinos in California, described in Carlos Bulosan's (see Appendix II) *America Is in the Heart* (1946), erupted most severely at Watsonville in January 1930. During five days of violence, gunmen firing from a passing car peppered a camp barracks with shots and killed Filipino farmworker Fermin Tobera as he lay in his bunk.

In California, Arizona, Idaho, Nevada, Utah, and Wyoming, as well as in Georgia, Mississippi, Missouri, and South Dakota, state legislatures passed

"Positively No Filipinos Allowed." In California in the 1920s and 1930s, Filipinos faced de facto segregation. Courtesy of the Filipino American National Historical Society, Seattle, Washington.

America Is in the Heart (1946) made its
author, Carlos Bulosan, famous among
later generations of Filipino Americans.
Courtesy of the Filipino American
National Historical Society, Seattle,
Washington.

anti-miscegenation statutes forbidding marriage between "white" and "Mongolian" partners. Recalling California in the 1930s, Paul Valdez remembered: "They used to pass out leaflets saying that the Japanese were taking the lands from the Americans, the Chinese were taking the businesses, and the Filipinos were taking the women" (Vallangca 1977: 113). If a couple lived in a restrictive state, they could circumvent the prohibition by marrying in another state, as did the Filipino father and English immigrant mother of Olympic gold medalist Victoria Manolo Draves (see Appendix II). Born in San Francisco in 1924, she was forced to hide her Filipino heritage and use her mother's maiden name, Taylor, when she began competing, because of hostility against Filipinos.

Filipinos also enlisted in branches of the U.S. military before World War II. By 1901, with the Philippine-American War still under way, over 5,500 Filipinos were serving as Philippine Scouts under American officers in the regular army. In 1904, 1,369 Scouts, on detachment from their regular post-ings in the Philippines, became a much-applauded part of the Philippine Exhibit at the St. Louis World's Fair.

In 1904, the U.S. Navy began recruitment of Filipinos—just over 300 in that year. Thereafter, Filipino numbers grew steadily, never falling below 3,900 between 1918 and 1933. In 1922, the navy's 5,018 Filipinos consti-tuted 5.7% of the enlisted force. Filipinos became known as "superior ser-vants"—so "superior" that the navy stopped its enlistment of African American messmen in 1919. In 1932, when Filipinos numbered 3,922, only 441 African Americans remained in the service. But Filipinos quickly found that their own race also circumscribed their opportunities for advancement. In 1920, the Bureau of Navigation informed the commanding officer of the Hampton Roads Naval Training Station "that it was 'contrary to the Bureau's policy to rate filipinos in any branches other than the messmen and musicians branches'" (Harrod 1978: 60, 180–81, 222). Despite such obvious discrim-ination, many Filipinos found lifelong careers and undoubtedly enjoyed more security in the navy than did most compatriots who lived in the United States during these years.

Despite their ability as U.S. nationals to migrate freely, those born in the Philippines were not eligible to become citizens of the United States. Nat-uralization had been "limited to free white persons" in 1790, a policy lib-eralized prior to the outbreak of World War II only for African Americans—by ratification of the Fourteenth Amendment in 1868—and for African immigrants—by passage of the Naturalization Act of 1870. Thus, although all children born in the United States to Filipino immigrants were U.S. citizens, before World War II, no matter how many years Philippine-born Filipinos had lived in the United States, they were ineligible for naturaliza-tion, and, therefore, could not vote, or be absolutely sure of their future status and security.

In the mid-1930s, Filipinos in the United States also faced a more tenuous legal situation. The Tydings-McDuffie Act of 1934 promised the Philippines independence after ten years (a pledge not kept, because of World War II, until 1946), but immediately restricted immigration from the Philippines to a fifty per year quota. After independence, Filipino immigrants, like all other Asians, were to be totally excluded, although a clause (invoked in 1946) permitted Hawaii's sugar planters to recruit labor in the Philippines if they could demonstrate a need. Filipinos already in the United States now knew that they could never visit their homeland, even to see a dying parent, without relinquishing their right to return to the United States. During the Depres-sion, Congress also passed the Repatriation Act of 1935, which allocated federal funds for the transport of Filipinos who would voluntarily return to the Philippines. Fewer than 2,200 Filipinos took the government's offer.

Despite such difficulties and an imbalanced sex ratio between Filipino men and women that left Filipinas in short supply, Filipinos struggled during the years prior to World War II to make lives for themselves in the United States. Bachelor Filipinos relied on each other for camaraderie in "Little Manilas" and farmworker camps. Filipino/Filipina and Filipino/American couples and bachelors alike created communities based on kinship, friendship, and mutual interest. They spent their time in various ways—caring for their purely Filipino and their racially mixed children; establishing clubs reflecting provincial origins, occupational affiliations, and the need for mutual assistance; founding American branches of fraternal organizations such as the Caballeros de Dimas-Alang, the Legionarios del Trabajo, the Gran Oriente Filipino, and the Knights of Rizal, as well as the Filipino Federation of America; holding queen contests to support their associations; affiliating with religiously sponsored groups such as the Protestant YMCA's Filipino Students' Christian Movement and the Catholic Gibbons Society; playing team sports such as baseball in Filipino leagues; cheering Filipino boxers; and hanging out in pool and taxi dance halls, in barber shops, in Chinese restaurants, and in space rented to function as Filipino community centers.

Hoping to better the work lives of their countrymen, some became activists in the labor movement. Among Filipino workers on Hawaii's plantations, Pablo Manlapit established the Filipino Federation of Labor in 1911, later known as the *Vibora Luviminda* under the direction of Antonio Fagel and Epifanio Taok in the 1930s; Moses Claveria recruited on Maui; and, in the most successful effort among Filipino sugar workers in Hawaii, Ricardo Labez and Carl Damaso organized for Local 142 of the International Longshoremen's and Warehousemen's Union after World War II. In the 1930s, Cypriano Samonte in Chicago and J. C. Brana in New York City helped to organize Filipino Pullman employees under the banner of the African American–led Brotherhood of Sleeping Car Porters, which won recognition in 1937.

Among *alaskeros*, "union organizer Chris Mensalvas tersely noted, 'there . . . [were] too many organizations' to create any unity among Filipinos" (Friday 1994: 138). In 1936, union leaders Virgil Duyungan and Aurelio Simon accepted an invitation to dinner at a Seattle restaurant and were "gunned down in cold blood" (Evangelista and Evangelista 1982: 166). Ethnic divisions among Filipinos, Chinese, and Japanese workers also segmented the labor force in the Alaska canned salmon industry. By the 1940s, Filipinos, ethnically dominant in a declining industry as Americans turned to canned

Margarita Bilar Ventura (center) and her daughters, Feling Bilar (left) and Catherine Bilar (right) wore Filipina dresses for this photograph taken in Stockton, California, in 1928. Courtesy of the Filipino American National Historical Society, Seattle, Washington.

tuna, soon resumed struggling "among themselves for power within the union" (Friday 1994: 195). In 1981, in an event that must have produced a sense of *deja vú* in many, union leaders Gene Viernes and Silme Domingo were murdered in Seattle, their deaths apparently tangled in intrigue involving leaders of ILWU Local 37, pro-Marcos sympathizers in the United States, and the Philippine government's National Intelligence and Security Agency.

In the fields of California before the mid-1960s, Filipino labor efforts also fragmented in an array of organizations that appeared and disappeared over time. Not until the "Great Grape Strike of 1965," did Filipino workers, under the leadership of Philip Vera Cruz (see Appendix II), Larry Dulay Itliong, Pete Velasco, Nacasio Campos, and Alfredo Vasquez, join across ethnic lines with Cesar Chavez' Mexican-American National Farm Workers

Association (NFWA) to form the AFL-CIO's United Farm Workers Organizing Committee (UFWOC).

Wherever they lived and however they earned their pay, Filipinos in the United States celebrated Rizal Day in late December as an affirmation of who they were as Filipinos and what they were becoming as Filipino Americans. From these roots, Filipino American communities would grow in size and stability during the years after World War II.

FILIPINO AMERICANS IN TRANSITION: 1945–1965

The two decades between 1946 and 1965 encompass an era of important transitions in Filipino American history. Previously established patterns changed in crucial ways—ways that charted the course later followed by post-1965 Filipino immigrants. Philippine independence, access to naturalized citizenship, the migration of Filipinas, the formation of new families, the arrival of Filipino professionals, the expansion of ethnic community institutions, and the maturation of the first generation of children of Filipino parentage born in the United States—together, these forces for change gave Filipino America a far different face in 1965 than in 1946.

The outbreak of World War II actually began the process of change. Hostility against Filipinos lessened; they were allies—and not Japanese. Less than a month after Pearl Harbor, a change in the Selective Service Act permitted Filipinos to serve in the U.S. Army even though they were not citizens. Thousands saw active duty in the Pacific in the 1st and 2nd Filipino Infantry Regiments, while others served in non-Filipino units fighting in Europe. The right of naturalization was soon extended to these Filipinos, and over four hundred took the oath of citizenship in a mass ceremony at Camp Beale in California in February 1943. During and immediately after World War II, 10,737 Filipinos in the military were naturalized (Barkan 1992: 201). Other Filipinos would have to wait a few more years.

Filipinos in the United States watched from a distance as Philippine independence on July 4, 1946, finally severed, at least legally, the almost half-century colonial bond. Almost simultaneously, in the Luce-Celler Bill passed on July 2, 1946, the United States granted access to naturalization to all remaining Filipinos who had come to the United States before passage of Tydings-McDuffie. Filipinos in America now faced the need to choose. Would they live their remaining years as citizens of the Philippines or the United States? During the 1947 fiscal year, the first after passage of Luce-Celler, 10,764 Filipinos became citizens (Barkan 1992: 201).

Even as it granted pre-1935 Filipino immigrants the right to become nat-

Finally eligible for naturalization because of their service in the U.S. Army, these soldiers of the 1st Filipino Infantry Regiment took their citizenship oath in 1943 at Camp Beale, California. Courtesy of the Filipino American National Historical Society, Seattle, Washington.

uralized citizens, the Luce-Celler Act also limited future Filipino immigration to a 50 per year quota. Despite their meager quota, Filipinos found expanded opportunities, opportunities based—as they would be for post-1965 immigrants—on family and on occupation. Filipina brides and nurses led the way.

Women from the Philippines had come to the United States in tiny numbers by comparison with their male countrymen before 1934. In 1930, for example, when foreign- and native-born Filipinos in the continental United States numbered 45,208, 67.4 percent lived in California, of whom only 6.5 percent were female. By contrast, Filipina numbers grew substantially between 1946 and 1965 (see Table 2.2). In 1960, 67,435 Filipinas were counted—37.1 percent of the Filipino American population. By 1970, their numbers more than doubled and their percentage increased to 45.6 percent. Two groups are especially crucial in accounting for this surge: brides, who immigrated after marrying either members of the United States armed forces or Filipino men who had arrived before 1934; and nurses, who came to the United States for post-graduate study and often remained to work and to marry.

During the closing months of World War II, American armed forces joined with their Philippine counterparts to free the Philippines from Japanese occupation. Even after Philippine independence, the presence of U.S. military personnel persisted on American-controlled military bases. Throughout this period, members of the U.S. Navy, Army, and Air Force stationed in the Philippines, some of whom were themselves Philippine-born, married

Table 2.2
The Filipino Population by Sex, 1950–1970

Year	Male	Female	Total
1950	NA	NA	61,645
1960	114,179	67,435	181,614
1970	183,175	153,556	336,731

Source: Roger Daniels, "Asian Americans: The Transformation of a Pariah Minority," *Amerikastudien* 40 (1995): 478; United States, Bureau of the Census, *U.S. Census of Population: 1960—Subject Reports—Nonwhite Population by Race* (Washington, D.C.: U.S. Government Printing Office, 1963): 5—based on sample data; United States, Bureau of the Census, *1970 Census of Population—Subject Reports: Japanese, Chinese and Filipinos in the United States* (Washington, D.C.: U.S. Government Printing Office, 1973): 119.

Filipinas who, in the immediate post-war years, were termed "war brides."

When husbands were transferred back to the States, difficult times for war brides left behind often followed. Several who ultimately settled in Seattle suffered vulgar comments and an especially nasty insult: they were called " 'hang-gang pier lamang,' or wives 'up to the pier only,' [whose] . . . husbands would never return for them" (Lawsin 1996: 50C). After filling out immigration forms, waiting for requisite approvals, and enduring delays ranging from a few months to several years, Filipinas were ultimately able to join husbands and fiancés in the United States. Legislation passed in 1945 and 1946 facilitated their migration. Under the War Brides Act of 1945 (Public Law 271) and the Fiancées Act of 1946 (Public Law 471), Filipina wives, children, and fiancées of U.S. servicemen were permitted entry into the United States despite quota restrictions then in force. Approximately 118,000 spouses and children arrived "quota free without visa or passport" (Acierto 1994: 70).

Wherever they settled, Filipina brides sought out other newcomers and participated in Filipino American community organizations. In Chicago, they became active in the Filipino American Veterans of Chicago Post Auxiliary #234 and the Fil-Am Woman's Club of Chicago. One of their number, Angeles (Ann) Llapitan supported her postal-worker husband Carmelito's long campaign to unite Filipino organizations in Chicago under the umbrella of the Filipino American Council and to purchase a community center. In Seattle, Filipinas founded the Philippine War Brides Association in 1949, first, to help its members to ease loneliness in an unfamiliar environment, and, over the longer term, to stimulate mutual self-help and encourage active participation in community life. Under its auspices, Seattle's war brides or-

Having come to the United States as war brides after World War II, these Filipinas continued to associate in the 1960s. Courtesy of the Filipino American National Historical Society, Seattle, Washington.

ganized a dance troupe and a glee club to preserve and disseminate Filipino culture, studied together to facilitate passing the U.S. citizenship exam, supported cash awards to members' children upon high school and college graduation, offered financial assistance when members' families experienced illness or death, and raised money to help finance the 1965 acquisition of a Filipino Community Center in Seattle.

Not all Filipinas arrived during these years as the war brides of military personnel. More typically, many unmarried, middle-aged Filipinos who became U.S. citizens after the war journeyed temporarily to the Philippines to find wives and then returned to the United States with their often younger brides to begin families. Like the war brides, these wives (and sometimes children) gained admission outside the limits of the 100-per-year Filipino immigrant quota.

The lives of two Seattle old-timers offer typical examples. Born in San Carlos, Pangasinan, Simeon A. Tamayo landed in Seattle in December 1929 and worked in Alaska during the summer, in California farm fields, as a bowling pin boy, and as a houseboy before he joined the U.S. Army in 1942. Early in 1930, Tamayo's townmate, Primitivo A. (Fred) Dimalanta arrived to join his brother Fortunato (Frank) who had come to Seattle in 1920. During the 1930s, Fred Dimalanta labored in restaurants and hotels before being hired at the Puget Sound Naval Shipyard in 1941. Twenty years after his arrival in the United States, Tamayo visited his hometown and married Teodora Valdez. Three years later, Fred Dimalanta repeated the process, marrying Purita Aquino, also from San Carlos.

Nurses became a second source for the increasingly noticeable migration of Filipinas during the post-war years. Those arriving during the 1950s came under the auspices of the State Department's Exchange Visitor Program (EVP) created under the Information and Education Exchange Act of 1948. The EVP offered foreign nursing graduates a two-year opportunity for post-graduate study and clinical experience in U.S. hospitals on the premise that they would return to their homelands with increased knowledge and skill. In practice, however, the EVP also became a convenient means for addressing the nursing shortage in many inner-city hospitals at a cost cheaper than hiring U.S.-trained nurses.

The Philippines soon became an important source for the EVP. Past co-lonial ties between the United States and the Philippines made Filipina nurses particularly welcome. The English-language schooling of Filipina nurses di-minished the language barrier experienced by nursing graduates from other countries. More importantly, dating from early intiatives in the Philippines in the early 1920s under the International Health Board of the Rockefeller Foundation, an American model shaped nursing education even after the American colonial period ended.

Over time, a symbiotic relationship between the Philippines as the sending country and the United States as the receiving country developed. From 7,000 nurses in the Philippines in 1948, the number surged to 57,000 in 1953. Choosing to be a nurse might guarantee under- or unemployment in the Philippines, while simultaneously opening new career possibilities in the United States. By 1973, 12,526 Filipina nurses had come to the United States under the Exchange Visitor Program (Brush 1995: 551).

Filipino men also continued to come to the United States after Philippine independence through their service in the U.S. Navy. In 1947, the U.S.-Philippine Military Bases Agreement permitted the U.S. Navy to continue enlisting Filipinos, a policy that expanded during the Vietnam War when the annual maximum was raised from 1,000 to 2,000 recruits per year ("Fil-ipinos in the Military" [1981]: 115). By 1970, the approximately 14,000 Filipinos serving in the U.S. Navy outnumbered the entire Philippine Navy (Rumbaut 1991: 220). As a result of the civil rights movement and changes in naval training programs, the relegation of Filipinos to steward and musician ratings began to diminish in the 1970s. But, even as some qualified for other ratings, the concentration of Filipinos in the "lower billets" remained. In the mid-1980s, Filipinos were still 45 percent of all those in the Mess Management (formerly steward) rating ("Filipinos in the Military" [1981]: 115). During and after their enlistments, Filipino navy men tended to raise families, buy homes, and put down roots in communities such as San Diego, Norfolk, Virginia, and Honolulu where post-retirement employment in ship-yards and defense plants proved lucrative.

Examination of one final aspect of the pre-1965 years remains essential to an understanding of the magnitude of Filipino immigration in the post-1965 period. In 1952, the United States undertook its first extensive modification of immigration policy since the mid-1920s. On the surface, the McCarran-Walter Act, appeared no step forward for Filipinos who continued to be restricted to the 100-per-year quota that the Philippines was given in 1946. But, the law also established the principle of family reunification as customary rather than extraordinary in U.S. immigration policy. Whether native-born or naturalized, U.S. citizens might henceforth bring their foreign-born spouses and children to the United States *outside* the limits of the quota system. Thirteen years later, the Immigration and Nationality Act of 1965 abandoned national origins quotas for a system of family and occupational preferences and continued to permit spouses and children of U.S. citizens to enter without limitation. Thus, McCarran-Walter first forged migration chains based fundamentally on the linkage between citizenship and family.

PART II

FILIPINO IMMIGRATION AFTER 1965

3

U.S. Law and Filipino Immigration

In 1960, the nation's 181,614 Filipino Americans were in fact, as well as in perception, a virtually "invisible" component in the national polity of 163 million persons. Passage of the Immigration and Nationality Act of 1965, which ushered in the era of the "New Americans," would soon bring thousands of newcomers from the Philippines.

THE IMMIGRATION AND NATIONALITY ACT OF 1965

The Immigration and Nationality Act of 1965 altered previous immigration policies in key ways. Over a three-year period, the legislation eliminated national origins quotas and instituted a series of preferences based largely on two goals: relieving occupational shortages and achieving family reunification. The 1965 law capped annual immigration from the Eastern Hemisphere at 170,000 per year and imposed a 20,000-per-country maximum; the Western Hemisphere received 120,000 slots per year.

Seven rank-ordered preferences based on "family" and "occupation," each allocated a percentage of the annual maximum, were established. Under "family" preferences, immigrants who became citizens might "petition" the U.S. government for immigrant visas for their adult unmarried and married children and their siblings. While waiting to become a citizen, a permanent resident might be joined by a spouse and unmarried children. Once these newcomers themselves qualified for citizenship, that family's "chain of migration" continued to lengthen.

Sponsors of the 1965 Act believed that the comparatively small numbers of Asian-born citizens present in the United States in the mid-1960s would limit the potential for immigration under family preferences. They were wrong. Although many new Filipino American families were initially established under the "professional" (third) preference when Filipino physicians and nurses immigrated in large numbers, family ties soon became even more critical.

Significant exceptions also permitted many Filipinos to enter *outside* of the preference system and the yearly country limit of 20,000. Despite the Philippine's 100-per-year quota, spouses and minor children of citizens had nonetheless qualified for immediate admission under the McCarran-Walter Act of 1952. The 1965 Act continued this practice and added parents of a citizen to those exempt from annual limits. Filipinos admitted as exempt actually exceeded the number admitted annually under the preference system in the late 1970s and early 1980s.

In practice, post-1965 Filipino immigrants combined use of exempt categories and both occupational and family preferences to move their extended family networks to the United States. Although only 2,000 "professional" visas were theoretically available each year, Filipinos who came under that preference soon brought not only immediate family members to join them, but also, like other new immigrants, enthusiastically sponsored other relatives, especially their siblings, prompting analysts to label the law "the brothers and sisters act" (Reimers 1991: 81). In addition, Filipinos who had become citizens after 1946 and their non-quota, immigrant spouses also became eligible to bring their siblings.

Between 1966 and 1991, the last year during which the 1965 Act remained in force, more Filipinos came under exempt and preference-driven family reunification provisions than under occupational preferences which accounted for no more than 10.3 percent of the annual total of immigration from the Philippines during the years between 1977 and 1991.

In addition to qualifying for immigrant visas prior to entering the United States, Filipinos could also become immigrants in two other ways. Many who originally arrived on temporary, non-immigrant visas as students, tourists, and temporary workers also became immigrants by "adjusting their status" and obtaining the "green card" given to permanent residents. In addition, the United States and Philippine governments jointly permitted Filipinos to continue to enlist in the U.S. Navy during these years. Recalling his "Coming to America," Nestor Palugod Enriquez, who enlisted in 1958 and scored higher than most Filipinos on the navy's occupational aptitude test, explained why: "I will never forget the first question: 'blank is to football, as this is to basketball' . . . My hours of junkie reading about sports and life in the U.S. paid handsomely that day. . . . I used my high-test score to win a place in the U.S. Submarine School in New London [Connecticut] and a better job" (Enriquez 1997: 13). Each year some of these men qualified for naturalization and thus became able to sponsor their family members' immigration.

During the ten years immediately after passage of the 1965 Act, over 230,000 Filipinos immigrated to the United States, more than doubling the Filipino American population of 1960. Finding positions in big-city hospitals and establishing practices in small towns, Filipino physicians were among the most visible of the newcomers. By the mid-1970s, however, doctors in the United States were no longer deemed in short supply, and the previously warm welcome extended under U.S. immigration law to foreign medical graduates (FMGs) from the Philippines disappeared.

THE IMMIGRATION OF FILIPINO HEALTH CARE PROFESSIONALS

A decade after the third wave of Filipino immigration began, the economic optimism of 1965, with its 4.5 percent unemployment rate, evaporated. The economy stagnated and unemployment reached 8.5 percent in 1975. The previously pressing need for foreign professionals now appeared to threaten American job seekers. Medical associations and lobbyists vigorously pressed a case against foreign medical graduates: bringing FMGs to the United States drained sending countries of badly needed health care providers; "high [FMG] failure rates" on national medical exams were used to question their competence; and, although doctors were still in short supply in some areas of the nation, uneven geographical distribution rather than overall scarcity was blamed (Ong and Liu 1994: 59–61).

Restricting the Entry of Filipino Physicians: The Eilberg Act of 1976 and the Health Professions Educational Assistance Act of 1976

In consequence, the United States modified the Immigration and Nationality Act of 1965 by enacting two laws that significantly affected the immigration of Filipino physicians: the Eilberg Act of 1976 and the Health Professions Educational Assistance Act of 1976. The Eilberg Act required immigrants entering under the professional preference to have a firm job offer in hand from an employer in the United States unless their occupation had been certified to be in short supply on the Department of Labor's Schedule A.

Although the Eilberg Act did not target foreign physicians by name, the Health Professions Educational Assistance Act (HPEAA) of 1976 did, declaring "there is no longer an insufficient number of physicians and surgeons in the United States" (Reimers 1991: 88). The Act mandated removal of FMGs from Schedule A and thereby subjected them to the provisions of the Eilberg Act. The HPEAA also required foreign physicians to pass either the National Board of Medical Examiners' Examination or the Visa Qualifying Examination and demonstrate "competency in oral and written English" before qualifying for admission (Ong and Liu 1994: 60).

The 1976 measures significantly curtailed the immigration of Filipino physicians. Annual numbers plunged by more than 50 percent—from over 700 per year before the 1976 acts to about 300 in subsequent years. Those who did come faced narrowing job options. Their first employers would now likely be the inner-city hospitals least attractive to U.S. medical graduates—hospitals able to qualify for waivers permitting them to hire FMGs because of their critical and continuing personnel shortages.

Expanding and Controlling the Supply
of Filipino Nurses

As discussed in Chapter 2, owing to operation of the Exchange Visitor Program, nurses from the Philippines had already become a presence in U.S. health care before 1965. After passage of the 1965 Act and the addition of foreign nursing graduates (FNGs) to Schedule A, their immigration soared far higher. Like Filipino physicians, most Filipino nurses came as professional preference immigrants during the decade following passage of the 1965 Act. Others migrated under a temporary visa and later had their status adjusted.

By 1970, 43 percent of the FNGs coming to the United States were from the Philippines, followed by 24 percent from Canada, 15 percent from Britain, and 4 percent from Korea. Between 1965 and 1972, the number of Filipino nurses working in U.S. hospitals grew by 400 percent and was typically more than double that of Philippine-trained doctors. In 1975, for example, the United States admitted 1,362 registered nurses from the Philippines, in contrast with 572 physicians.

By 1976, the same forces working to limit migration of Filipino physicians began to affect Filipino nurses, although never to as great an extent. In that year, the Department of Labor removed all health care professionals, except dieticians, from Schedule A. Nurses, like doctors, would need a job offer in the United States before qualifying for an immigrant visa. To an even greater extent with nurses than with physicians, inner-city hospitals retained a strong interest in recruiting nurses in the Philippines. Sometimes employers relied on those already on staff to recommend family members and friends for vacancies, but many metropolitan hospitals, faced with ongoing shortages, especially in the 3:00 P.M. to 11:00 P.M. shift and in critical care units, placed ads in Manila newspapers, worked with Philippine employment agencies, and sent their own recruiters across the Pacific.

After 1976, temporary work visas became the major route into the United States for migrating Filipino nurses. In fact, because the immigration of FNGs has been severely restricted since 1976, some Filipino physicians have acquired nursing degrees in the hope of making $26,000 as a beginning staff nurse in the United States and ultimately finding a way to become a permanent resident. In 1988, 6,239 nurses from the Philippines arrived on temporary work visas.

The migration of Filipino FNGs under temporary work visas continued in the 1990s under a pilot program that gave U.S. hospitals the ability to recruit an unlimited number of nurses under a new, temporary work (H1A) visa category. The nurses were in turn promised that they could apply for a green card once in the United States. In 1995, 5,306 registered nurses from the Philippines were admitted on H1A visas—81.5 percent of the 6,512 registered nurses who entered in that year. Recruited by a Houston hospital in the early 1990s, Rachel explained both her decision to become a nurse and to work in the United States: " 'Since I was small, I liked nursing. I used to take care of my grandmother, and she always said I would be a good nurse. . . . [But] it was the lure of money' that drew [Rachel]" to the United States. Soon after arriving, she was sending $600 home each month (Kolker 1996: 6A).

The prospect of building a new life in America, or, at the very least, of earning money with which to improve their own and their families' lives in the Philippines continued to entice Filipino nurses into temporary employment in the United States until the mid-1990s. But, after Congress refused to extend the H1A visa program, Filipino nurses with H1A visas who had not yet obtained a green card faced the prospect that they would have to return to the Philippines. A backlog of two years in applications for the coveted card, as well as stricter penalties for "overstaying" one's visa, seemed likely to force many back to the Philippines—for most an unwelcome prospect. Said Rachel, thinking of herself as lucky to have a green card, but also worrying about her less fortunate colleagues: "If you have tasted a good life, I don't think somebody else would want to go home (either), . . . If you can afford to buy good food, dress nicely, and buy a car, it's like the movies—something only rich people can do in the Philippines. . . . In a way, you can't blame Filipinos when they want to stay" (Kolker 1996: 6A).

More generally, although Filipino nurses working in the United States do earn far more than nurses in the Philippines, not all who have migrated as registered nurses have been able to practice their profession at that level because of licensing requirements. In addition, despite long years of work in U.S. hospitals, Filipino nurses are only half as likely as nurses in general to secure management-level positions.

UNDOCUMENTED AND FRAUDULENT ENTRY

Simultaneous with the persistent need for Filipino nurses as temporary workers in the early 1980s, critics of changing national demographics raised an alarm over the scale of immigration to the United States and the number of undocumented aliens present illegally in the country. Immigrants from the Philippines were by no means a major target of concern—that dubious distinction fell to Mexicans and Central Americans. But government efforts to remedy the perceived crisis affected thousands of Filipinos. Unlike Mexicans and Central Americans who typically entered "without inspection" by walking or wading across the U.S.-Mexican border, Filipinos generally arrived as visitors or temporary workers and "overstayed" the limits of their temporary visas. Other Filipinos, along with Mexicans and Caribbean and Latin Americans, bought false marriage papers or contracted fraudulent marriages as costly solutions to entry problems.

The Immigration Reform and Control Act (IRCA) and the Immigration Marriage Fraud Amendments, both enacted in 1986, sought to check these practices. The IRCA took a three-part approach to the problem of illegal immigration: increased enforcement, employer sanctions, and legalization. Most important for Filipinos, the legalization program permitted undocumented aliens who had resided in the United States continuously but illegally since January 1, 1982 to apply for temporary residency, and then, after a nineteen-month interval, for permanent residency. Between 1989 and 1996, 27,696 Filipinos were legalized and received immigrant status under the IRCA—a minuscule fraction of the almost 2.7 million legalized under IRCA and 6.7 percent of Filipino migration during these years. The Immigration Marriage Fraud Amendments made those qualifying for immigrant status on the basis of a marriage of less than two years "conditional immigrants" and required a Filipina seeking to become the "mail order" bride of an American citizen to have met him in person before their marriage.

The Immigration Marriage Fraud Amendments of 1986 neither kept Susana Remerata, a businessman's daughter and a college graduate, from emigrating, nor did they prevent her death at the hands of Timothy Blackwell, the husband she met after having her photograph published in *Asian Encounters* (a mail-order bride magazine). Soon after her arrival in the United States, twenty-five-year-old Susana Remerata Blackwell charged her husband with assault. Claiming that she was "cold, distant, wouldn't talk much and slept fully clothed," he, in turn, filed for an annulment, a move that could have jeopardized her immigrant status, and demanded that she repay the $10,000 that his travel and her immigration had cost him. In March 1995, outside the courtroom where their case was being heard, Blackwell shot and killed Susana, then seven months pregnant by "a Filipino gang member who had molested her." Two other Filipinas, including forty-seven-year-old Phoebe Dizon who had taken her in, also died. In May 1996, Blackwell was convicted and sentenced to life in prison (Wilson and Byrnes 1995: 1, 16, 17; Egan 1996: 12; "Veloria Applauds Regulations . . ." 1997: 4).

Of course, not all mail-order brides court disaster. In her mid-forties, "widowed and alone," Lourdes "Lory" Jung bought space and placed her own photo in a magazine. After corresponding with eight men, she talked with Ewald Jung by telephone, met him in the Philippines, and married him within the year. "[I]n time, she got bored. All she did was sit around the house all day." Contemplating the "barely landscaped" yards of their home in Sarasota, Florida, Lory Jung decided to plant a garden—"banana trees, bromeliads, apple trees, peppers, papaya trees, sweet potatoes and a sea of pineapple plants . . . beneath an immense jacaranda tree" in the front, and "huge gourds hanging from vines, plus grapes, melons, okra, strawberries, citrus, garlic, yucca, avocado and several exotic vegetable varieties . . . from the Philippines" in the back. "When I go outside and look at the garden, . . . it makes me proud." Ewald Jung remarked philosophically, "She works too hard, but she doesn't listen to me, . . . I can't stop her from playing in the mud" (Levy 1996: 1–2E).

Despite Lory Jung's happy outcome, the experiences of Susan Remerata Blackwell and other abused mail-order brides have typically received more extensive media coverage, thus prompting the federal government to intervene once again. In the late 1990s, Congress enacted legislation requiring mail-order bride businesses to provide prospective brides with written information, in their native language, concerning "laws dealing with residency status, penalties for marriage fraud, rights of immigrants who suffer spousal battery, and about the mail order business itself" ("Veloria Applauds Regulations . . ." 1997: 4). Whether such provisions can stop Filipinas from following their dreams for a better life, if not their hearts, to the United States remains unlikely.

THE IMMIGRATION ACT OF 1990 AND ITS IMPACT

In the late 1980s, even as the IRCA began the process of legalization for almost 2.7 million undocumented aliens, analysts and lawmakers turned to broader questions of immigration policy and law. Although some called for restriction on cultural and racial grounds, those concerned with keeping the United States well positioned in a highly competitive world economy through easier importation of highly skilled foreign workers carried the day. At the same time, post-1965 immigrants and their advocates argued for the retention of family reunification as a central premise of U.S. immigration. The Immigration Act of 1990, like the 1965 Act, combined these two strands into law.

Changes in the Preference System

Since passage of the Immigration Act of 1990, immigration to the United States from the Philippines has remained a substantial component in annual immigration totals. In both 1994 and 1995, the Philippines continued to be the second largest source of U.S. immigration, trailing only Mexico.

From 1992 through 1996, 275,826 Filipinos immigrated to the United States under exempt, family-sponsored, and employment-based categories, an increase of 32,250 over the 243,576 who arrived between 1987 and 1991. Immediate family members of U.S. citizens accounted for 51.5 percent of the total. Under family-sponsored preferences, an additional 30.3 percent entered. Under employment-based preferences, 18.2 percent qualified for admission.

Since enactment of the 1990 law, the numbers arriving under employment-based preferences have grown substantially. After the migration of health care professionals was limited in 1976, Filipino immigrants arriving under occupational preferences failed to surpass 4,100 in any year between 1977 and 1991. By contrast, the number of employment-based preference immigrants who arrived in 1993—11,882—is larger than the number for *any* year recorded under the 1965 Act—even during the peak years of the early 1970s. Under the 1990 Act, 9,800 Filipinos can be admitted each year on the basis of job skills—more than double the 4,000 admitted annually under the 1965 Act. Currently, Filipino immigrants use all the employment-based slots available to them. While *all* countries now have a backlog of unskilled workers waiting for visas, only the Philippines and the People's Republic of China also have a backlog of skilled workers awaiting admission.

To a lesser extent, the change from the 1965 Act to the 1990 Act also altered the pattern of annual admissions under family-sponsored preferences. Fewer immigrant visas are available each year for the brothers and sisters of U.S. citizens, a reduction likely to dishearten countless siblings in the Philippines whose wait for a visa is now approaching twenty years. In contrast, Filipino immigrants who have permanent resident status will find it easier to bring spouses and children to join them because of a substantial increase in this category.

The Naturalization of Filipino World War II Veterans

The Immigration Act of 1990 contained one additional section of vital interest to Filipino Americans. Section 450 made naturalization available to surviving Philippine-born World War II veterans of the U.S. Armed Forces in the Far East, the Philippine Army, the Philippine Scout Rangers, and recognized guerilla units who served during the period between September 1, 1939 and December 31, 1946.

The question of citizenship for Filipinos serving in *Philippine* units has long been at issue. Becuase President Franklin D. Roosevelt incorporated the Philippine military into the U.S. armed forces by executive order, proponents argue that Filipino veterans are entitled to citizenship and its benefits. Advocates also maintain that Filipino veterans fought side-by-side with Americans in defense of the Philippines, which, although a "commonwealth," was still a possession of the United States, not an independent nation during the war. In 1948, the prospects for veterans in the Philippines worsened when they were specifically precluded from claiming citizenship on the basis of the World War II service.

The continuing quest for justice for Filipino veterans gained momentum during the 1980s, becoming, in effect, a Filipino American redress movement, a counterpart to the Japanese American movement for redress stemming from the wartime relocation of Pacific Coast Japanese Americans. The provision in the 1990 Act giving Filipino veterans the right to naturalize constituted a partial victory for redress advocates.

During the first two years of the program's implementation, aged Filipino veterans, some virtually penniless, were required to come to the United States to apply for citizenship. Seventy-five years old in 1992, Pablo Dungo "sold his house and his farm to come . . . [W]hen he reached San Francisco International Airport, he . . . had no friends, and no family to contact." His intent was clear. Once a citizen, he would be able to "petition his wife and ten children." Another Filipino veteran, former Philippine police department colonel Demetrio C. Dela Cruz, who at the age of 14 joined the U.S. 45th Infantry Regiment in the Philippines, said: "I didn't want to come here really, . . . but I eventually decided to do it for my children, . . . They really want to come here" (Picache 1992: 24–29). On October 6, 1992, Filipino veterans became eligible for naturalization in the Philippines and the deadline for application was extended for two years.

Citizenship did not, however, confer full veterans' benefits on those newly naturalized under Section 450. The issue remains intertwined with the continuing problems associated with 1996 retrenchments in benefits for legal immigrants, and will be discussed in Chapter 8, "The Future of Filipino Immigration."

Irrespective of how they have come, once in the United States, these Filipino immigrants and their children have together created new lives, combining the imported with the acquired to produce new, multiple, and diverse meanings subsumed within the label, "Filipino American."

4

Filipino Values and Customs in an American Setting

Transported from the Philippines and altered in America, Filipino values and customs serve multiple functions in the lives of Filipino Americans by simultaneously preserving, reinterpreting, and reinventing Philippine cultural elements into the redefined, varied identity that is Filipino American. This chapter explores five cultural elements that contribute to that ongoing definition of Filipino American: values; names and naming practices; foods; social gatherings, festivals, and religious celebrations; and dress and domestic decor.

VALUES

Deeply rooted in culture and religion, Filipino values and customs emphasize respect for, loyalty to, and dependence upon the family. The Philippine bilateral kinship system traces descent and defines blood kin through both paternal and maternal lines. Ideally, maintaining kin bonds takes precedence over achieving individual goals, for personal identity and self-worth flow directly from familial relationships. While the nuclear family of parents and children establishes primary loyalties, the inclusion of extended family members who are related by blood and fictive family members who are related by rights and obligations can enlarge the Filipino family well beyond the size of the typical American family. Given the centrality of family relationships and networks, the striving of recent immigrants to bring their relatives to the United States is not surprising.

As they raise their children, Filipino parents strive to cultivate a sense of *hiya* (shame) within each child's *loob* (inner self). Properly internalized, *hiya* will function as a mechanism of self-control throughout life, encouraging a Filipino to avoid unacceptable actions which might cause the loss of *amor propio* (self-respect) in the eyes of others. Labelled *walang hiya* in slang, the Filipino who lacks that sense of shame that places high value on winning the approval and avoiding the censure of others within the family or larger community will risk losing acceptance. The withdrawal of such approval is considered a severe sanction.

Parents also encourage their children to acknowledge their debts to others with appropriate gratitude and respect. First and foremost, an internalized debt of gratitude, called *utang na loob*, is owed to one's mother (*inay* or *nanay*) and father (*itay* or *tatay*), whom one can never adequately repay, and to others within and outside the family from whom one has received unsolicited favors. Traditionally, *utang na loob* is given visible form in the customary greeting offered to an older person and in speech. The younger person takes the hand of an older person and brings it to his or her own forehead as if asking for a blessing while saying *mano po* in greeting. A younger person will also use the interjection *po* or *ho* in talking with an elder to show respect. Such forms of respect would be typical in a young Filipino's relationships with parents, grandfather (*lolo*) and grandmother (*lola*), an aunt (*tita*) or an uncle (*tito*), a godmother (*nanang*) or a godfather (*ninong*), and other older relatives. A debt of gratitude, defined as *utang na loob*, requires that appropriate, continuing repayment in the form of deference, obedience, cooperation, and sacrifice be made to family members who are owed the debt.

The bonds of family in the Philippines extend beyond blood and marital relationships by the practice of *compadrinazgo*, which creates fictive kin ties through sponsorship at important events in a person's life such as baptism, confirmation, and marriage. For example, at a baptism in the Philippines, as in many other countries, a spiritual bond is established between the godparent and the godchild. Godparenthood establishes a vertical relationship called *padrinazgo*. But, the ties being created at a baptism do not stop with this familiar relationship. In addition, the parents of the child being baptized become ritually linked to the sponsors as ritual co-parents in a horizontal relationship among adults called *compadrazgo* and refer to each other in future interaction as *compadre* and *comadre*. Typically, those chosen as sponsors in Filipino American families include blood kin and those who are already close family friends, but, as in the Philippines, sponsors may also be chosen in the hope of forging relationships that can later prove socially, economically, or politically useful.

Rights and obligations flow from these ritual kinship bonds. Filipinos expect kin group members to be loyal to and supportive of one another. In his 1970s research on Filipino Americans living in Salinas, California, anthropologist Edwin B. Almirol noted that, in addition to buying a baptismal gift and paying part of the expenses for a baptism, *compadres* and *comadres* typically continued to give their godchildren gifts on birthdays, at Christmas, and on other important occasions such as graduations and weddings. In addition, they often assisted in preparations for parties for their godchildren and brought food and provided help when their godchildrens' parents became ill. Kin group members were also crucial to the process of immigration—signing immigration petitions and affidavits of support promising that a newcomer would not become a public charge, sending money for transportation, providing housing for new arrivals, and assisting in their search for employment.

Filipinos also prize *pakikisama*, the ability to get along with others. Filipinos are expected to seek consensus and defer to the wishes of the group rather than pressing individual preferences. To preserve group accord, Filipinos typically try to avoid confrontation and abstain from expressing opinions or providing information that might be disruptive of cohesion.

Although *compadrinazgo* and *pakikisama* would appear to promote harmony among Filipinos in the Philippines and the United States, the customs associated with these values can also exclude as well as include. Whether defined as family, extended kin network, club or voluntary association, or in any other way, the group includes only those considered a part of that group, and, thus, excludes others—even if those outsiders are themselves Filipinos or Filipino Americans. Hence, the strictures of rights and obligations and of loyalty and harmony can simultaneously encourage both harmony and discord. For example, Filipinos customarily hold that because family and kin groups take precedence over other loyalties and associations, the demands of anyone or anything outside should necessarily be subordinate. Loyalty to one's own group may, in consequence, foster rivalry with other groups. In Filipino American organizations, for example, bonds based on kinship or on provincial origin can sometimes define preference for or opposition to candidates for office in acrimonious election contests.

Little actual research on the transfer, perpetuation, adaptation, and abandonment of Filipino values among Filipino Americans has been conducted, but anthropologist Enya P. Flores-Meiser suggests that the rapid pace of change experienced by Filipinos in the Philippines has brought Western notions of "competition, individualism, and material success" into conflict with traditional Filipino values (Flores-Meiser 1995: 468). One may speculate that such conflicts permeate the values carried by Filipino immigrants to the United States and that additional conflicts are generated in the United States when the differing values of Filipino parents and their American-reared children collide.

NAMES AND NAMING PRACTICES

Formal Filipino names reflect parentage, kinship ties, national heritage and customs, and ethnic blending. At birth, each Filipino typically receives three names—a first or given name, a middle name, and a family or surname. In addition, Filipino boys and girls often acquire nicknames that follow them into adulthood and are sometimes considered ethnically distinctive by non-Filipinos.

Filipino family names reflect the nation's diverse heritage. Some can be considered indigenous—for example, Bacdayan and Macapagal. Other names, such as Cojuangco and Sylianco, derive from the Chinese and reflect centuries of Chinese trade with the islands. The Spanish, too, added their surnames, not typically through intermarriage, for relatively few Spanish or *peninsulares* either came to the Philippines or married *indios*, but rather through custom and edict. During the first two and a half centuries of Spanish control, some Filipinos acquired family names having religious significance, such as *Cruz* (cross) or *Santos* (saints). After 1849, non-religiously connected Spanish surnames such as Gonzales, Alamar, and Lopez came to predominate. In that year, the Philippines' Spanish governor mandated the adoption of surnames by all Filipinos to facilitate colonial administrative matters. Each Filipino family without a surname chose one from the specific pages of an alphabetical listing of Spanish surnames sent to their town. Thus, if a town was sent the "B" and "C" pages of the list, the Filipinos in that town all acquired surnames beginning with "B" and "C." Of course, a century and a half of marriage and migration have virtually eliminated the possibility of matching surnames to places of origin.

As in Spain and in other countries colonized by the Spanish, the family name of a Filipino's mother becomes part of the name of each of her children. During the Spanish colonial era, the mother's family name was added to the end of the child's name. The Philippine national hero, José Rizal y Mercado, took "Rizal" from his father and "Mercado" from his mother. Thus, in Filipino families, brothers and sisters share both a middle and a last name. After the United States' acquisition of the Philippines, the mother's family name typically became the child's middle name. Hence, since the beginning of the twentieth century, José Rizal's full name usually appeared as José

Mercado Rizal or José M. Rizal. After marriage, a Filipino wife customarily adopts her husband's family name as her surname, drops her mother's family name as her middle name, and moves her own surname to the middle position. Thus, Corazon Sumulong Cojuangco became Corazon Cojuangco Aquino upon her marriage to Benigno S. Aquino, Jr.

Like family or surnames, Filipino first names also reflect the religious and cultural differences of the islands' past. A given name such as Ali Muhamad testifies to the continuing strength of Islam as religion and culture in the southern Philippines, despite the fact that only five percent of the Filipino population is Islamic. Early in the twentieth century, Filipino Catholics often consulted a religious calendar and gave a newborn the name of the saint celebrated on the day of the baby's birth. Less typically, a son might be given his father's first name. Thus, because of the Philippines' religious and cultural heritage, most Filipino first names have typically been Spanish, but in both the Philippines and in the United States, English or "American" versions have become increasingly popular: Antonio, now Anthony; Juan, now John. After World War II, a number of grateful parents gave a son the name "MacArthur," after the famous general. Sometimes, all children in a family are given alliterative first names starting with the same letter or syllable— Arturo, Arnelle, and Arleen—or a child may be given a name which combines syllables from parents' or grandparents' first names—for example, Arlyn, the daughter of Arturo and Erlinda, and her sister, Carmel, named after their grandmothers, Carmen and Eluteria.

Few Filipinos reach adulthood without becoming known by a nickname. A girl's nickname often ends in "ing"—Purita becomes "Puring"; Trinidad is called "Trining." In contrast, a boy's nickname frequently ends in "oy"— Benigno is known as "Ninoy"; Pablo responds to "Pacoy." Some Filipino nicknames shorten a name while retaining a recognizable root, as American nicknames often do—"Cory" for Corazon; "Berto" for Roberto; "Mo" for Guillermo. At other times, the connection disappears—"Popsy" for Perpetua; "Bimbo" for Sabas; "Pido" for Pedro. Or, a "junior" might be known by a nickname combining a diminutive with "Boy"—Teodoro Locsin, Jr., a Harvard Law School graduate and advisor to Philippine President Corazon Aquino, is called "Teddy Boy" by his friends. While nicknames continue to be given in Filipino American families, adolescents growing up in the United States often prefer "American" ones—nicknames which do not label them as "different." Ethnically distinctive naming practices may also decline over time as young Filipino Americans intermarry with others.

Because of the Spanish derivation of many Filipino first and family names, Filipinos have sometimes been confused with Spanish-speaking Americans.

Almost every Filipino American family has received bulk mailings printed in Spanish rather than English, despite the fact that few Filipinos speak, read, or write Spanish.

FOODS

Like Philippine history, Filipino cuisine reflects the blending over time of Malay, Islamic, Chinese, Spanish, and American influences. Owing to colonial ties that flourished for more than two hundred years under Spanish rule, elements deriving from Mexico have also been detected.

The Philippines' Malay past is most apparent in preparations using coconut and coconut milk, and in *lechon*, a whole pig roasted over charcoal and hot stones and served with a tangy liver sauce which was prepared in the pre-Spanish era after the harvest or hunt. In the Philippines and the United States, *lechon* still ranks as the most celebratory of Filipino dishes, but today it is more often catered than prepared in a backyard pit. Three well-known regional specialties may also be Malay in heritage: *kare-kare*, oxtails stewed in peanut sauce; *pinakbet*, a boiled stew of vegetables, greens, and pork seasoned with *bagoong*, a fermented shrimp paste; and *dinuguan*, a rich, dark stew made with pork meat and blood flavored with hot peppers and *patis*, a thin, salty shrimp or fish sauce called *nuoc mam* by the Vietnamese and *nampla* by the Thai.

Chinese influence is tasted in several well-known dishes: *pancit*, typically made with *sotanghon*, transparent bean noodles, is cooked with so many combinations and variations of meat, seafood, and vegetables that contests have been held in the United States to award the best; *lumpia*, resembling the Chinese egg roll, can be "Shanghai" or fried as in typical Chinese restaurants, "fresh" as a spring roll, and *ubod*, made with hearts of palm. The dipping sauces served with *lumpia* also parallel Chinese accompaniments.

The Spanish brought tomatoes, garlic, and the technique of sautéing (*guisado*) them with onions in oil. *Paella Valenciana*, a melange of meats and seafood generally reserved for special occasions, and *leche flan*, an egg custard dessert made in a caramel-lined pan, are also Spanish in origin. The Spanish connection may have further influenced Filipino cooking by bringing Mexican influences to the Philippines. For more than two hundred years, galleons regularly sailed between Manila and Acapulco. Culinary historians suspect that the paste of vinegar, oil, chili, herbs, and spices, which flavors such Mexican dishes as *puerco en adobo* and *chuletas de puerco adobadas*, made its way to the Philippines to be used in the veritable Filipino national dish, *adobo*, a pork, chicken, and/or seafood stew cooked in vinegar, soy sauce, garlic and pepper.

The Filipino version of stuffed chicken, *rellenong manok*, combines ground meat such as ham, pork, chicken, and frankfurters with raisins, bread crumbs, onion, and sweet relish for the stuffing that is baked with whole hard-boiled eggs and pieces of hot sausage in the chicken. All of these ingredients are readily available. Less so is the goat meat needed for a favorite Filipino stew, *kalderetta*; lamb or beef is usually recommended as a substitute. Craving bittermelon (*ampalaya* or *amargoso*), a green, wrinkly skinned, gourd-like vegetable, some Filipinos have proudly grown their own in the United States, carefully nurturing seeds from year to year, rather than settle for the canned variety.

Popular desserts at Filipino American gatherings include *bibingka*, a sweet, sticky rice cake made with coconut milk and topped with a broiled layer of thick coconut cream and brown sugar, and *halo-halo*, a sundae made with sweetened garbanzo and kidney beans, sweetened fruit such as jackfruit (*nangka*), strips of sweetened, preserved coconut in syrup (*macapuno*), crushed ice, vanilla or mocha ice cream, and evaporated milk.

As the Filipino population in the United States has grown, the complexity of Filipino cooking and the availability of Filipino ingredients have increased dramatically. Early in the twentieth century, within almost entirely male enclaves, Filipinos reconstructed dishes tasted in memory, using ginger and souring agents such as vinegar, tamarind, or lemon juice. Since the 1970s, recipes developed from pre-migration memories, clipped from Philippine magazines, and hand-copied for friends have been supplemented by Filipino cookbooks such as Eleanor R. Laquian and Irene D. Sobreviña's *Filipino Cooking Here and Abroad* (1977) and and Marilyn Ranada Donato's *Philippine Cooking in America* (1977). More recently, Manhattan-based cook, caterer, author, dancer, and choreographer Reynaldo G. Alejandro has set a high standard and penetrated the trade book market with *The Philippine Cookbook* (1985), which also examines the cultural heritage of Filipino foods and lists mail-order sources for ingredients in eleven states and Canada. Recipes also appear regularly in Filipino American magazines and newspapers throughout the United States.

Filipino American restaurant options have also expanded. Although they do not rival Chinese, Thai, and Vietnamese restaurants and groceries in number, Filipino counterparts can now be found in most major and many smaller American communities. Joni's and Elena's, two Philippine restaurant chains, have opened popular branches in Honolulu. Goldilocks, a Philippine chain of restaurant and bake shops, has expanded operations to California.

Chef Reynaldo G. Alejandro demonstrates the preparation of a Filipino dish. Courtesy of Reynaldo G. Alejandro.

Said satisfied customer, Jose Vivar, who headed to a Goldilocks Restaurant directly after flying back with his wife and daughter from a visit to the Philippines: "It (Goldilocks) reminds me of home. . . . The food here is just as good as the Goldilocks in Manila" (Orquiola 1992: 31–35). At New York City's hot "Filipino *moderne*" Cendrillon, chef/owner Romy Dorotan and his wife, Amy Besa, observe that their rave-review-winning restaurant "isn't about authenticity. . . . We capture the flavor and spirit of filipino food, but we're more broadly based and would like to be more inventive" (Kiester 1996: 41).

Filipino food products processed and packed on the West Coast have also become popular alternatives to mother's cooking. Goldilocks sells its U.S.-processed and -packed porridge, soup, sauce, and cake mixes via mail order and advertises "A Tradition of Good Taste" and "authentic home-cooked flavors" within reach of Filipino American kitchens anywhere in the nation ("Goldilocks Goes Mass-Market" 1996, 72). Specializing in frozen Filipino foods, Primo Quesada's Ramar International Corporation has brought mango, *macapuno* (sweetened coconut), and *ube* (purple yam) ice cream under the Magnolia/Mr. Sorbetes brand, *tocino* (cured pork), *longganisa* (Filipino-style sausage), and *lumpiang Shanghai* (fried Filipino egg roll) to California consumers—not all of them Filipino American—since 1978.

Today, in both the Philippines and the United States, complex traditional dishes most likely appear at special occasions and on restaurant menus. In everyday cooking, boiled rice, fish, simple stews, and noodle dishes compete with hamburgers, french fries, fried chicken, convenience products, and franchise food in the busy households of immigrant parents and American-reared children.

SOCIAL GATHERINGS, FESTIVALS, AND RELIGIOUS CELEBRATIONS

Because of the centrality of the family, Filipino Americans make important family events and milestones the occasion for celebration, just as they do in the Philippines. Parties mark baptisms, first communions, graduations, and birthdays. Although wealthier Filipino Americans sometimes utilize hotel or commercial party facilities, these gatherings are generally held at home and often inspire more elaborate food preparation than typical in a household's daily routine. Mothers make their own versions of *pancit* and *leche flan, comadres* bring *lumpia* and *bibingka,* and, where skill and feasibility coincide, fathers and their *compadres* tend a *lechon* slow roasting in a backyard pit. The Philippines' San Miguel beer may even replace ever-popular American brands for the day. Relatives living at some distance often time vacations to coincide with parties being given at the homes they will visit, knowing that family members not seen on a regular basis will be there.

For most Filipino Americans who are predominantly Catholic, a family wedding combines religious devotion and gala festivity. The wedding itself is typically a religious ceremony held in a church, although in the case of a "mixed" marriage—Filipino American Protestant bride and Jewish American groom, for example, the ceremony, presided over by both a minister and a rabbi, might take place on "neutral" turf—in a hotel ballroom or a community center. If preserving traditional Filipino customs is important to the bride and groom and their families, a Filipino American church ceremony is likely to include the tying of a cord around the couple as a symbol of their union. Unlike customary practice in the United States that makes the bride's parents responsible for much of the expense of a wedding, the reverse is true in the Philippines where, traditionally, the groom's parents are expected to pay for the reception. Anecdotal evidence appears to indicate that Filipino American families typically follow the American custom of the bride's parents paying, especially if the groom is not a Filipino American, or less frequently the bride's parents share the cost with the groom's parents. Regardless of who pays for it, the reception will usually include a lavish dinner, live music

American-born Ray Paul Dimalanta and Ruby Mendoza incorporated the Filipino cord tradition into their 1979 Seattle, Washington, wedding ceremony. Courtesy of Purita Aquino Dimalanta.

for dancing, and perhaps even the traditional custom of pinning of cash to the clothes of the bride and groom.

In the Philippines, where goings and comings across the Pacific have long been occasions of sorrow and joy, Filipinos give *despedida* (farewell) and *bienvenida* (welcome) parties when someone special departs or arrives. As they have grown old in the United States, some Filipino immigrants have marked the progress of their aging by planning a final trip "home." In 1987, eighty-two-year-old Filipino Methodist minister Fernando A. Laxamana, who arrived in the United States in the mid-1920s to attend Dakota Wesleyan College, planned a trip that, given his failing health, he expected would be his last. He happily anticipated the dinner for 150 that his sister intended to host in his honor. (Rev. Laxamana died in DeKalb, Illinois, on February 11, 1996.)

Filipino American festivities also include national, provincial, and religious celebrations that bring community members together. First and foremost among these is Rizal Day, celebrated on December 30 in memory of Dr. José M. Rizal (1861–1896), an ophthalmic surgeon, novelist, sculptor, poet, and linguist who focused national and international attention on the particulars of Spanish misrule and became the Philippines' national hero after his execution in Manila by a Spanish firing squad on December 30, 1896, at the onset of the movement for Philippine independence. Since 1898, Filipinos in the Philippines and abroad have commemorated the anniversary of Rizal's death. Since the 1920s each major center of Filipino residence in the United States has hosted a Rizal Day banquet and dance—sometimes more than one if sponsoring clubs and organizations were unable to agree on the site or the arrangements. In more recent years, the growing numbers of Filipino Americans within a metropolitan area can necessitate multiple locations in the city and its suburbs. Typically, the festivities have always included a lavish dinner, live music, the playing of national anthems, speeches by dignitaries, songs and performances, and, without fail, a dramatic recitation of Rizal's farewell, his "Ultima Adios." The crowning of a Rizal Day queen from among the candidates of rival organizations has also long been an important tradition. Philippine Independence Day on June 12 and Philippine-American Friendship Day on July 4 are often marked in Filipino American communities with programs combining patriotic and cultural elements.

Provincial loyalties also remain significant among Filipino immigrants. Many join a club or association on this basis. In the Chicago area, for example, Filipinos from the province of Aklan founded the Aklan Cultural and Educational Foundation in the early 1980s to sponsor humanitarian projects in Aklan and in other parts of the Philippines and to preserve the customs of the province for themselves and for their Filipino American children. The most important is *Ati-Atihan*, a raucous festival held annually in Kalibo, Aklan, which combines commemoration of a legendary meeting in the year 1213 between aboriginal Atis and Bornean emigres with the Feast of the Holy Child, celebrated on the second Sunday in January. In Chicago, Aklanons have brought *Ati-Atihan* to the Philippine Week parade.

Roman Catholic celebrations are also prominent among Catholic Filipino Americans who practice their religion with some fervor and live in communities where their numbers make the continuation of Philippine ethnoreligious customs feasible. The Christmas season begins on December 16 with a series of pre-dawn masses, the *Misas de Aguinaldo*, or gift masses, a tradition imported from Mexico during the Spanish colonial period. After the *Misa de Gallo*, the final pre-dawn mass which is held at midnight on Christmas Eve, families typically gather for the opening of the Christmas gift-giving season and for the *Noche Buena*, a joyous post-midnight supper and the calendar's most important dinner, although some families prefer to feast on Christmas Day rather than eat a heavy meal in the middle of the night. On Easter Sunday, in a ceremony called *Salubong*, statues of the Blessed Virgin, wearing a black shroud of mourning, and of the Risen Christ are carried in a procession. *Flores de Mayo*, a month-long celebration in May, is dedicated to the Blessed Virgin. During May, *Santa Cruzan*, the rite commemorating the discovery of the true cross, is re-enacted as a religious procession with beauty queens dressed as biblical characters. New immigrants may also continue to celebrate the feast of the patron saint of their town of origin.

DRESS AND DOMESTIC DECOR

From power suits to jeans and t-shirts, Filipino Americans reflect contemporary American fashion styles as they dress for their daily lives. Similarly, in their homes, Filipino American decorating choices run the gamut from traditional to contemporary to eclectic combinations of current and past trends in domestic decor. In dress and home furnishings, Filipino Americans, like other Americans, exhibit both individual preferences and relative levels of affluence or poverty. Yet, on occasion, Filipino Americans use ethnically identifiable items in both these areas.

When deciding what to wear for special events and celebrations, Filipino American men and women, especially those of the immigrant generation, sometimes choose distinctive clothing styles worn by their contemporaries in the Philippines. Rather than donning jacket, shirt, and tie, especially on a hot, humid day, men can opt for the *barong tagalog*, an embroidered, pocketless, collared shirt that is typically natural in color, is made of lightweight material, buttons in a placket from the neck to the waist, and is cut straight across the bottom with side-slits for ease of movement and access to trouser pockets. Always worn over a white, short-sleeved undershirt, never tucked into the pants, and never worn with a jacket over it, the *barong* varies in cost and level of formality on the basis of fabric, extent of embroidery, and sleeve length. (Ironically, during the Spanish colonial period, natives of the Philippines were barred from tucking their shirts into their pants, a privilege reserved for Europeans.) A wash-and-wear, short-sleeved version in a polyester or cotton blend with minimal embroidery is considered correct attire for informal occasions or casual business wear in the Philippines and can substitute for a short-sleeved, casual shirt in the United States. By contrast, the formal *barong* is always long-sleeved and cuffed. The most expensive versions are made from *piña*, a cloth woven from pineapple leaf fibers, or *jusi*, a fabric made from the inner fibers of the *abaca* plant. *Barongs* of this quality are elaborately embroidered on the front and sleeves and can be worn in place of a suit or a tuxedo at Filipino American galas.

Filipino American women enjoy more options for ethnically distinctive dress than do men who are limited to the *barong tagalog*. Ethnically identifiable clothing worn by Filipinas usually derives from the styles popular among elite women during the first half of the twentieth century. At the turn of the century, such dress consisted of a *baro* or blouse, with *sinamay* or wide, often transparent, "angel-like" sleeves that sloped over the shoulders and were typically stiffened to reveal their width, and a *saya* or skirt, either with or without *kola* or train. Sometimes, a *tapiz* or a piece of fabric was tied around the waist and worn over the *saya* or skirt, leaving only the bottom of the skirt visible. Alternatively, in a style more typically adopted by contemporary Filipinas, the *tapiz* was omitted, leaving the skirt loose and billowing, as in early twentieth-century European fashions. Another element that continues to be worn on occasion is the *pañuelo*, a triangularly folded, sometimes ornately embroidered, scarf-like piece of fabric that is draped around the neck and shoulders. Still worn by contestants in annual Maria Clara "queen" contests in the United States, a distinctive variation most closely associated with Rizal's fictional heroine, Maria Clara, combines a *baro* of fine, embroidered, white material, a *pañuelo* of the same fabric, and a long, shirred skirt of checked or striped black and white material. In the 1930s, the sleeves of the *baro* were shortened to elbow-length and flattened against the arms while standing stiff and "butterfly-like" above the shoulders. By the 1940s, these separate elements were combined in one gown called the *terno* which, over time, has been modified to reflect current fashion. When Filipina migration to the United States began to grow after World War II, most women either brought or sent for a *terno* with butterfly sleeves to wear at Filipino American celebrations. Today, most Filipinas in the United States typically special order their garments or purchase predecorated fabric, usually while on a return visit or through a relative still living in the Philippines. Or, on occasion, visitors will bring pieces of native cloth as gifts for those in America. When confronted with unsewn fabric, Filipina Americans will call upon their own or a family member or friend's sewing skills, or search for a seamstress of Filipina heritage who, in the absence of a pattern, is capable of turning yard goods into a finished garment. Thus, elaborate Filipina dress remains much a part of female networks and is most easily accessible to those who are themselves relatively recent immigrants or their daughters. Although Filipino catalogs published in the United States now regularly offer *barongs* of varied style and cost, along with women's garments termed "traditional *barong* dress," lavish, carefully fitted women's attire remains more difficult to obtain (*Tatak Pilipino* 1997: 49–53).

Fabrics chosen for Filipina garments range from silks, satins, and brocades for heavy skirts to those materials native to the Philippines, such as *jusi* and *piña*, which can be used for all of the separate elements of a costume or combined in a single dress. In contrast with *barongs*, color, ranging from pale pastels to rich primary shades, knows no limit in women's wear. Today, the butterfly sleeve is no longer ubiquitous; many Filipina Americans choose evening wear, which is not easily identifiable with their Philippine heritage— even if designed and made in the Philippines. Nonetheless, the Filipino American gala becomes a visual kaleidoscope when Filipina Americans celebrate their ethnicity by wearing gowns of traditional styling, lavish fabrics, lush colors, or intricate combinations of embroidery, lace, beading, and sequins.

Items displayed in Filipino American homes often remind residents and visitors of the importance of ethnic identity. Although few can afford the cost of importing heavy pieces of furniture from the Philippines, most Filipino Americans add Filipino elements to their decor. The ubiquitous wooden *carabao* (Philippine water buffalo), paintings of Filipino scenes, dolls in traditional dress, wall hangings of carved wood or woven fabric, *piña* cloth placemats and napkins, capiz shell trays and lamps, maps of the Philippines, and even the Philippine flag can recall the old home in the new. At Christmas, decorations brought from the Philippines or sent by relatives and friends will be hung on the family Christmas tree along with the latest collectibles from the local Hallmark store. The Filipino American family whose dwelling reveals nothing of its Philippine heritage is rare indeed.

Irrespective of ongoing modification by time and location in the United States, the values and customs discussed in this chapter remain important to countless immigrant and native-born Filipino Americans and define important facets of Filipino American ethnic identity. In addition, ethnic identity is also built locally and nationally by association and communication among Filipino Americans. These community-focused aspects of Filipino American identity are discussed in the next chapter.

5

Creating and Transforming Ethnic and Cultural Identity

Wherever Filipinos have settled in the United States, they have sought companionship and support through clubs, societies, and associations. In larger centers of residence, community-wide umbrella organizations often knit these groups together, both to provide readily available space and to give Filipino Americans a public presence within the larger locale. With considerable success in recent years, others have utilized mass communications to create a national identity among diverse Filipino Americans through print sources such as magazines, newspapers, and through electronic forms—radio, television, film, and, most recently, the Internet.

CREATING ETHNIC IDENTITY THROUGH ASSOCIATION

Because Filipino Americans are diverse, it would be misleading to assume that there is a single Filipino American "community" or that "community" is perceived by all Filipino Americans in the same way. For some, community is linked strongly to the specific location in which they now live—the ubiquitous "Philippine or Filipino American Association of 'our place' "; for others, community flows from the bonds of provincial origin, school attendance in the Philippines, occupational, business and professional affiliation, and/or belief; for still others, community is defined transnationally, by residence in the United States combined with continuing interest in the Philippines; and, for many, community is exhibited in varying combinations of these forms of

Choral members of "Young Once," a performance group comprising Filipino
American seniors, entertain at ethnic festivals in the Seattle, Washington, area.
Courtesy of the Ethnic Heritage Council, Seattle, Washington.

association. Despite this diversity—perhaps because of it—Filipino American ethnic identity has taken shape and continues to evolve through ever-
changing patterns of personal affiliation and connection into a broader notion
of what it means to be of Filipino heritage and living in the United States.

At this point, a word of caution is in order. Even limiting the task to the
post-1965 era, an exhaustive examination of organizations and associations
created by Filipino Americans would be a monumental, if not an impossible,
task. In the early 1980s, Filipino American organizations in Hawaii alone
numbered 147. Far from a comprehensive survey, this section sketches the
contours and the importance of Filipino American ethnic identity as forged
through association and through forms of communication accessed in private
and in public.

Patterns and Problems of Association

Does every Filipino American belong to an organization? Probably not,
but more than enough do to give Filipino Americans an undoubtedly well-
deserved reputation as organizers and joiners. As officers and members of
innumerable associations, Filipino Americans define and re-define attach-

ments outside of their family networks. This brief treatment highlights the bonds connecting Filipino Americans through provincial, alumni, occupational, charitable, fraternal, historical, and umbrella associations.

Being born and growing up in a Philippine town, province, or region establishes a central basis for organization-building among Filipinos in the United States. Town, provincial, and regional loyalties often remain strong, in part because of shared memories of experiences "at home," but also because the nationwide effort to transform Tagalog, the provincial language of the Manila area, into a national language called *Pilipino*, has not obliterated the other seven principal Philippine languages: Bikol, Cebuano, Hiligaynon, Iloko, Pampango, Pangasinan, and Waray. Recent immigrants typically understand and speak both *Pilipino* and English in varying degree, but many remain more comfortable in the language in which they were raised.

Whether these local ties and languages provide a basis for segmented ethnicity among Filipino Americans has yet to be systematically explored, but, from the earliest years of the century to its close, organizations that tap provincial loyalties have endured among Filipino Americans. In 1992, an editorial in Honolulu-based *Mabuhay International Monitor* proclaimed: "Communities of Filipinos both in Hawaii and in the US mainland are known to socialize among themselves only, often speaking Ilocano, Visayan or Tagalog, as the case may be. Because the predominant group in Hawaii is Ilocano, one hears Ilocano being spoken in the market, in the grounds-keeping areas, in the fastfood outlets, etc." ("Social Adjustment" 1992: 3).

Attendance at a specific Philippine college or university and membership in a specific profession also fosters group formation in the United States. "Old school ties" bring graduates together to talk of old times and new lives and to generate support for *alma mater*. For example, in the United States, alumni of the University of the Philippines are organized into state and regional chapters under the national umbrella of the University of the Philippines Alumni Association of America (UPAAA), which was founded in 1981 and holds an annual national reunion.

Occupational identity also spawns association. Trained at various medical schools in the Philippines, Filipino physicians practicing in the small cities and rural communities of the southern half of "The Land of Lincoln" came together to found the Association of Filipino Physicians of Southern Illinois in 1978 to provide for "continuing medical education and camaraderie . . . as well [as] to counter discriminatory practices in the profession" (Pilapil 1995: 3). Across the Mississippi River, Filipino physicians and nurses gather under the banner of the Philippine Medical Association of Greater St. Louis, Missouri. Many members of such local organizations also belong to the Association of Philippine Physicians in America (APPA) that dates from 1972.

Over the years, successful Filipino immigrants have also provided assistance to "needy *kababayans*" (countrymen) in the Philippines through organizations begun in the United States. For example, medical missions are a voluntaristic staple among Filipino immigrant physicians. After the 1991 joint annual meeting of APPA and the Philippine Medical Association, alumni of the Far Eastern University of Medicine in Manila spent a week together bringing medical care to Nueva Ecija, while Greater St. Louis area physicians brought their skills to Mindanao (Pilapil 1992: 21).

Fraternal organizations have a particularly rich and lengthy history among Filipino Americans, among them the Caballeros de Dimas-Alang, the Legionarios del Trabajo, the Gran Oriente Filipino, and the Knights of Rizal, all originally offshoots of Philippine organizations and all begun in the United States prior to 1965. All stress the need for solidarity, protection, and mutual assistance.

Founded in the Philippines in 1906 to continue revolutionary goals in the face of American rule, the Gran Orden de Caballeros de Dimas-Alang derives from the late nineteenth-century legacy of both Dr. José M. Rizal, who wrote from Europe under the pseudonym "Dimas-Alang," meaning "cannot be touched," and the revolutionary *Katipunan* movement led by Andres Bonifacio and Apolinario Mabini. The Caballeros de Dimas-Alang (CDA) drew its rituals and procedures from its founders' experience with masonry which had been banned and driven underground by the Spanish, but flourished under American rule.

In 1920, the Caballeros de Dimas-Alang began organizing in the United States. Within two years, six lodges located in California joined together as the Grand Lodge in America. Although pursuit of Philippine independence took center stage among Caballeros at home, the CDA in the United States quickly emerged mainly as a vehicle for camaraderie and mutual assistance and came to number almost seventy lodges and 2,000 members in the 1930s. CDA members fought the repatriation (deportation) of Filipino workers during the Depression, raised money to build two Mustang fighter aircraft during World War II, launched a project to bring modern farm technology to the Philippines in Cotabato after the war, and outlawed communism in its ranks in 1948. The CDA also built Dimas-Alang House in San Francisco for low-income, aged Filipinos, which became the focal point of a three-year court battle by rival CDA factions for control in the late 1980s. In 1990, continuing controversy over alleged mismanagement of funds led 84 members representing 14 lodges to pursue "reconciliation" rather than risk the destruction of one of the nation's oldest Filipino American fraternity ("Plan for CDA Unification" 1990: 1, 10).

Brought to San Francisco by members of the Gran Oriente Filipino in Manila in 1920, the Gran Oriente Filipino (GOF) was part of the "ancient and accepted Scottish rite of Freemasonry." The GOF established lodges in Filipino population centers throughout the mainland and in Hawaii, and formed an East-West Ladies Chapter "in order to inspire the wives and families of the members." ("75th Diamond Jubilee" 1995: n.p.) In the 1930s in San Francisco, the Gran Oriente Filipino purchased a 24-room hotel and two apartment buildings which continued to serve the community in the mid-1990s, offering a "comfortable and happy environment" to "predominantly Filipino-American, low-income senior citizens and families" ("1994 Annual Grand Lodge Convention and Banquet and Ball" 1994: n.p.). In 1995, the Gran Oriente Filipino also owned temples in San Francisco, Seattle, and San Jose, California.

The Legionarios del Trabajo (LDT) was imported into the United States when members of the Philippine organization created Worshipful Mayon Lodge No. 459 in San Francisco in 1924. Spreading throughout the United States, the fraternity sought to "unite and extend effective protection" to "Filipino workingmen and laborers" and claimed "approximately 1,000 members" prior to World War II. Fifty years after its founding, the LDT persisted, with its Brothers and Sisters—"teachers, lawyers, doctors, nurses, accountants, government and civil service employees, businessmen, farmers, contractors, artists, and housewives"—"receiv[ing] health, hospitalization, mortuary and legal benefits" and supporting cash scholarship awards (Esteban 1974: 14). Headquartered in Stockton, California, the LDT numbered forty-three local lodges in California and Washington and more than 1,200 members in 1991.

The Knights of Rizal, another ritualistic fraternal organization with its roots in the Philippines, has also been active in the United States since the first decade of the twentieth century. Young Filipinos studying at Chicago-area schools established both a "North Chicago Branch" and a "South Chicago Branch" of the Knights of Rizal in 1906 ("Chicago Boys Active" 1906: 21). In 1928, on behalf of the Knights, Filipino student-turned-immigrant Francisco Alayu presented a bust of Rizal to the Newberry Library in Chicago. Almost a half century later, after having disappeared from view, the Knights were reestablished in Chicago in August 1977, eight months after Sir Quirico Evangelista, the Order's Supreme Commander, arrived from the Philippines and attended the first Rizal Day held at the the city's new Rizal

Center. Alayu, nearing the end of his life, became the chapter's first Commander. By the mid-1990s, the many new chapters formed in North America required a deputy supreme commander for the Americas and a coordinator for each of five regions—Central USA; Eastern USA; Western USA; Hawaii, Guam, Alaska USA; and Canada—whose members periodically come together in an "International Assembly."

Although membership statistics in the early 1990s indicate persistent vitality among these fraternal organizations, recent photographs showcasing elderly members suggest a different story. Dean T. Alegado notes about Hawaii: "[V]ery few among the younger join these masonic lodges and they are, therefore, in danger of going out of existence" (Alegado 1991: 106). Whatever their twenty-first century prospects, Filipino American fraternal organizations have been a vital part of community life during the last third of the twentieth century.

One aspect of Filipino American associational life verges on the ubiquitous. Countless fraternal, provincial, or community-based organizations sponsor queen contests that derive from both the town fiesta of the Philippines' Spanish heritage and from more commercialized American ventures such as the first Manila Carnival in 1908. Queen contests provide constituent clubs, chapters, and lodges with an opportunity to show off, for the selection of the queen and her court is, more often than not, based on a group's ability to raise more money than the rest, thereby entitling its candidate to the crown. In the 1920s and 1930s, with few Filipinas, queens and princesses were typically the white girlfriends of single Filipinos. Between the late 1930s and 1965, Filipina newcomers and the daughters of earlier couples took crowns.

Among post-1965 Filipino immigrants, their wives and daughters have taken center stage. Each year, the Knights of Rizal choose a Miss Maria Clara in honor of Rizal's heroine. At triennial conventions, both the Caballeros de Dimas-Alang and the Legionarios del Trabajo honor a woman sponsored by a member lodge as either Mrs. Dimas-Alang or Miss Legionarios del Trabajo, respectively. Local-level queen contests also abound. In 1992, *Heritage* published five photographs taken when, as part of a fundraising effort, the Filipino Community of Carson, California, named Fe Ero "Mrs. Philippines, USA" and designated three runners-up—Mrs. Luzon, Mrs. Visayas, and Mrs. Mindanao—from the local representatives of various Philippine provinces. Carson's "Mrs. Philippines USA" was not likely the only woman so designated an equivalent "queen" by Filipino Americans in that year, for contests are held in many locations. In Seattle the Mrs. Filipino Community of Seattle contest has been held since 1968.

Escorted by her husband, Fred, and an honor guard of
the Caballeros de Dimas-Alang, a fraternal order, Purita
Aquino Dimalanta becomes "Mrs. Dimas-Alang," the
order's queen, in 1979. Courtesy of Purita Aquino
Dimalanta.

Since the mid-1980s, historically conscious immigrant and native-born
Filipino Americans have begun, as never before, to research, preserve, and
make known their history in the United States. At the national level, Seattle
community activists Fred and Dorothy Laigo Cordova, second-generation
Filipino Americans, established the Filipino American National Historical
Society in 1982. Building on twenty-five years of contacts made through the
Filipino Youth Activities of Seattle, Inc., which they founded in 1957, and
the Young Filipino People's Far West Conferences, which were held annually
between 1971 and 1976, the Cordovas work to encourage the formation of
local chapters throughout the country. On the local level, also founded in
the early 1980s, the Filipino American Historical Society of Chicago drew
together American-born offspring of Filipino old-timers. By contrast, im-

migrants who came to the United States in the 1960s and 1970s founded the Filipino American Historical Society of Springfield, Illinois, in 1988.

Over the years, umbrella organizations have emerged in many locations to foster closer contact among Filipino American organizations and to encourage local recognition of Filipino Americans as an ethnic and political presence. Since 1959, the United Filipino Council of Hawaii (UFCH) has served as a state-wide umbrella for separate island councils, which are themselves umbrellas for myriad local organizations. Under the UFCH, Filipino Americans in Hawaii started Fiesta Filipina, an annual festival extending over several days and featuring "native Filipino games" and "a program of folk dances and songs" which is now considered comparable to the Chinese Hawaiian Narcissus Festival and the Japanese Hawaiian Cherry Blossom Festival (Domingo 1983: 342).

Founded in 1935, Seattle's community-wide organization, now called the Filipino Community of Seattle, Inc., has persisted for decades. In 1965, the organization, which enrolls individual members rather than constituent associations, purchased its own building, the Filipino Community Center, and retired its mortgage in 1974. Seattle's Filipinas, many of whom came to the United States as brides during the years immediately after World War II, played a crucial role in the building-purchase campaign through the Mrs. Filipino Community of Seattle Pageant which has been held since 1968. Although only the contestant who raised the most money could wear the crown, all benefited financially, with each candidate keeping 55 percent of the money she solicited, and 45 percent going to the Filipino Community of Seattle, Inc. (Dimalanta [1986]: 159). In 1997, the Filipino Community Center housed a variety of services: free martial arts, chess, aerobics, ballroom dance, and Tagalog classes, lunch for seniors twice a week, and youth activities each Friday evening. As in Hawaii, Seattle's Filipino Americans also have held an ethnic festival, the *Pista sa Nayon*, during Seattle Seafair each August since 1990.

In smaller communities and in regions characterized by dispersed residence, Filipino Americans have also attempted to coordinate their associational efforts. In 1984, led by Maximo Fabella, Jacksonville, Florida's "three major Filipino organizations" founded the Filipino American Community Council of Northeast Florida. Courtship by local politicians soon followed, as did appointment of "Fil-Ams . . . to local commissions and community advisory boards. . . . Philippine Week and Rizal Day are now recognized and celebrated by the city" ("Maximo Fabella: Maximum Resource" 1997: 48).

Cut-throat competition and inter-community conflict can result when Filipino American joiners aim at leadership and recognition. When the 3,500-

member Filipino Community of Santa Clara County [CA], Inc., ran its decades-old Mrs. Philippines of Santa Clara County contest in August 1993, contestants sold 46,000 two-dollar ballots, bringing in $92,000. Selling 10,325 ballots, the winner and her campaign manager husband garnered $10,944, 53 percent of the money they raised, while unsuccessful candidates netted $15,290 and "four board members on the pageant committee divided another $5,095." At most, $5,000 "went to youth scholarships." The remaining $55,671? Missing. The queen? "Furious." She "had to pay $250 for her own rhinestone tiara and four-foot trophy . . . [in part, because] the chairwoman of the board who brought those items doubled the price she had paid when asking the sponsoring organization to reimburse her." Defending herself, the chairwoman retorted: " 'She wanted the nicest, biggest one, . . . None of the other princesses did. They wanted simple ones.' . . . [And] she justified the markup because she bought the items wholesale through her family's San Jose jewelry business." Another board member opined: "I'm just hoping it won't happen again. . . . People won't trust us" (Jung 1994: 3).

Although such controversies are typically known only within the local Filipino American community, conflict over electing the president of the Filipino-American Community of Los Angeles, Inc., made front page headlines in the *Los Angeles Times* in May 1989: "Hostile rivals lock a president out of his office. The press dubs it a 'bloodless coup.' The embattled leader summons his followers and tries to regain control of headquarters. The air seethes with mistrust and intrigue. As angry opponents mass outside, police cars race to the scene." In previous elections, candidates for the office mortgaged homes and borrowed "huge sums" to expand their war chests. A Manila-born L.A. police officer reported: "There's a lot of vote buying." A very public indicator of persistent rivalries, the 1989 dispute reminded some that discord often gives the community a bad name: "We were here ahead of the Koreans and the Vietnamese and the Cambodians. All of them have accomplished a lot by getting together and asserting their rights" (Peterson 1989: 1, 14).

Whether over queen contests, elections, seats at a banquet's head table, or countless other causes, dissension is commonplace—sometimes seemingly endemic—among Filipino Americans. Jockeying for position and power can fracture whatever ephemeral unity Filipino Americans share. The proliferation of organizations can itself fragment Filipino Americans into diverse and discordant clusters uninterested in defining or pursuing common goals. Their time consumed by the elements of daily life—family, kin, work, and worship—as well as by the groups they join, most Filipino Americans take ethnic identity as a personally defined given, even as the multiple meanings of "Filipino American" evolve over time and in different circumstances.

TRANSFORMING CULTURAL IDENTITY THROUGH COMMUNICATION

In Private: Newspapers, Magazines, Radio, Television, Video, Film, and the Internet

In addition to face-to-face association in their organizations, Filipino Americans also construct their ethnicity in private through their encounters with ethnically defined communication forms. The ethnic magazines and newspapers that they read; the Philippine-language radio and television stations that they listen to and watch; the Philippine-made CDs and videos that they purchase or rent; and the e-mail and the Internet groups in which they participate—all simultaneously help to shape the meaning of "Filipino American" for those within and outside the group.

The explosion in scope of such communication forms during recent decades has transformed the experiences of post-1965 immigrants from the Philippines by contrast with their predecessors. Filipinos in the United States before and immediately after World War II had little beyond letters to maintain ties with those left behind in the Philippines. Even as they attempted to report on developments affecting both the Philippines and Filipinos in the United States, Filipino American newspapers and magazines were typically short-lived and limited in scope and distribution. To keep abreast of events "at home," some Filipinos in the United States subscribed to *Philippine Free Press* or *Graphic*, magazines published in the Philippines which occasionally covered the doings and the difficulties of Filipinos in America. Little in either Philippine or Filipino American publications helped build a collective identity grounded in residence in the United States. Instead, ethnic identity emerged as a by-product of Philippine nationalism, by continuing reference to Philippine issues—from the quest for national independence, to the war in the Pacific, to the prospects for the homeland after liberation.

In the late 1990s, those who are of Filipino heritage can employ multiple forms of mass communication in private to create identity. With their large and diverse population and their wide geographical distribution, Filipino Americans are necessarily selective in what they absorb. By making personal choices, Filipino Americans shape their own lives as well as a composite group identity. This section can only highlight the vitality of Filipino American publications and media at the century's close.

In the late 1980s, Fred Cordova explained the sorry state of Filipino American periodicals: their lack of "reputable advertisements displaying consumer goods and services . . . Philippine Airlines consistently . . . [being] the sole big-time advertiser," and their poor, unprofessional quality. "Fifty percent of their editorial perspective is bound by a canned-release, you-send-me-stuff, [while] the remaining 50 percent shows sloppy journalism" (Cordova 1987: 5). Cordova's criticism still applies today. Aimed at offering education, information, entertainment, and services, Filipino American newspapers have appeared in—and have disappeared from—most major population centers. Published on a weekly basis since 1962, the *Philippine News* is a notable exception. Its publisher and editor-in-chief Alex A. Esclamado utilized "regional make-over pages to satisfy its nation-wide readership," and thereby "set Pinoy journalism on its ear" (Cordova 1987: 5).

Magazines have also come and gone in Filipino America. Before World War II, student publications such as the YMCA-sponsored *Filipino Student Bulletin* published campus and community news for a limited national audience, while Hilario Moncado's *Filipino Nation* stressed the expansion of his quasi-religious Filipino Federation of America. In the 1940s, Diosdado Yap's *Bataan* in Washington, D.C., and Felisberto R. Villar's *Philippine Quarterly* in Chicago offered a broader perspective but were long gone in the early years of the post-1965 immigration.

More recently, two newer magazines have become staple reading in many Filipino American households. Since June 1987 when he put Philippine President Corazon Aquino on his first cover, Victor P. Gendrano, who arrived in the United States in 1963, has published four, essentially ad-free issues of *Heritage: Magazine of Filipino Culture, Arts and Letters* each year. Cory Aquino also adorned the first cover of Mona Lisa Yuchengco's *Filipinas: A Magazine for All Filipinos* when it debuted in May 1992. Published monthly by Yuchengco and current editor-in-chief Rene P. Ciria-Cruz, *Filipinas* is undoubtedly the most ambitious of current Filipino American magazines with its size—almost 100 pages—and cover photos reminiscent of *Time* and *Newsweek*, its slick, glossy pages, its well-written articles reporting on Filipinos on both sides of the Pacific, and its hard-hitting coverage of such issues as Filipino racism, AIDS, and teenage pregnancy that other publications avoid.

In locales with considerable numbers of immigrants from the Philippines, various forms of non-print media—radio, television, CDs and videos—are regularly available to Filipino American households. Every Sunday afternoon from noon until 3 P.M. for over five years, Filipino immigrants in Seattle have tuned their radio dials to "Radyo Manila" to hear Conrado "Sluggo" and Roger Rigor, Manny Uson, Gerry Grutas, and "Lola Maharlika" Balisi broadcast " '*balitang seryoso-balitang artista, musika, kuwentuhan-interviews, dyoks na pang Pinoy lamang*' (serious news-showbiz news, music, storytelling-interviews, jokes for Pinoys only), local politics and community issues, Pili-pino legends and cultural-historical trivia," gossip, dedications, and "immortal Pilipino tunes" (Morente 1997: 22).

Utilizing "cable, over-the-air and satellite broadcasting," Filipino televi-sion programming is also becoming available in various U.S. markets (Sreen-ivasan 1997: D-11). The 4,700 Filipinos living in Anchorage, Alaska, can tune in "Fil-Am Showtime," a half-hour news program taped weekly by Juliette and Nez Danguilan "in a converted bedroom above their little cof-feehouse and restaurant, Cafe D'Amor" (Toomey 1997: A-1, A-8). On KCNS, "The #1 Asian Station in the San Francisco Bay Area," Philippine news is "received [the] same day via satellite" and broadcast in "Taglish" each weekday evening, while six and a half hours of Tagalog and Taglish programming each Saturday include "the very best in television drama," a musical variety show, investigative reports, "Manila, Manila"—a weekly magazine program, and "*Ober Da Bakod*"—"Family feud-Filipino-style!" ("The #1 Asian Station in the San Francisco Bay Area" 1996: 53). Its Bay-area competition, KTSF runs an hour of local and Philippine news each weekday evening and three hours of Saturday programming featuring im-ported as well as Filipino American satire, variety, drama, and public affairs shows.

Even more ambitious, since 1994, ABS-CBN, the "most watched of all local networks" in the Philippines, has offered "The Filipino Channel" to Filipino American subscribers over cable in such metropolitan markets as New York, Chicago, and San Francisco and by "direct-to-home via satellite dish anywhere in the U.S." ("TFC: The Filipino Channel" 1995: 33). Writ-ing in 1994, John L. Silva observed: "Homesickness will be but a dream as you are lulled to sleep by an up-and-coming crooner from Manila" (Silva 1994: 36).

Other media forms are even more readily accessible to Filipino American consumers. Mail-order catalogs offer CDs and laser discs appealing to diverse tastes in Philippine music—love songs, famous artists of yesterday and today, and classical, inspirational, religious, swing, jazz, ballroom, cha-cha, kids, and regional collections. Philippine-made movies, scenic videos, and language CDs and tapes are also available through mail-order distributors and from stores catering to a Filipino clientele.

New in the 1990s, e-mail and the Internet are only the most recent con-duits for communication among Filipinos, at least those having access to the latest technology. Subscribers to "soc.culture.filipino"—a Usenet newsgroup located on the World Wide Web—receive UPI news stories about the Philippines and can chat with others interested in Filipino and Filipino American identity and culture. Organizations with World Wide Web homepages—for example, Gabriela, which "works on issues arising from US policy decisions which impact negatively on women and children of the Philippines"—can reach browsers across the globe, post upcoming events, and communicate with the committed who visit their site (http://www.gabnet.org). All these media can be brought directly into the home. Other forms are more public.

In Public: Dance, Music, Theater, Art, and the Martial Arts

Access to Filipino culture in the United States expanded during the years after World War II as newly formed families and second-generation Filipino American adults worked to develop ethnic pride in those growing up during the post-war years. In the early 1960s, members of the Bayanihan Philippine Dance Company, founded in 1957, ranked as visiting royalty in the United States. During the short span of the dancers' appearance, Filipinos long distanced from the Philippines by time and space proudly celebrated the cultural richness of their homeland. Since 1957 in Seattle, teenaged Filipino American girls and boys have worn "traditional" garb as they perform intricate maneuvers in Fred and Dorothy Cordova's Filipino Youth Activities (FYA) Drill Team. If they lived near countrymen, many Filipino Americans learned at least a few folk dance steps in their youth.

In the late 1990s, community-based efforts have become more extensive. Professional performances of culture are not necessarily imported—much is as Filipino American as it is Philippine—but rather constructed and reconstructed in the United States by Filipino immigrants and Filipino Americans working in dance, music, theater, art, and the martial arts. Though these forms are most accessible to those living in major metropolitan areas who choose to be interested, still, their expansion across the country manifests a growing cultural affluence that simultaneously generates a genuine pride-in-group in which Filipino Americans can more generally partake.

Through the years, dance has likely been the most persistent form of cultural preservation and renewal. Whether given in ornate hotel ballrooms, functional school auditoriums, or drab rented halls, virtually all "cultural programs" include traditional Philippine dance—the *pandanggo sa ilaw* (dance of lights), the *singkil* (a Muslim Filipino court dance), or, most typically, the *tinikling* (bamboo or bird dance) in which dancers simulate "the

The Filipino Youth Activities Drill Team performing in Seattle in 1996. Since 1957, Seattle's Filipino Youth Activities drill teams have delighted audiences with their colorful costumes and precision movements. Courtesy of the Filipino American National Historical Society, Seattle, Washington.

nimble movements of the *tikling* bird avoiding the farmer's field traps. The barefoot dancers hop as though skipping rope double-dutch, to escape the bamboo poles clashing dangerously close to their toes." At *Iskwelahang Pilipino* (Filipino Schoolhouse) in Boston, students also learn to play the *rondalla*, a "simple and direct form of Filipino music" utilizing stringed instruments such as *banduria, laud, octavina, gitara* and *báho* (Dowdy 1993: 12). *Kulintang*, an orally transmitted form of traditional music from Mindanao and the Sulu Archipelago in the southern Philippines that is played on gongs and drums, has also been introduced to Filipino Americans in the last twenty years.

Finding his "roots," first in the late 1970s from old records, then at the University of Washington, and subsequently during a stay at Mindanao State University, Robert Kikuchi-Yngojo brought *kulintang* and other aspects of Asian culture to the San Francisco Bay area—"When I was a kid, we never had Filipino role models in the schools. . . . Sometimes, a hush comes over the crowd when the teacher announces that I'll be playing music from the Philippines. . . . I know I've really made my mark when the kids run up after

Dancing the *tinikling* is a staple of Filipino American cultural performances. Courtesy of the Ethnic Heritage Council, Seattle, Washington.

all the others have left to tell me, 'Mister, you know I'm Filipino, too' " (Alba 1992: 28).

Just as Filipino dance and music have become part of the cultural landscape, so too Filipino Americans can see their experiences interpreted on stage and in film (see Films and Videos section in Bibliography). Produced by Seattle-based theater group Sining KilUSA, Timoteo Cordova's "Across Oceans of Dreams," a musical "showcas[ing] Filipino American males of the *manong* generation," played to "packed houses throughout the American Northwest" in the early 1990s ("Across Oceans of Dreams" 1993: 31). In Chicago, since the early 1990s, the Pintig Cultural Group, a Chicago-area Filipino arts organization, was formed by young Filipino Americans searching for their identity. After mounting an art exhibit that raised $3,000 for victims of the Mt. Pinatubo volcanic eruption, Pintig staged Chris Millado's "America Is in the Heart," a play based on the novel by Carlos Bulosan (see Appendix II) with Larry Leopoldo in the lead role. Promotions director Jerry Alfafara explained its goal: "We want to present art and music that reflect our unique experiences as Filipinos in America, yet remain rooted in Philippine history" (Garza 1992: Sec. 2, 7). Pintig's latest of six productions,

"The Bells of Balangiga," written by Rodi Vera, with music and direction by Louie Pascasio, "tells the true story of how a little town in Samar rose up against colonization in 1901" in an ambush of American troops signaled by the ringing of the bells. Retaliatory U.S. forces "stole the bells . . . [which] now reside in a monument inside a military camp in Wyoming." Pintig's production was part of an unsuccessful campaign for the return of the bells during the Philippine centennial in 1998 (Montreal 1998: 16–17).

Films dealing with Filipino American subjects are increasingly available (see Films and Videos section in Bibliography). Although these films have achieved national distribution, the work of other Filipino American film-makers is often more difficult to encounter. In 1996, *Waiting in the Wings*, "a short film about the conflicting values between immigrant Filipino parents and Fil-Am children," garnered awards from both the School of the Visual Arts in New York City and the Director's Guild of America for twenty-one-year-old filmmaker Charles Uy ("Charles Uy: Visualize More Awards" 1996: 57). Arkipelago, "a community based cultural organization that strives to promote, explore, and comment on the Philippine diaspora through arts related projects and programs," works to raise awareness of such talent. In November 1997, Arkipelago held *"Sa Pinilakang Tabing"* (on the Silver Screen), a "film and video festival of established and emerging Filipino and Filipino American filmmakers," which screened fourteen short films on the Barnard College campus (http://www.columbia.edu/~eth6,arki.html).

In the visual arts, several Philippine- and American-born artists have won recognition, either for work done years ago, or for work of recent vintage. Perhaps the most currently celebrated is eighty-seven-year-old Venancio C. Igarta (see Appendix II), a "colorist" whose vibrant canvasses have explored Philippine and Filipino American themes since the late 1930s. Two years after the fall of Bataan and Corregidor, Manuel Rey Isip won widespread distribution with his poster, "The Fighting Filipinos: We Will Always Fight for Freedom!" when the Philippine government-in-exile commissioned 15,000 copies for distribution throughout the United States. Today, Jordin Isip, Manuel Rey Isip's grandson, a graduate of the Rhode Island School of Design, is an illustrator whose work has appeared on the cover of *Time* for the magazine's story on "The War on Welfare Mothers" and in *The Atlantic Monthly, The New York Times Magazine, GQ, The Progressive,* and *Rolling Stone.*

For some young Filipino Americans, Philippine martial arts has involved an exploration of their heritage. Traceable to the Philippines' pre-Spanish era, *arnis, kali,* and *eskrima* (or *escrima*) stress the use of the hands, either empty or armed with a stick or a bladed weapon, as well as the cultivation of physical, mental, emotional, and spiritual qualities. Banned by the Spanish, Filipinos practiced martial arts in secret, sometimes passing on their training within the family. In the United States, Filipino martial arts first arrived with early Filipino immigrants—Floro Villabrille in Hawaii, Angel Cabales on the West Coast, and Florendo Visitacion on the East Coast— who passed their knowledge on to their students. Among other more recent practitioners, Dan Inosanto "introduced Filipino stickfighting" to famed martial arts practitioner Bruce Lee and founded the Filipino Kali Academy in his backyard in Carson, California, in 1974, a year after Lee's death (Jundis 1993: 66). In 1989 in Cebu, at the first World Tournament of Filipino martial arts, participants founded the World Eskrima Kali Arnis Federation (WEKAF) to sanction tournaments held around the world and whose members represent twenty-five countries.

More readily than during the years before World War II, and even than prior to 1965, contemporary Filipino Americans can partake, as they choose, of a far wider range of opportunities for association, communication, and culture within the borders of their heritage. This said, it necessary to stress that Filipino American is regarded as "ethnic," rather than "mainstream." Take, as a final example, "Pistahang Filipino," held symbolically, no doubt, on the centennial weekend of June 13–14, 1998: "Featuring—*Parada ng Musilong Bumbong at Litson*—Filipino Folk Dancers and Choirs—Santa-Cruzan—Star Studded Special Presentation of Filipino Entertainers in Concert Direct from the Philippines—See the Finest Philippine Products in Trade Booth Exhibits. Taste and enjoy sumptuous Filipino Fiesta Foods! and much, much more!" Where!?! At Paramount's Great America Theme Park in Santa Clara, California ("Pistahang Filipino" 1998: 27).

6

Economic and Political Power

Often viewed as "forgotten" or "invisible" within the larger American context, immigrants from the Philippines and their American-born children have begun to secure heightened economic comfort, if not power, and to achieve increased political recognition, if not clout. Filipino American magazines such as Victor Gendrano's *Heritage* and Mona Lisa Yuchengco's *Filipinas* build group pride by calling attention to special achievements of Filipino Americans in the American economic and political arena. Yet, these successes do not tell the whole Filipino American story. Financial instability and political impotence mark the lives of some. These Filipino Americans and their difficulties, which will be explored later in this book, are no less a part of Filipino America's identity.

OCCUPATIONS

The U.S. Census of 1990 provides the most recent collective, national portrait of Filipino American participation in the American economy. In 1990, 750,613 Filipino Americans over the age of 16 were employed in the civilian labor force, of whom 151,012 (20.1 percent) were native born, and 599,601 (79.9 percent) were foreign born. Of these foreign born, 327,701 (54.7 percent) entered the United States prior to 1980; 271,900 (45.3 percent) arrived after that year. By 1990, 348,424 (58.1 percent) had become naturalized citizens.

No occupations are more closely associated with post-1965 immigrants

Table 6.1
Occupations of Filipino Americans in 1990

Occupational Category	Native-Born		Foreign-Born	
	#	%	#	%
Managerial and professional specialty occupations	32,428	20.8	167,521	27.1
Technical, sales, and administrative support occupations	61,497	39.5	213,626	34.6
Service occupations	23,497	15.1	102,288	16.6
Farming, forestry, and fishery occupations	2,167	1.4	9,081	1.4
Precision production, craft, and repair occupations	13,981	9.0	41,725	6.8
Operators, fabricators, and laborers	17,442	11.2	65,360	10.6
Armed forces	4,708	3.0	18,189	2.9
TOTAL	155,720	100.0	617,790	100.0

Source: United States, Bureau of the Census, *1990 Census of Population, Asians and Pacific Islanders in the United States* (Washington, D.C.: U.S. Government Printing Office, 1993): 115–116.

from the Philippines than are physicians and nurses. Filipino American health care professionals veritably define the ethnic group in the minds of many Americans. The 1990 Census supports this impression. More Filipino Americans reported occupations in the health service industry than in any other category. In 1990, 150,460 Filipinos—20 percent of the 750,613 Filipinos over age 16 who were employed in the civilian labor force—listed health care–related employment. Immigrants predominate in this category. Ninety-one percent of Filipinos in the health care services industry were born in the Philippines, 57 percent of whom arrived in the United States before 1980. However, a word of caution is in order. The census does not distinguish one health care occupation from another. All health services workers, from physicians to nursing home attendants, appear in this category. Indeed, Filipinos illegally in the United States who work at the bottom of the ladder of health care–related occupations are probably undercounted by the census.

Filipino Americans working in other professions and related services constitute another important category. In 1990, these Filipino Americans numbered 71,574 or 9.5 percent of Filipino Americans employed in the civilian labor force. Of these Filipino Americans, 30,697 were employed in "educational services," a category ranging from university administrators to teachers' aides.

The 1990 census also permits division of the 750,613 Filipino Americans over age 16 who were employed in the civilian labor force into six occupational categories. Table 6.1 provides this breakdown for native and foreign-born Filipino Americans, and adds to it the 22,897 Filipino Americans in the armed forces. Several points revealed by the numbers and percentages deserve emphasis. As already noted, the Filipino American work force is overwhelmingly immigrant rather than native-born—79.9% as opposed to 20.1 percent. Of these foreign-born Filipino Americans in the work force, 61.7 percent are concentrated in jobs subsumed under "managerial and professional specialty occupations" and "technical, sales, and administrative support occupations." While this statistic does not reveal the range of income or status associated with the diverse occupations captured in these categories, it does indicate that 6 of every 10 foreign-born Filipino Americans do non-manual work. Conversely, 35.4 percent of foreign-born Filipino Americans are engaged in manual work in "service," "farming, forestry, and fishery," and "precision production, craft, and repair" occupations and as "operators, fabricators, and laborers." The tiny percentage—1.4 percent—of both foreign- and native-born Filipino Americans employed in "farming, forestry, and fishery occupations" makes clear that the *manongs* and the *alaskeros* who largely defined early twentieth-century Filipino America are now part of the Filipino American past.

Other 1990 census statistics indicate a lack of entrepreneurial activity among Filipino Americans. In 1990, only 23,819 (3.2 percent) Filipino Americans were self-employed—52.8 percent male and 47.2 percent female—80.1 percent foreign-born and 19.9 percent native-born. Filipino Americans, the second largest Asian American population group in the United States in 1990, ranked fifth among Asian and Pacific Islander groups owning their own businesses and, in comparison with Koreans who ranked first, were sixth in ownership of retail businesses. In asking why, population analysts James T. Fawcett and Robert W. Gardner suggest that Koreans, who migrate from a more prosperous nation than do Filipinos, are likely to arrive in the United States with considerably more capital with which to start a business than are Filipinos—on average $14,500 for Koreans as opposed to $1,700 for Filipinos. Further, Filipinos, unlike Koreans, are more likely to view starting a business as an individualistic rather than a family-based endeavor and may view entrepreneurship as "running counter" to ingrained Filipino values emphasizing family bonds over individualism. Most importantly, "many Filipino immigrants feel that they are doing very well indeed, in comparison with their life in the Philippines" (Fawcett and Gardner 1994: 211–238; quotations appear on 235 and 223). Stability, for many, is linked to the public sector. Indeed, 95,379—15.9 percent of foreign-born Filipino Americans—held local, state, or federal government jobs in 1990.

Moving beyond statistics to capture the variety and the richness of contemporary Filipino American identity can only be done impressionistically and selectively. Each Filipino American life, whether native- or foreign-born, intersects with those of family members and friends, of classmates, townmates, and provincemates, and of other fellow Filipino Americans. In addition, each Filipino American has a separate tale of interaction outside of the ethnic group with Americans who are not of Philippine heritage.

Filipino physicians have often established practices outside major metropolitan areas. The earliest to settle permanently in the United States have now lived for over a quarter of a century in America's small cities and towns. Since 1969, for example, Virgilio Pilapil has practiced in Springfield, Illinois' state capital. Over the years, other Filipino physicians joined him in central Illinois—most in Springfield, but others in smaller, surrounding communities—Gloria and Virgilio Dycoco in Pana, Alfredo Jocson in Decatur, Virginia Caballero-Dauz in Shelbyville, and Lemuel G. Villanueva in Jacksonville. Their careers as physicians in these midwestern communities, sometimes as the only Filipino physician in town, bear little resemblance to the work lives of Filipina hotel housekeepers in San Francisco, immigrants who, like many physicians, arrived in the 1970s and see "their employment primarily as a bridge to greater stability and comfort," even as they too take pride in the income they earn (Santa Maria 1994: 5–7). Nonetheless, the differing patterns of Filipino American rural and urban life in the nation's small towns and largest cities, as well as the inherent differences in the income and status which mark their jobs, make the experiences of these two Filipino immigrant groups different in ways that historians have only begun to investigate.

Filipino Americans have also entered occupations and have achieved career successes less typical of others in their ethnic group. A few examples only touch on the variety. A Dayton, Ohio, area resident for more than twenty-five years, Rodolfo "Rudy" S. Bernardo began implementing a "Character

Education" program at Dayton's Allen Elementary School when he became its principal in 1989. During the next six years, Bernardo, his staff, and the students and their parents raised Allen from 28th to first among Dayton's 33 elementary schools in standardized achievement test scores, making Bernardo a national leader and spokesman for the "character education movement."

Now scattered throughout the United States, five Rivera brothers, Terry, Dindo, Atab, Al, and Joseph, the sons of a physician, were already building varied careers—in agriculture, scrap metal, and aircraft maintenance, and as a stock broker—before they migrated in their late twenties to the United States or Canada between 1968 and 1977. Since then, all have worked in various supervisory or managerial capacities for the Marriott Hotel chain. "This sure beats working with pigs," thought Dindo, who abandoned work on a masters degree in agriculture to earn one in hotel and restaurant management. Although Dindo left Marriott in 1976 for IBM, the others have moved up the hotel chain's corporate ladder, while simultaneously moving from city to city. Currently, at Marriott's flagship hotel near the White House, Al declares: "Someday, when the Marriott opens a hotel in Manila, I want to be its general manager" (Almendrala 1995: 23–24).

In 1997, Hawaii-born Byron Acohido, three of whose grandparents were Filipino immigrants, while the fourth was from Korea, and Alex Tizon, who was only four years old when his family left the Philippines, each won Pulitzer Prizes in journalism for their work at the *Seattle Times*. Acohido collected the prize in the "beat reporting category" for his articles about a faulty rudder mechanism on Boeing 737 aircraft, which led to mandatory inspections of all the jetliners. Tizon and two colleagues won in the "investigative reporting category" for a series that showed federal Housing and Urban Development housing subsidies intended for poor Native Americans on reservations "being siphoned off to the more well-to-do tribal leaders serving on the housing authorities or operating million-dollar casinos" (Almendrala "The Pulitzer Two" 1997: 26–28).

Two examples also illustrate the diversity among the small number of native- and foreign-born Filipino Americans who are self-employed. Self-described " 'Texapino' (half-Texan, half-Filipino)," Neal McCoy was born in Texas in the late 1950s to a Filipina mother and an Irish father. During long years spent pursuing his dream of becoming a country music singer, McCoy mowed lawns and sold shoes. His last two albums, "No Doubt About It" and "You Gotta Love That," sold more than a million copies. Colet Lahoz, a Philippine-trained nurse who had worked in the United States for more than a decade, returned temporarily to the Philippines in 1980 to train in "Eastern medicine." At the clinic that she has operated since 1984 in White Bear Lake, a prosperous St. Paul, Minnesota, suburb, Lahoz utilizes Philippine folk medicine and herbal remedies in addition to acupuncture.

Other entrepreneurs have achieved wider prominence in the larger society by virtue of their financial success. Philippine-born fashion designer Josie Cruz Natori, CEO of an $80 million New York City–based firm specializing in lingerie, ready-to-wear, and perfume, considered "dozens of ideas (from selling fertilizers and diving gear to buying a hamburger franchise)" before launching her firm (Daspin 1997: 150). Loida Nicolas Lewis (see Appendix II) is the Chair and CEO of TLC Beatrice, an international food conglomerate, which is the 68th largest privately held company in the United States.

INCOME LEVELS

Based on the occupational successes of many, but by no means all of their group, Filipino Americans enjoy a collective reputation associated with comparatively high income levels. In 1989, with a median household income of $43,780, Filipino Americans ranked third in the nation among sixty ancestry groups, falling behind only immigrants from Russia ($45,778) and India ($44,696) (Hacker 1997: 159).

The economic strength of households headed by foreign-born Filipino Americans is especially striking. Filipino Americans arriving prior to 1980 had the highest median household income among all Filipino Americans— $49,051—in 1989. But even those who came to the United States during the 1980s, whose median household income was $38,764 in 1989, topped native-born Filipino Americans with a median household income of $37,943.

Why were Filipino immigrants who came to the United States between 1965 and 1980 so successful? Likely, they were then and continue to be among the best prepared by education and professional training to position themselves and their families on the upper rungs of the American economic ladder. Those who came to the United States under the occupational preference provisions of U.S. immigration law made effective use of their English-language, American-style Philippine educations, especially in careers in heavy demand such as those in the health service professions. By contrast, the lesser earning power of the Filipino immigrants of the 1980s probably derives from a combination of three factors. First, by the 1980s, the continued migration of highly skilled medical professionals had been made more difficult by changes in U.S. immigration law. Second, arriving under family preference provisions, many Filipino immigrants of the 1980s joined highly skilled family members who had arrived earlier. Even if well educated, these immigrants were not as likely to find that their training could command high incomes in the United States. And, third, having come so recently, the 1980s immigrants from the Philippines may not have had sufficient time to establish their careers and reach their peak earning power in the United States.

Another comparison is worth making. In 1989, households headed by a native-born Filipino American lagged behind those of immigrants from the Philippines, irrespective of the time of the immigrant's arrival. Households with foreign-born heads enjoyed an average income of $45,289; households with native-born heads, $37,943. Almost 19 percent of foreign-born–headed Filipino American households enjoyed incomes over $75,000, whereas only about 12 percent of households headed by native-born Filipino Americans did. At the bottom, 29.3 percent of households headed by native-born Filipino Americans, as opposed to 22.4 percent of households headed by an immigrant, had incomes of less than $25,000.

Although no single explanation is possible, one can speculate that native-born Filipinos, some the children of first-generation immigrants who found less than lucrative employment, entered adulthood without the college degrees and professional training that have given many post-1965 immigrants from the Philippines a distinct advantage in the U.S. economy. In Hawaii, for example, the closing of the Oahu Sugar Company, once the largest employer on the island, displaced 355 workers in 1995, who on average earned only $8.50 per hour. Second-generation Filipino American Joseph Anguay, who worked for Oahu Sugar for 40 years, had dreamed as a young man of becoming a lawyer, but explained—"I had 14 brothers and sisters so I had to help my Dad" (Vinluan and Pajaron 1996: 36).

In 1990, 15,267 Filipino American families were in poverty (defined as $12,674 for a family of four in 1989), including 3,967 (8.3 percent) of 47,691 families with native-born heads and 11,300 (4.6 percent) of 245,538 families with immigrant heads. The 3,967 poor families headed by a native-born Filipino American were typically young—48.3 percent headed by a female having children under 18 years of age. By contrast, 29.8 percent of poor immigrant families were headed by husbandless women with children under 18 years of age. Two-parent, poor families with children under age 18 were 30.1 percent of poor families with native-born heads and 34.6 percent of poor families with immigrant heads.

How might these experiences of Filipino Americans at the bottom of the ladder be explained? The youth of both native- and foreign-born single mothers and Filipino American families in poverty (68.1 percent of the 15,267 Filipino American families below the poverty level) indicates that by 1990, and probably thereafter, Filipino Americans born and/or raised in the United

States were showing the strains of American life. Many of these poverty-stricken, young Filipinos probably came of age during times of economic dislocation, especially in California, during the late 1980s and 1990s. Those who, to the dismay of their Philippine-educated parents, did not finish school have subsequently faced the same difficulties as have other less-educated Americans. The "Americanization" of young Filipino Americans, their assimilation of American culture, norms, and values, has also been accompanied by problems—at least for some. Teenage pregnancy, followed by single motherhood or early marriage, is a sure predictor of economic and occupational insecurity whatever one's ethnic origin. These, and other problems affecting Filipino Americans, will be discussed more fully in Chapter 7.

POLITICAL PARTICIPATION

To Filipino Americans the word "politics" can call to mind images from both sides of the Pacific. For Filipinos who settled in the United States after 1965, vivid memories from the Philippines undoubtedly persist. But long years spent in the United States have added other dimensions to their political consciousness—some coming through personal experience; the rest, through mass media. For U.S.-born Filipino Americans, stories of Philippine politics usually come second hand. Their personal politics, unfractured by migration, are drawn from the multifaceted politics of contemporary America. Many remain indifferent.

During the twentieth century, American colonial rule and its lingering legacy shaped Philippine politics in countless ways—by creating the institutions of representative self-government, by strengthening the power of elite landowners, by supporting the rituals of Filipino party politics, by influencing Philippine election outcomes in the interests of American foreign policy, by bolstering the regime of Ferdinand Marcos, by contriving in the quiet revolution that ultimately brought Corazon Aquino to the Philippine presidency, and by relinquishing, at long last, U.S. military bases on Filipino soil. All these elements, and many more, have molded the ways in which the Philippine-born, especially those raised in the Philippines, encounter politics in the United States.

Not all elements of Philippine political life are American derived. Traditional values and customs also play an important role in Philippine politics. Candidates seeking votes for national office typically claim voter support by appeals to common provincial or regional loyalties. Politicians deliberately utilize the *compadrinazgo* system to build a popular following. Contemplating his many election victories, Ninoy Aquino, whose assassination in 1983 ignited the turmoil that ultimately toppled Marcos, "once reckoned that he had amassed some ten thousand *compadres* who would recruit their *compadres* and the *compadres* of their *compadres* to work for him during elections" (Karnow 1989: 21).

Organizational Politics

In the United States, the heritage of the Philippines is most visible in organizational politics. To quote an anonymous Filipino mixing truth with wry humor: "It has been said that whenever two Pinoys had gotten together, they formed a club. Further it has been said that whenever those two Pinoys had gotten together in the past with a third, the three Pinoys immediately organized themselves into a Filipino Community" (Alo and Uy 1995: 43). Filipinos in the United States have sought camaraderie, support, and protection through association on the basis of student status, collegiate and provincial loyalties, occupational and professional identities, religious fidelities, and charitable and fraternal concerns, sometimes mixing goals in a single organization and often coming together under a multi-organizational community umbrella designed to advance the collective interests and goals of Filipino Americans.

While elections in many Filipino American associations proceed smoothly, more a matter of who is next willing to do the job, rather than a contest for prominence or control, other contests are vigorously fought battles. Disputed outcomes have led to violence, legal challenge, and secession. Filipino Americans and those concerned with their fate often bemoan the consequences of splintered groups and fractured unity for the larger community, sometimes labelling it as all too typical. Some have called for change, as did Philippine president Fidel Ramos in May 1997—"Filipino Americans must unite and put an end to the community's fragmentation" ("From the Editor" 1997: 4).

Interest Group and Coalition Politics

Filipino Americans have joined among themselves and, to a much lesser extent, with other Asian American groups to address contemporary political, economic, and social concerns. Although Filipinos had engaged in labor activism prior to World War II, Filipino American interest group politics directed toward community empowerment became visible in the late 1960s, especially in California where the population of Filipino Americans remains heavily concentrated, but also in other metropolitan centers of Filipino American life and at colleges attended by Filipino American students.

Interest group politics first flared among Filipino Americans on college campuses during the late 1960s and early 1970s, especially during strikes at San Francisco State College and at the University of California, Berkeley. The activism in which they and other minority group members participated ultimately led to the formation of "ethnic studies" programs, notably at Berkeley, UCLA, and San Francisco State, and to ongoing work within their ethnic communities. Just as others sought knowledge of and pride in their roots, so too did Filipino American students who sought simultaneously to learn about their heritage and to return something to the Filipino American communities from which they had come. The call to combine knowledge and action fueled their efforts, not only then, but during the decades to come.

At San Francisco State, Filipino American students founded the Philippine-American College Endeavor (PACE) and participated in San Francisco State's Third World Liberation Front to ensure that Filipino American culture and history would be taught in Ethnic Studies. While PACE leaders tried to build a "revolutionary consciousness," the organization's less politically oriented members concentrated on recruiting and tutoring Filipino American college students (Wei 1993: 18–19).

At Berkeley, Filipino American students organized the Pilipino American Alliance (PAA) and joined other students in an Asian American Political Alliance (AAPA) to work for change on campus. Seeking to expand into the community, PAA recruited "a large anti-Marcos grouping from the Filipino [American] community," and, as participants in the Asian Community Center established in 1970, fought to save the International Hotel which housed low-income, elderly, bachelor *manongs* in what remained of San Francisco's pre–World War II, ten-block Manilatown (Wei 1993: 21). Although the I-Hotel finally fell in 1977, many retained a commitment to political activism within the community.

Helping fellow community members emerged as an ongoing goal. Filipino Americans in Los Angeles created Search to Involve Pilipino Americans, Inc. (SIPA) in 1972 to combat problems confronting Filipino American youth and to foster knowledge of and pride in the Filipino American experience. Funded by Los Angeles County, the United Way, and its own efforts, SIPA has offered "fun activities" and workshops on contemporary issues for over twenty years ("Search to Involve Pilipino Americans, Inc. (SIPA)" 1991: 24).

In Oakland in 1973, Filipinos for Affirmative Action (FAA), also a United Way–funded organization, came into being to address an agenda broader than its name would imply. A wide range of social, economic, and political issues, all having an impact within the Oakland Filipino American community, have been addressed: racism, discrimination, immigration law revision, gangs, teen pregnancy, AIDS, and youth concerns "involving family, academics, relationships, peer pressure, cultural identity, and substance abuse" ("About Rebay" 1992: 3). Most recently, FAA has opposed both the changes enacted in the nation's welfare system and the mandated ending of affirmative action under California's Proposition 209, also known as the California Civil Rights Initiative.

Opposition to California's Proposition 187, which denies a wide range of publicly funded programs and services to those unable to prove U.S. citizenship, or permanent or temporary residency but has yet to be fully implemented, and to Proposition 209 also spawned a national organization, Filipino Civil Rights Advocates (FilCRA) in Berkeley in December 1994. FilCRA's July 1997 national conference in Washington, D.C., aimed at "Forging a Civil Rights Agenda for the Filipino American Community" with sessions on affirmative action and employment; civil rights and education; immigration, welfare reform and English-only legislation; Filipino World War II veterans; issues confronting labor; domestic violence, dual discrimination, and methods of empowerment; census 2000; and attacks on gay and lesbian rights ("National Membership Meeting" Schedule, FilCRA, July 25–27, 1997).

Unlike organizational politics, which is the realm of immigrants from the Philippines, interest group politics is overwhelmingly the arena of those born or reared in America. The interest group activists of today, many the children of pre–World War II Filipino immigrants, matured in an era of protest against economic, political, and racial inequality, in an era of feminism and ethnic power. Over the years, in careers in social welfare, in legal services, and in education, these now-aging campus protesters and others recruited to the cause have continued to address persistent problems in Filipino American communities.

The legacy has also been continued by more recent students. Some have continued the labor activism of the pre-1965 generations. Quezon City–born Joanne Bunuan joined the AFL-CIO as an organizer following her graduation from the University of Massachusetts in the early 1990s and has participated in organizing drives in Grand Rapids, Michigan, and Yazoo, Mississippi. In the Bay area, former UCLA undergraduate activist, Jaime Geaga, who arrived in the United States with his family at age eleven, founded the Filipino Task Force on AIDS (FTFA) after learning that he was HIV-positive in 1985. FTFA works to educate the Filipino community about AIDS and safe sex, to offer social support for gay Filipino men, to "provide medical care access, social services and housing programs to individuals with AIDs" through a network of volunteers (Silva 1995: 47–48).

While working within their communities and nationally, Filipino American activists wondered whether to make common cause with other Asian American groups. Indeed, the inclusive term, "Asian American," emerged after "brown" Filipinos rejected use of "yellow" in the "Yellow Power" equivalent of "Black Power" (Espiritu 1992: 32–33). While recognizing the advantages of diversity and larger numbers, some Filipino Americans have strongly questioned the extent to which a panethnic construct, "Asian American," can meet their specific needs. Identifying Filipino Americans as "the group most outspoken against the pan-Asian framework," Yen Le Espiritu records a litany of Filipino American complaints: "Even though we're the fastest growing Asian community, we're still getting crumbs"; "We should be getting the directorship and the funding"; "Filipinos are not getting enough of the pie. The issues being addressed have always been Japanese and Chinese issues" (Espiritu 1992: 79, 105–6).

Others, however, believe that coalition politics can help Asian Americans do as well as African Americans and Hispanic Americans. Some Filipino Americans argue that, despite their position as the nation's fastest growing and second largest Asian American group, Filipino Americans are not yet able to build sufficient mainstream interest in their specific causes and goals. As Richard Gurtiza, national secretary of the Asian Pacific American Labor Alliance, put it: "As Asians in the trade union movement . . . we haven't received the recognition we deserve. Now we have our own organization, which ensures a place at the table" (Bacon 1997: 20).

Like interest group politics, coalition politics can also harken back to the world of the *manongs* and to campus activism. As executive director of the Asian Law Caucus, the oldest non-profit legal services organization for Asian Americans in the San Francisco Bay area, Angelo Ancheta, Jr., speaks out on issues of concern to Asian Americans—anti-Asian violence, California Propositions 187 and 209, anti-immigrant trends, and cuts in social service funding. The son of an Ilocano who arrived in the United States in 1928 intending to go to college and married a Filipina teacher in 1959, Ancheta "remembers the beating he got in grade school for being 'different' and the taunts of 'chink,' 'nip' and 'jap' " that he endured. A poster of a pre–World War II sign in the doorway of a Stockton, California, hotel proclaiming "Absolutely No Filipinos Allowed" hangs prominently in his office, a reminder of the racism that his parents and other Filipino Americans suffered and survived. While a UCLA law school student in the mid-1980s, Ancheta co-chaired UCLA's Asian Pacific Law Students Association to make common cause with others from "marginalized communities." Given Ancheta's background, his vehement opposition to the University of California regents' decision to end affirmative action in university admissions, employment, and contracts is not surprising (Ayuyang, "Angelo in America" 1996: 39–41).

Filipino Americans are less conspicuous in the work of Leadership Education for Asian Pacifics (LEAP). Based in southern California, LEAP was created by "a cross section of the Asian Pacific community leadership in Southern California" in 1982 "to mobilize the talents and resources of Asian Pacific communities, nurture its leaders and foster public understanding of Asian Pacific Americans" ("The Filipino American Community in Southern California," LEAP Forum Registration Form, September 29, 1990). LEAP's Asian Pacific American Public Policy Institute (APA-PPI) addresses public policy issues through its nationally distributed publications and "by holding regional symposia" ("Facts About LEAP" 1996). Declaring "We Won't Go Back," Lillian Galedo, executive director of Filipinos for Affirmative Action and co-chair of Filipino Civil Rights Advocates, argued against Proposition 209, the "California Civil Rights Initiative," on behalf of all Asian Pacific Americans, not just Filipino Americans: "Ending affirmative action . . . is aimed at giving an advantage back to those who benefit from inequality and racism. As Asian Pacific Americans, we can't let that happen. We must defend affirmative action so that when the dust settles . . . we will not be at the bottom" (Galedo "We Won't Go Back" 1996: 35). On November 3, 1997, the U.S. Supreme Court refused, without explanation, to hear the challenge to Proposition 209.

The organizations through which Filipino Americans have participated in interest group and coalition politics—some of them examined in this section—have mixed accomplishment with frustration. Yet, a reminder is in order. The activism of a few is by no means typical of the many. Countless Filipino Americans, like innumerable Americans in general, remain oblivious to causes and campaigns, preferring to define their lives in personal, rather than political terms.

Mainstream Party Politics

Filipino Americans have also participated in mainstream party politics as voters, as elected and appointed officials, and as political party supporters. To what extent do Filipino Americans value and engage in the processes that give life to government in the United States?

Despite several notable exceptions to be discussed shortly, Filipino Americans are not, as a group, viewed as politically active or aggressive—perhaps because so many are not yet citizens or are under 18 years of age and, therefore, cannot vote; or perhaps because Filipino Americans eligible to vote are not perceived as voting in large numbers; or perhaps because ascribed Filipino character traits—being *mahinhin* or coy and exhibiting *delicadeza* or tact—can make Filipino Americans reluctant to appear too forward, especially outside their own circles. Challenging Filipino Americans to "become more assertive" in a 1997 editorial entitled "Meek Is Weak," *Filipinas* editor Rene P. Ciria-Cruz opined, "If we're still an invisible minority it's partly because we're still inaudible" ([Ciria-Cruz] "Meek Is Weak" 1997: 4).

Although numbers tell only part of the story, numbers do reveal two major factors contributing to the perceived lack of Filipino American political power in the national arena—age and citizenship. In 1990, 27.3 percent of Filipino Americans were under the age of 18 and unable to vote. In addition, Filipino Americans unable to cast a ballot also included 25.6 percent who were over age 18, but were not citizens. Thus, 52.9 percent of the nation's officially recorded 1,419,711 Filipino Americans could not vote in that year—nor could 57 percent of Chinese Americans and 59.4 percent of all Asian Americans. By contrast, only 38.7 percent of Japanese Americans and 29.6 percent of all Americans could not cast a ballot because they did not meet the nation's age and citizenship requirements.

No data on the percentage of eligible Filipino Americans actually voting are available, but the perception of their "low level of participation in 'mainstream politics' " persists ([Ciria-Cruz] "Honor Our History—Vote" 1996: 4). Irrespective of whether Filipino Americans typically vote, some of their compatriots are nonetheless entering and winning elective office, and many Filipino Americans take pride in these successes as symbolic of the progress of an immigrant group that was barred from citizenship little more than a half-century ago. In addition, a handful of Filipino Americans have positioned themselves within governmental circles and political party networks.

As might be expected, Filipino American candidates appear most frequently in areas with substantial concentrations of Filipino Americans. In Hawaii, for example, the American-born son of Filipino immigrant parents, Benjamin J. Cayetano (see Appendix II) captured the governor's office in 1994, thereby becoming the highest-ranking Filipino American elective official in U.S. history. In November 1996, twelve other Filipino Americans in Hawaii also won office. In Washington, Velma Veloria, and in West Virginia, Jon Amores won re-election in state house races ("Pols Progress" 1997: 15). And, in early 1997, Pete Fajardo defeated Carson, California's incumbent mayor, Mike Mitoma, by 155 of 11,381 votes cast in a four-way race. But, Pete did not thereby become the first Fajardo to head a local government. In 1995, Juventino B. "Ben" Fajardo won the village presidency of Glendale Heights, Illinois, 25 miles west of Chicago. In this community of about 30,000, 7 percent are Filipino American (Pilapil 1997: 32).

Despite these success stories, a serious dilemma typically plagues Filipino American office seekers. Although some communities can claim large numbers of Filipino Americans, their electoral strength is rarely sufficient to win victory only by mobilizing fellow Filipino Americans. While not alienating Filipino American voters who place primary value in shared ethnicity, a candidate must simultaneously convince a broader constituency that issues matter more than heritage—a task which has sometimes seemed easier for the American-born rather than the immigrant.

When he won election to the city council in Daly City, California, in 1993, San Francisco–born Michael Patrick Guingona, whose great-grandfather was a governor of Batangas, defeated Mario Panoringan, an immigrant from Pangasinan, and three other candidates to become the first elected official in a community in which Filipino Americans numbered 24 percent of the eligible voters. During the previous fifteen years, ten Filipino Americans had run and lost in various contests, including Guingona, who failed in his first council bid in November 1992. When Guingona, a 1989 University of San Francisco law school graduate and former public defender, ran a mainstream, grassroots, issue-oriented campaign rather than "as a 'Filipino' candidate that was only concerned with the Filipino community," he "drew fire" from many immigrants for his "lack of Filipinoness," but responded forcefully in an unaccented voice that some considered an "advantage": "We have to be able to survive in this system. I don't even want to take any of the vestiges of the system in the Philippines and bring them here because they don't work here." Second-place finisher Panoringan, who polled 28 percent to Guingona's 38 percent, suffered from the "apathy" of his presumed supporters, many of whom did not keep their promises to vote (Torres 1993: 12–16). Mike Guingona is now Daly City's mayor.

Filipino Americans also secured appointive governmental positions during the 1990s, especially because of the Clinton Administration's efforts to include women and minorities in its ranks. Philippine-born, European-educated Maria Luisa Mabilangan Haley, who lived in the president's home state for over twenty years after she met and married an Arkansas attorney while running a finishing school in Manila, became a Clinton appointee focusing on international trade development during his gubernatorial years and later did extensive volunteer work during his presidential campaign. After the 1992 election, Haley served on Clinton's transition team and, as a member of the board of directors of the Export-Import Bank, came to be "considered the highest-ranking Fil-Am in the White House" (Ayuyang "Capital Gains" 1996: 60).

Others among Clinton appointees include liberal Democrat Paula Bagasao as a senior policy advisor at the U.S. Agency for International Development; Ferdinand "Danny" Aranza, who was raised in Guam, as the Interior Department's deputy director of insular affairs; Irene Bueno as deputy to the assistant secretary for legislation of the Department of Health and Human Services; Eugene Bae as senior program analyst in environmental security at the Defense Department; Christian Baldia as senior policy analyst in domestic finance at Treasury; Tyrone Cabulu as confidential assistant in the Bureau of Export Affairs at Commerce; and Bob Santos who, after thirty years of activism in Seattle's Filipino American community, became head of the Northwestern/Alaska office of the Department of Housing and Urban Development. Raised in Canada and the 1971 valedictorian at Long Island University where she worked in Eugene McCarthy's 1968 presidential campaign, Irene Natividad served from 1985 to 1989 as the first Asian American chair of the National Women's Political Caucus which works for the election of women candidates; chaired the National Commission on Working Women which worked to better women's economic status during the early 1990s; and became a member of the Student Loan Marketing Association under Clinton.

Thus, in recent years, Filipino Americans have become more visible in U.S. governmental circles. Like those chosen from other nationalities and racial groups, Filipino American appointees achieved their positions after years of experience in their communities or in their professions. Some share an almost life-long commitment to traditional Democratic political values and consciously aim at using their power to achieve the outcomes they have long sought. For example, Bob Santos used his clout at HUD to prevent the closing of a homeless shelter in Seattle. "Twenty years ago, I led a group from the International District to demand action from the HUD office. . . . Now I run the HUD office" (Ayuyang "Capital Gains" 1996: 31, 32).

The Filipino American commitment to the Democratic Party has a long heritage, one that predates 1946 when immigrants from the Philippines were finally allowed to become citizens and voters. As Emil Guillermo, an independent journalist who formerly hosted National Public Radio's "All Things Considered," explained it: "Republicanism is as alien to the Guillermos as *patis* is to white folks. My family arrived here in the '20s. They know firsthand what happens when you mix immigration with an economic depression: racism. . . . Only the unions and the labor movement saved them. . . . That's been the bond to the Democratic Party, as well as to the civil rights movement" (Guillermo 1996: 25). Many second-generation Filipino Americans and their old-timer parents identify the Democratic Party with changes that continue to affect the quality of their lives—unions, civil rights legislation, student loans, social security, federal deposit insurance on savings, and Medicare.

Although they are not an immediate threat, the Republican Party has made inroads among Filipino Americans, especially among those with high incomes, such as small business owners and medical professionals, and those with strong connections to the military. Filipino American Republicans tend to espouse reliance on family rather than government, and identify GOP "core conservatism" with "traditional ('Filipino') values of hard work, self-responsibility, respect for authority, family cohesion and love of God" ([Ciria-Cruz] "Its the Values, Stupid" 1996: 17). Those with ties to the U.S. military value the Republican commitment to high military budgets that long kept communities, such as San Diego, strong, as well as GOP support for citizenship and veterans benefits for Filipino veterans of World War II. For example, retired Chief Petty Officer Bob Medina helped to organize the Filipino-American Republican Council of California in the late 1970s after he retired from the U.S. Navy, worked for Republican candidates in San Diego County, and served on the staff of Republican congressman Duncan Hunter from 1979 until 1993.

Affirmative action has been a more divisive issue among Filipino American Republicans. Despite their general belief "that equal opportunity for all isn't a reality yet," some reject affirmative action, fearing the forced hiring of the unqualified and a backlash among white Americans. Others joined with Democratic Filipino Americans in California to oppose Proposition 209. Philippine-born and educated Hernando Caampued, a San Jose, California, civil engineer who owns his own consulting firm, a Republican since 1986, and a member of the Presidential Commission on Minority Business Development during the Bush Administration, worked against the measure: "I don't like handouts, . . . but let's face it. Women are discriminated, minorities are discriminated, what more without affirmative action? It's a program to outreach more minorities, qualified minorities. . . . We must also remember the sacrifices of other minorities for civil rights. Do we want blacks and Hispanics to do all the fighting? What will they think of us? That we just sit back and then enjoy all the benefits from their efforts?" Some say that that is precisely the point. Democrat Rodel Rodis candidly states: "Some racist Filipinos go to the GOP because they associate the Democratic Party with blacks and Hispanics" ([Ciria-Cruz] "Its the Values, Stupid" 1996: 17, 19).

In the future, Filipino Americans willing to make a political commitment are likely to remain predominantly Democratic. Current Democratic Filipino American party loyalists will likely be strengthened by the addition of newly naturalized voters who blame anti-immigrant legislation on the Republican Party. Filipino Americans, whose Philippine relatives have spent futile decades waiting for immigrant visas, associate immigrant-bashing with extremists in the GOP. Despite what some current Filipino American Democratic activists see as an unfortunate conservative turn by the Democratic Party during the Clinton Administration, Filipino Americans on the eve of the twenty-first century are still more likely Democrats than Republicans, if—and that's a big if—they play politics at all.

Sexual Politics

In addition to organizational, interest group, coalition, and mainstream politics, one final aspect of Filipino American political involvement deserves attention—sexual politics. In recent decades, many Filipino American gays, lesbians, and bisexuals have deliberately chosen activism, taking pride in their identity and participating in organizations such as Kambal sa Lusog, a Filipino American lesbian and gay group, or Kilawin Kolektibo, a Filipina American lesbian collective, both in New York City; in Asian Lesbians of the East Coast (ALOEC); in Asian and Pacific Islander Queer and Questioning Under 25 Altogether (AQUA[25]A) in California; and in the Asian/Pacific Islander Parents and Friends of Lesbians and Gays (A/PI-PFLAG) Family Project in San Francisco. In New York City in the early 1990s, Filipino gay men were drawn into the controversy over the Broadway musical *Miss Saigon* when some participated in the Gay Asian Pacific Islander Men of New York (GAPIMNY) protest of the show. By contrast, others came to regard the success of *Miss Saigon* star Lea Salonga and other Filipino-American cast members as "a collective triumph" (Manalansan 1994: 65–67).

Filipina American lesbians have also been active in claiming recognition. The women of Kiliwan have marched in the Philippine Independence Day Parade in New York City and have been interviewed on *Radyo Pinoy*, a Filipino radio program. Yet, many continue to feel marginalized. "To be visible, we also need some political consciousness. The *bakla* [gay men] are already known" (Lipat, Ordona, Stewart, and Ubaldo 1997: 241). "People just don't want to talk about it, . . . If they don't talk about it, it doesn't exist" (Almendrala "The Sound of Silence" 1997: 26).

Like homosexuals and bisexuals throughout American society, Filipino Americans often confront their most serious challenges in dealing with their own families, often waiting years before "coming out," and sometimes never doing so explicitly. Filipino American parents also react in varied ways—from "no real problem" to "very hostile" (Lipat, Ordona, Stewart, and Ubaldo 1997: 238). Other parents blame themselves or comfort themselves with the belief that their child's homosexuality is just a passing phase. Still others can never be reconciled, even to a child dying of AIDS. Thus, in New York City, Filipino American gay men have come together to help their sick friends, raising money for medical expenses and "*Abuloy* or alms for the dead" by running "fashion shows and drag parties" (Manalansan 1994: 69).

Whatever their interest group, coalition, mainstream, or sexual politics, Filipino Americans, as individuals and as family members, confront multiple, often difficult issues in contemporary America. These matters are examined in the next chapter.

PART III

FILIPINO AMERICANS ENTERING THE TWENTY-FIRST CENTURY

7

Contemporary Issues among Filipino Americans

Under an umbrella of national citizenship, Filipinos in the Philippines generally define their identities by reference to class, religion, and province. By contrast, Filipinos in the United States partake in a sharply defined ethnic identity made collective by their contrast with Americans of other ethnicities and races. Yet, Filipino Americans are themselves amazingly varied. Class, religion, and provincial origins still matter greatly among Filipino Americans. Filipino Americans differ in age, in their time of arrival or birth in the United States, in the depth of their connections to non-Filipino Americans, and in their occupational attainment, economic status, and political attitudes and commitments.

For some, immigration from the Philippines and settling into America is remote—part of a family past connected to parents, grandparents, and even more distant ancestors who came long ago and may now be dead, unable to answer their descendants' myriad questions about their circumstances and their experiences. Just as these native-born Filipino Americans with deep roots in the United States contrast with contemporary America's more numerous Filipino immigrants, the newcomers also differ among themselves, initially, because of who they were and what they experienced in the Philippines prior to their migration, and, subsequently, because of the disparate choices they make and the dissimilar experiences they have after coming to the United States. Their children also vary. Some are themselves immigrants, with different memories of their homeland based on the age at which their transplantation to America occurred. Other children of immigrants, born and raised in the United States, have little against which to contrast the lives they now live.

Precisely because of their diversity, not all Filipino Americans are directly and personally enmeshed in the concerns and difficulties of Filipino American youth, adults, and elders that are examined in this chapter. Still, because Filipino Americans typically perceive a collective Filipino American identity based on ethnicity and race, irrespective of how they construct that identity broadly and within the context of their own lives, their grappling with contemporary issues plays an important role in the ongoing process of self- and group-definition. As such, these situations and predicaments challenge not only those Filipino Americans who experience them personally, but also those Filipino Americans who seek to understand who they are—as Filipino Americans—on the eve of the twenty-first century.

INDIVIDUAL ASPIRATIONS, FAMILY CLAIMS, AND THE FILIPINO AMERICAN HOUSEHOLD

As discussed in Chapter 4, the family plays a central role in defining personal identity in the Philippines. Individual aspirations and needs are expected to give way to the good of the family group. Immigration to the United States has not diminished the family as the central reference point for vast numbers of Filipino Americans. Given the place of family within Filipino American lives, household structure is a crucial component in understanding the lives of Filipino Americans.

In 1990, Filipino American households more typically included members other than spouses, children, and even parents and parents-in-law of the householder, than did American households in general. Whereas 8.5 percent of American households in 1990 were "extended" by the presence of sub-families—related members other than spouses, children, and parents and parents-in-law of the householder—and roomers, boarders, or foster children over the age of 15, 28.5 percent of Filipino American households contained such persons. These extended household living arrangements characterized 30.6 percent of all foreign-born Filipino American households, in contrast with 18.8 percent of native-born Filipino American households.

The ramifications of this pattern defy precise interpretation. On the one hand, one might argue that, because almost 70 percent of the households captured by the 1990 census were *not* extended, a nuclear household composed of parents, children, and a grandparent or two remains the norm. On the other hand, one must still wonder about the extent to which household extension might in the past or in the future be a part of the experience of many of the nuclear households as well. If, at some point, Filipino Americans do share their homes with others outside their immediate, nuclear families, what will that mean? Will familial and fictive kinship ties thereby be strengthened and perpetuate those Filipino values which emphasize the importance of the family over the individual? Or, might tensions among members of these enlarged households, especially between generations, foster future rejection of traditional norms? No single outcome can be predicted.

The traditional Filipino emphasis on family solidarity can also generate a countervailing reluctance to share difficulties with anyone outside of the family circle, except perhaps a priest. An outsider's knowledge of trouble within the family brings *hiya* or shame to the family. Explaining Filipino reluctance to seek help, Monsignor Oscar Aquino of St. Francis Church in New York City asserts: "If your son or daughter is not good, he or she is told '*nakakahiya ka* (you are an embarrassment).' A Filipino doctor talked to me about his son, but he never sent the child for therapy or psychiatric help, even if he could afford it. To ease their conscience, parents come to church, [and] light a candle" (Quimpo 1994: 51). In addition, because Filipinos value *pakikisama*, "smooth personal relationships," they tend to avoid that which disrupts harmony or causes confrontation (Berganio, Tacata, and Jamero 1997: 281).

The sections that follow highlight issues and concerns of particular relevance to Filipino American youth, adults, and elders, thus targeting these cohorts as separate components within Filipino America. Teens don't worry about the medical care they will receive when they are old, and the elderly don't join gangs. But, of course, such artificial categories blur constantly in practice, for teenaged and elderly Filipino Americans generally confront such matters within their families.

FILIPINO AMERICAN YOUTH

In 1990, 437,648 (30.8 percent) of the nation's 1.4 million Filipino Americans were under the age of 20—329,538 born in the United States and 108,110 born abroad. Most lived in the nation's 356,375 Filipino American households, of which 65,623 (18.4 percent) were classified as native born, and 290,752 (81.6 percent) as foreign born. Whether native-born or foreign-born, Filipino Americans under the age of 18 more likely lived in two-parent households than did Americans under the age of 18 in general—80.9 percent, as opposed to 73.0 percent. No doubt, these young Filipino Americans face issues common to many of the nation's youth. But, growing up American and Filipino also presents special challenges, especially with regard to education, social issues, generational tension, and cultural conflict.

In researching the assimilation of the children of immigrant parents into American society, Alejandro Portes and Min Zhou have offered a model of "segmented assimilation"—"three possible patterns of adaptation most likely to occur among contemporary immigrants and their offspring" (Zhou 1997: 975). "One of them replicates the time-honored portrayal of growing acculturation and parallel integration into the white middle-class; a second leads straight into the opposite direction to permanent poverty and assimilation into the underclass; still a third associates rapid economic advancement with deliberate preservation of the immigrant community's values and tight solidarity" (Portes and Zhou 1993: 82). How many second-generation Filipino Americans will adapt along the lines suggested by each of these patterns—or according to other patterns—is impossible to predict. Zhou notes that "major determinants" include both external or societal factors—"racial stratification, economic opportunities and spatial segregation," and internal or ethnic group factors—"financial and human capital upon arrival, family structure, community organization, and cultural patterns of social relations" (Zhou 1997: 999). The diverse backgrounds and varied lives of Filipino American parents will likely create multiple contexts in which their children will mature.

Education in the United States

Since the beginning of the twentieth century and the expansion of education under American colonial rule, the desire for education has been a pervasive goal among Filipinos. "Education has always been immensely important to Filipinos. It was not and is still not uncommon for all children in a family to be professionals—or for one elder brother or sister to take any job in order to allow the younger ones to acquire higher educations" (Vallangca 1987: 138). Education has, in fact, been the single most compelling reason for migration to the United States since the end of World War II, and bleak job prospects continue to fuel a massive diaspora of Filipino labor around the world in the late twentieth century.

Given this history, the tremendous significance of education to Filipino Americans, especially recent immigrants, should not be surprising. Having arrived with diplomas in hand, many Filipino newcomers simultaneously pursue two education-related goals in the United States—securing their children's educations and utilizing their own. For some, the achievement of these goals has come only with great difficulty—if at all. Indeed, the two objectives have, at times, been in conflict in daily life. As Philippine-educated parents have struggled to build their own careers, their long hours at work and their depleted energy levels at home have cut some youth adrift from the very goals so clearly defined in their parents' minds. As this has occurred, many Filipino Americans have personally and collectively struggled with self-doubt, seeking answers sufficient to explain why many young Filipino Americans have neither followed in their parents' footsteps nor become the "model" Asian Americans celebrated by superficial observers of contemporary American life.

The "Model Minority" Myth and Filipino American Educational Attainment

In recent years, scholars have spent considerable energy debunking the stereotypical notion of Asian Americans as a "model minority," a construct that emerged during the civil rights turmoil of the late 1960s and stressed the success of Asian Americans, especially Japanese Americans and Chinese Americans, with regard to education, occupation, and income. Emerging during years when many college-educated Filipino professionals began to arrive, the myth of the model minority soon came to encompass Filipino Americans as well. Recent immigrants themselves fostered—and continue to foster—the notion of education as central to success by paying lavish attention to the educational achievements of their children—their high school valedictory addresses, their college admissions, and their graduations with honors. The typical pride of parents and kin is transformed into a celebration of triumph in a new land.

Two sets of statistics drawn from the 1990 U.S. Census can help to probe Filipino American educational attainment. In 1990, 83.8 percent of Filipino Americans between 18 and 24 years of age had completed high school or its equivalency; for native-born Filipino Americans, 84.2 percent, and for foreign-born Filipino Americans, 83.6 percent. For this age cohort as a whole in the United States, the comparative percentages were 76.5 percent for all Americans, 78.4% for native-born Americans, and 57.1 percent for foreign-born Americans. In contrast, however, the high school-or-better percentages for 18- to 24-year-olds in other Asian American groups were higher—91.4 percent for Japanese Americans, 86.6 percent for Asian Indians, and 84.6 percent for Chinese Americans.

Data on Filipino Americans 25 years of age and older who have completed a bachelor's degree or higher are especially revealing with regard to the differences between native- and foreign-born Filipino Americans and, when compared with similar data for other Asian American ethnic groups, also highlight differences within contemporary Asian America: 39.3 percent of all Filipino Americans hold a bachelor's degree or higher, in contrast with

58.1 percent of Asian Indians, 40.7 percent of Chinese Americans, and 34.5 percent of Japanese Americans. However, the difference between foreign-born and native-born Filipino Americans is especially striking. While 42.4 percent of the foreign born in this cohort hold a bachelor's degree or higher, only 22.3 percent of the native born do—a gap of 20.1 percentage points. In no other group is this gap so large—14.5 percent for Asian Indians, 0.9 percent for Japanese Americans, and, in a reverse gap, native-born Chinese Americans exceeding the foreign born by 12.3 percent.

Rank ordering the data by place of birth and by sex makes the position of native-born Filipino Americans especially dismal. Native-born Filipino American men and women trail other Asian Americans. Native-born Filipino American men hold last place; only 22.1 percent of those 25 years of age and older possess a bachelor's degree or better. The place of native-born Filipino American females is scarcely better—third from the bottom, with 22.4 percent. Only foreign-born Japanese American females do worse.

Two conclusions can easily be drawn. First, the myth of the model minority with regard to educational attainment is hardly an appropriate depiction of the situation of Filipino Americans in general, but especially not of American-born Filipino Americans. As a group, Filipino Americans lag behind native- and foreign-born Asian Indians of both sexes, behind native-born Japanese Americans and Chinese Americans of both sexes, and behind foreign-born Japanese and Chinese American men. Second, within Filipino America, the divergence between native- and foreign-born educational attainment has likely set the stage for severe tension between the generations. The anger, alienation, and dismay present in families whose children have not reached the educational goals set for them by their parents is likely to be considerable, and is likely to be made manifest in countless ways, now and in the future.

Educational Prospects: High School Test Scores and Dropouts; and College Admissions, Affirmative Action, and the California Civil Rights Initiative (Proposition 209)

In 1990, of 167,259 Filipino Americans between 18 and 24 years of age, 27,023—11,060 (15.8 percent) of the native born and 15,963 (16.4 percent) of the foreign born—did not hold a high school diploma or its equivalent. Such numbers are not viewed with equanimity, especially in locales where heavy concentrations of Filipino Americans make the problem of low educational achievement and its consequences especially visible. Citing an Educational Testing Services study, *Filipinas* bannered Filipino Americans as a "Not So Model Minority" in June 1997: "dropout rates for Filipinos are 46 percent." Fifty percent of Filipino American high school seniors scored at or below "the 50th percentile among all seniors in reading" in contrast with South Asians among whom 79 percent scored above the 50th percentile ("Not So Model Minority" 1997: 68). Poor educational achievement is likely to affect not only those who drop out of high school or those who decline, after graduation, to go on to college, but perhaps also those who enter college—and find the work difficult.

Concern over Filipino American college attendance has also become an important issue for many, especially in California where Filipino Americans tend to be lumped together with other Asian Americans and where the statewide ending of affirmative action programs through the California Civil Rights Initiative (Proposition 209) is generally viewed by community leaders as simply the latest blow weakening Filipino American chances for equitable access to higher education. Because they are often assessed not as a separate group, but rather as a component in the more diverse, combined category of "Asian American," Filipino Americans have often been denied consideration for special programs targeting "underrepresented" groups on campuses. Asian Americans, as a whole, have generally not been seen as needing special assistance, as have African Americans, Hispanic Americans, and Native Americans. "The considerable success of some Asian Americans in gaining access to college and in graduating masks the academic and economic difficulties of others" (Magner 1993: A32).

At the University of California, Filipino American admissions have long been in question. Operating under the 1960 Master Plan for Higher Education, University of California campuses have selected most of their incoming freshmen from a large pool comprised of the top 12.5 percent of public high school graduates, but "because of educational disparities between rich and poor schools, the process often favors students from suburban schools and works against those from urban and rural schools" (Haynes 1997: 3). Thus, although technically in the pool of qualified applicants, Filipino American students did not necessarily win admission. Their situation worsened after 1990, when the number of Filipino American high school graduates able to meet the university's admissions standards exceeded 12.5 percent of all Filipino American students graduating from high school. Filipino American students then became ineligible for the affirmative action efforts in admission that previously gave them a competitive edge in the pool. The number of Filipino American freshmen on the Berkeley campus "dwindled from 227 in 1989 to 54" in 1993 (Guillermo 1998: 39). At UCLA, "without the benefits of affirmative action, Filipino Americans . . . [had] among the very lowest rates of admission at UCLA of any ethnic group . . . [and, according to UCLA's director of undergraduate admissions were] 'being beat out in the admissions game by students who are smarter and those who are poorer' " (Magner 1993: A34). In 1996, only 26 percent of the 1,377 Filipino Americans who applied for admission to UCLA won acceptance, while at Berkeley, only 16 percent of 979 applicants gained places in the freshman class. On both campuses, these were the lowest acceptance rates for any group. Because the U.S. Supreme Court refused to hear a case challenging the California Civil Rights Initiative (Proposition 209) in November 1997, the abolition of affirmative action in college admissions will now spread from the University of California system with its pool including the top 12.5 percent of the state's high school graduates to the California State University system with its pool containing the top 33.5 percent.

Only time will write the final chapter to this story. As access to college and to other avenues of mobility become more problematic for other groups, especially African Americans and Hispanic Americans, the impact of California's Proposition 209, and of similar efforts in states such as Texas, will remain hotly contested. In California, politicians have already begun proposing alternative ways based on geography and income to remedy the consequences of Proposition 209. Whether Filipino Americans will benefit from such efforts remains to be seen.

Generational Tension and Cultural Conflict over Gang Membership, Premarital Sex and Teen Pregnancy, and the Choice of a Spouse

In addition to concern over their educational prospects, Filipino American youth also confront issues stemming from generational tension and cultural conflict as they move through adolescence toward adulthood. They are not, of course, alone in facing these matters. Many American adolescents, especially the children of immigrants, also do. Undoubtedly, countless Filipino American adolescents reach adulthood scarcely touched by the traumatic concerns that can come to dominate others' lives. But, when parent-child clashes over gang membership, premarital sex and teen pregnancy, and the choice of a spouse occur, permanent rifts and lasting consequences can result.

As their children become more American than Filipino, at least in their eyes, many Philippine-raised parents bemoan their accents and their idiomatic English, their lack of respect, their tendency to talk back, and their late hours, and they worry about the financial costs of higher education in the United States and who their children will marry. Raising his children in Hopkinsville, Kentucky, Rufy Virata opined: "My younger boy has a Southern accent now. . . . I'm not really happy with it. I don't think it's appropriate. I'd rather that my boys have a Filipino accent because I would like them to identify with me" (Virata 1993: 72). In suburban New Jersey, eighteen-year-old Christina Hernandez's mother reminded her: "You should remember we are still Filipinos. Though we are in America, *you* are not American." When Christina talked of studying sports medicine, her mother broached sending her back to the Philippines where college tuition would be less costly, but, after eight years in the United States, Christina announced: "I couldn't stay there for more than a month. It's not home anymore" (Quimpo 1994: 51). Growing up in a small Kansas town as the only child of a Filipino doctor and nurse, Janette Bustos, who ultimately left Herington to attend Georgetown University, recalled disagreements during her high school years with her mother who would say: " '[W]hen I was growing up back home in the Philippines,' . . . We just had a lot of struggles trying to . . . adjust between the Filipino culture and the American culture and find the middle ground there" (*Green Pastures: Filipinos in the Heartland* 1997: video). Recent research on second-generation Filipino Americans, most of them living in California, suggests that their parents typically apply considerable pressure as they move through high school and college, urging them relentlessly to succeed in school and "to choose 'safe' professions" (Wolf 1997: 465). Because of "gendered notions of propriety," parents pressure their daughters to excel academically, yet simultaneously insist that they live at home and commute to college, so that their whereabouts can be monitored and their sexuality controlled (Wolf 1997: 467). On the other hand, sons, encounter more parental laxity.

For many Filipino American youth and their parents, adolescent difficulties will fade with time. In contrast, other predicaments—gang membership, premarital sex and teen pregnancy, and the choice of a spouse—can cause repercussions well past adolescence.

In the Philippines, where gangs focusing on criminal activity have been a phenomenon since the end of World War II, a more benign form of association is also typical among Filipino peers with common interests—the *barcada*. Members of a *barcada* typically share similar backgrounds—for example, in social class or school ties—and pursue solidarity through joint activities and mutual assistance. Over time and in varied settings in the United States, the Philippine *barcada* (or *barkada*) has become the Filipino American gang—sometimes still more a clique devoted to social activities than a gang, sometimes crossing ethnic boundaries to link with those who are not Filipino American, sometimes limiting their activities to "graffiti vandalism, shoplifting, and street violence," and sometimes involved in major criminal activity such as drugs and gun sales, theft, arson, murder, and rape (Pulido 1991: 12). No single force seems to generate Filipino gangs. Parental neglect, culture and language differences, poverty, racism, boredom, the absence of role models, the need to belong, and the fear of other gangs are but some of the reasons offered to explain Filipino American gang activity. Gangs can be found in suburban as well as inner-city settings, up and down the West Coast, in Chicago, and in the East.

In 1991, an article in a local newspaper about a shootout in suburban Virginia Beach, Virginia, ostensibly made public what had "been whispered among Filipino teenagers for years," the existence of at least three "Filipino gangs"—the Diego Boys, the Pretty Boys, and the Barcada Boys—whose members were from "solidly middle-class, hard-working families." One of those arrested explained from his jail cell: "People join the gangs to be cool, to say you're in it and don't mess with me" (Waltz 1991: B1, B4).

For some, the consequences of gang membership have proven fatal. "Death is part of the drama of living the gang life in L.A. Police say there are at least 60 Filipino street gangs in Los Angeles County," wrote Bangele "Nonoy" Alsaybar in 1993. Giving fictional names to the informant and the gang, Alsaybar interviewed Benjie, a member of Los Demonios: "I'll be eighteen four months from now. I'd like to take up nursing, get a good job, raise a family and help my Mom and other brothers and sisters, too." On the night after he spoke with Alsaybar, Benjie took a fatal blast to his chest, shot by a member of a rival Filipino American gang (Alsaybar 1993: 11, 67).

While young men are usually the focus of attention when Filipino American gangs are discussed, young Filipina Americans are not free of gang involvement. Because they usually arouse less suspicion than do young men, female gang members sometimes serve as drivers, decoys, and accomplices who gain the trust of intended victims, or hold weapons for male gang members who are more likely to be searched. By the early 1990s on the West Coast, Filipina American gangs "totally independent from the Filipino gangs" had also appeared (Pulido 1991: 12).

Some parents have responded to the threat of gang involvement in their children's lives by trying to move away from communities where Filipino American gangs are especially prevalent. Others have supported Filipino youth organizations, such as Filipino Youth Activities in Seattle, which, since 1957, has targeted "at risk" adolescents with drill team, dance, and martial arts programs designed to counteract the pull of gang membership. Still others have sent their children "back home" to the seemingly safer, less permissive environment of the Philippines—but with mixed success.

Rather than actual gang membership, parental fear of a child becoming "a little American nightmare" can also prompt "exile." In one instance, a Filipino American mother living in Los Angeles panicked over her daughter's "heavier make-up" and "shorter" skirts and the pregnancy of a sixteen-year-old girlfriend. She returned the girl to her father and an all-girls school in Manila. Now enrolled in college and hoping to become a lawyer, the young woman intends to remain in the Philippines (Galang-Macaraeg 1997: 25–26). Fear for her daughter's future in the face of adolescent sex and possible pregnancy was not unwarranted; 36 percent of 254 Filipino American high schoolers surveyed in Vallejo, California, in 1992–93 were sexually active.

Data on adolescent pregnancy among Filipino Americans is fragmentary. In 1991, in San Francisco, they recorded "the highest pregnancy rates among Asians (6.7%)," as well as "the highest rate of increase in the number of births (65%) compared to African Americans, Latinas, whites, and other Asian groups" with numbers that rose from 34 in 1990 to 56 (Tiongson 1997: 257–258).

Although no group in the United States is without some incidence of teen pregnancy, the phenomenon sometimes poses an especially difficult dilemma for Filipino Americans. Coming, for the most part, from a Catholic background which places high value on abstinence from premarital sex and rejects both divorce and abortion, and from a cultural tradition which fosters both *hiya* (shame) and *pakikisama* (getting along with others), Filipino American adolescents often find it difficult to discuss their situation with their parents. Many fear fury and outright parental rejection or, at the very least, continuing stigma within their families. Some are, in fact, surprised by the support that their families offer when their "predicament" is finally revealed. The extent to which abortion is utilized by Filipino Americans is unknown. In one family, an elder daughter chose that option, while a younger sibling decided, instead, to raise her baby as a single mother—and found that her "parents blamed her for the pregnancy more than the father" (Tiongson 1997: 266). Whether they become single parents—single mothers or non-custodial single fathers providing financial and/or emotional support—or marry and begin to raise a child within a two-parent household, these young Filipino Americans generally find their futures fraught with difficulties rooted in lack of schooling and poverty, as well as in the late twentieth century decline of the U.S. system of social welfare.

Choosing a spouse can also cause problems between young Filipino Americans and their parents, typically, when a child marries someone who is not a Filipino American, but especially if the intended partner seems lacking in "prospects." Of course, not all out-marriages provoke ire. Countless Filipino American parents extend a warm welcome to sons- and daughters-in-law of many nationalities and proudly note the arrival of multi-ethnic grandchildren in birth announcements and Christmas photos and letters. For example, by the late 1990s, three daughters of Arturo and Erlinda Apolinario, a physician and nurse who immigrated to the Philadelphia area from Manila in the early 1970s, had married non-Filipino Americans in elegant weddings after which the family and friends of both bride and groom dined and danced at lavish receptions.

Parental distress over a child's marriage is most typical when the child is deemed "too young" or when the spouse seems inappropriate. One San Diego immigrant mother tried to stop her daughter's marriage to "a white person she met at work . . . because . . . [she] wanted her to finish school first," but noted, "I did my best for her wedding." In this mother's eyes, her daughters' choices could have been far worse: "Honest to goodness, I don't mind whom my daughters marry, I just hope that it is not going to be colored *baluga* [black] people. I am not saying that I have anything against them. . . . But I keep praying to God, 'Don't let my kids marry *baluga*' " (Espiritu 1995: 124).

In the late 1980s, when Filipina American Beth Logan decided to marry her African American Oakland-born husband Chris a few years after coming to the United States with her family at the age of twenty-one, her parents asked disapprovingly: "*Bakit itim pa* (Why a black guy of all people)?" After almost a decade and the birth of two sons to the couple, her mother, Raphaela could admit: "when I got to know my son-in-law, I realized not all blacks are bad." Still, during the planning for the Logan family's first trip to the Philippines, Beth warned Chris: "People will call you *negro, egot* or G.I. Joe and most will think I'm a prostitute" (Kobylarz 1997: 22–23). The anti-black racial attitudes of Filipino immigrant parents, "deeply rooted in the home country's colonial past" and frequently reinforced in the United States, have been difficult to confront and change. Made more conscious of race and racism through multicultural courses and through interaction with African Americans, U.S.-raised Filipino American children sometimes try to convince their elders that racism against African Americans is no different from racism against Filipino Americans. But, long-ingrained attitudes die hard (Kobylarz 1997: 20–22).

FILIPINO AMERICAN ADULTS

The concerns challenging Filipino American youth in contemporary America obviously also affect their parents. But Filipino American adults, especially post-1965 immigrants, also face unique issues. Life in the United

States brings tribulation as well as triumph. Educated in the Philippines to expect professional employment, many have nonetheless faced a continuing struggle to "make it" in America through the practice of their professions. Others without specialized training have similarly found unanticipated difficulties in the quest to earn their daily bread. The trauma generated by the confluence of leaving so much behind, struggling so hard to get ahead, and dealing with a new milieu has left considerable numbers of immigrant Filipino Americans grappling, like their children, with often painful matters.

Struggling to Make It in America

Among the 647,487 foreign-born Filipino Americans counted in the 1990 Census, 77.3 percent held employment of thirty-five or more hours per week; 15.3 percent were employed less than thirty-five hours per week (whether by choice or through under-employment is not known); 4.6 percent were unemployed; and 2.8 percent were members of the armed forces. However these relatively positive statistics tell only part of the story. In 1985, sociologist Antonio J. A. Pido contended: "[N]ew Pilipino immigrants are competitive in the labor market, especially for lowerlevel jobs for which they are overqualified" (Pido 1985: 87). Possessed of good educations and sufficient proficiency in English, immigrants from the Philippines get jobs—hence, their comparatively low level of unemployment. Yet, despite a persistent image which portrays most Filipino immigrant adults as well-educated, generally successful professionals, making it in America remains far from easy.

For many Filipino newcomers, winning employment commensurate with their training has proven problematic. Immigrants with Philippine-acquired degrees and credentials have faced varying, state-imposed requirements with regard to education, citizenship, and experience as prerequisites for obtaining the licenses and certificates necessary for professional practice. During the 1970s, licensure as a physician in California required either an internship at a California hospital or U.S. citizenship. As a result, Filipino immigrant physicians sometimes took jobs far beneath their training—as "medical aides, clerks, waiters, or dishwashers"—just to remain in California, or they began to practice medicine in other states, even if they hoped to move to California in time (Allen 1977: 202). On the East Coast and in the Midwest, urban public hospitals without medical school programs and the labor supplied by physicians-in-training regularly turned to foreign medical graduates (FMGs) to fill their staff rosters. State licensing boards cooperated by waiving full medical licensing for hospital staff employment while simultaneously limiting movement from these jobs to private practice "by holding unusually difficult licensure examinations" (Allen 1977: 201). Today, state licensing require-ments together with federal immigration policies continue to limit options for Filipino physicians wishing to practice medicine in the United States.

Other Filipino professionals—accountants, dentists, lawyers, teachers, ar-chitects and engineers among them—have faced similar hurdles when state- and nationwide boards of professional certification have refused to accept Philippine study and experience as equivalent to American preparation. Until 1970, for example, California required foreign-educated dentists to complete two additional years of schooling in the United States prior to taking the California licensure examination. Because "Philippine jurisprudence is based on Roman law, while the U.S.'s is based on Common or Anglo Saxon Law," Filipino lawyers confront the most dire prospects (Pido 1985: 88). Immi-gration to the United States means either starting over by attending a U.S. law school or choosing another calling.

However, such stories of woe are not without exception. Two years after his 1969 arrival in Seattle, veterinarian Camilo De Guzman passed veterinary board examinations in both Washington and California. "One advantage I had over other foreign veterinarians was that the University of the Philip-pines' curriculum is recognized by the American Veterinarian Medical As-sociation. . . . I did not have to further my schooling" (Chew 1993: 21, 60).

Whatever their occupations, Filipino immigrants have sometimes also con-fronted discrimination based on "English-only" rules in the workplace. In 1974, a Filipina nurse at Illinois Masonic Hospital in Chicago quit her job of seven years after an American nurse challenged her for speaking Tagalog with a Filipino physician during her lunch hour. Rather than contest the situation, the Filipina nurse observed that she "want[ed] to forget the whole thing" (Lacson 1974: 7).

In a more recent California case, nurse Aida Dimaranan fought discrim-ination. After she was reassigned to a lesser job because of her campaign "against an unwritten English-only rule" in the Pomona hospital department where she worked, Dimaranan sued her employer (Mydans 1990: A10). In a 1991 court decision, she won back pay and a transfer to a position com-parable to the one she had originally occupied.

Not all immigrants from the Philippines bring professional skills such as nursing with them. An 8 percent sample of adults aged 18–69 who were issued immigrant visas at the U.S. embassy in Manila in 1986 indicates that these 2,077 predeparture immigrants included 240 credentialed profession-als—11.6 percent of the total. By contrast, in reporting skills which might be useful to them in the U.S. job market, 18.3 percent of the men in the sample mentioned driving/auto mechanic skills; 8.4 percent, secretarial skills;

8.0 percent, electrical skills; and 7.8 percent, farming/gardening skills, while 20.9 percent of the women indicated secretarial skills; 15.5 percent, baby-sitting/nursemaid skills; 10.1 percent, sewing/dressmaking skills; and 7.3 percent each, midwifery/nursing and housekeeping skills. These Filipino Americans will find places far beneath the top rungs of the American occupational ladder.

Near the bottom of this ladder, employment in the United States can generate concern over wages and benefits. One example may suffice. In California in the mid-1990s, Filipino Americans were estimated to be more than 10 percent of the state's 5,000 to 6,000 homecare workers. Providing services to elderly Americans who prefer to be in their own homes rather than in nursing homes, homecare workers often earn the minimum wage with no benefits. Once an elementary school teacher in the Philippines, one Filipina homecare worker declared: "I love this work because the elderly are very kindhearted; I feel I belong." But, she also opined: "It's really time to change. We're already receiving low wages. The most important is medical care because if something happens to you. . . . To be a good worker is to be good to yourself" (Cinco 1994: 17). While some homecare workers in San Francisco have resisted organization, believing that a union is "just a bother," others have joined a local of the Service Employees International Union, which offers partial medical coverage (Cinco 1994: 17).

The 1990 Census provides the most recent, comprehensive portrait of overall Filipino American workforce participation. Derived from 1990 census data, Tables 7.1 and 7.2 present the overall occupational patterns for Filipino American males and females, respectively, and, in addition, provide for comparison among native-born Filipino Americans, Filipino immigrants who arrived in the United States prior to 1980, and Filipino immigrants who came during the 1980s, the decade immediately preceding the census. Of slightly over three-quarters of a million Filipino Americans 16 years of age and older who were employed in the civilian labor force in 1990, 45.2 percent were men and 54.8 percent were women. The foreign-born constituted an overwhelming majority—just under 80 percent of all employed Filipino American adults—76.9 percent of the men and 82.4 percent of the women.

Two categories, very roughly approximating white and blue collar jobs, can be derived from the more specific occupational classifications of the 1990 Census. For these purposes, white collar is presumed to include managerial and professional specialty occupations and technical, sales, and administrative support occupations, while blue collar encompasses service occupations; farming, forestry, and fishing occupations; precision production, craft, and repair occupations; and operators, fabricators, and laborers. Slightly more

Table 7.1
Males Employed in the Civilian Labor Force—16 Years of Age and Older

Occupation	Native-born		Foreign-born Arrived Pre-1980		Foreign-born Arrived 1980–90		All	
	N	%	N	%	N	%	N	%
Managerial	7,355	9.4	19,189	13.3	9,742	8.3	36,286	10.7
Professional/ Specialty	7,691	9.8	23,077	16.0	10,583	9.1	41,351	12.2
Sub-Total	15,046	19.2	42,266	29.3	20,325	17.4	77,637	22.9
Technical/Sales	12,605	16.1	20,752	14.4	17,438	15.0	50,795	15.0
Administrative Support/ Clerical	10,173	13.0	23,775	16.5	19,971	17.0	53,799	15.8
Sub-Total	22,778	29.0	44,507	30.9	37,309	32.0	104,594	30.8

Service	12,695	16.2	17,879	12.4	23,821	20.4	54,395	16.0
Farming, Forestry, and Fishing	1,787	2.3	3,432	2.4	2,947	2.5	8,166	2.4
Precision Production, Craft, and Repair	12,487	15.9	17,708	12.3	12,199	10.5	42,394	12.5
Machine Operators, Assemblers, and Inspectors	4,208	5.4	8,978	6.2	10,817	9.3	24,003	7.1
Transportation/ Material Moving	4,571	5.8	4,281	3.0	3,651	3.1	12,503	3.7
Handlers, Equipment Cleaners, Helpers, and Laborers	4,840	6.2	5,071	3.5	5,617	4.8	15,528	4.6
Sub-Total	13,619	17.4	18,330	12.7	20,085	17.2	52,034	15.4
TOTAL	78,412	100.0	144,122	100.0	116,686	100.0	339,220	100.0

Source: United States, Bureau of the Census, *1990 Census of Population: Asians and Pacific Islanders in the United States* (Washington, D.C.: Bureau of the Census, 1993): 106, 115.

Table 7.2
Females Employed in the Civilian Labor Force—16 Years of Age and Older

Occupation	Native-born		Foreign-born Arrived Pre-1980		Foreign-born Arrived 1980–90		All	
	N	%	N	%	N	%	N	%
Managerial	8,840	12.2	19,799	10.8	12,202	7.9	40,841	9.9
Professional/ Specialty	8,542	11.7	44,637	24.3	28,292	18.2	81,471	19.8
Sub-Total	17,382	23.9	64,436	35.1	40,494	26.1	122,312	29.7
Technical/Sales	14,887	20.5	27,156	14.8	24,365	15.7	66,408	16.1
Administrative Support/ Clerical	23,832	32.8	43,657	23.8	36,632	23.6	104,121	25.4
Sub-Total	38,719	53.3	70,813	38.6	60,997	39.3	170,529	41.5

Service	10,802	14.9	26,539	14.4	34,049	21.9	71,390	17.4
Farming, Forestry, and Fishing	380	.5	1,224	.6	1,478	1.0	3,082	.8
Precision Production, Craft, and Repair	1,494	2.1	6,703	3.7	5,115	3.3	13,312	3.2
Machine Operators, Assemblers, and Inspectors	2,267	3.1	11,503	6.3	10,791	6.9	24,561	5.9
Transportation/Material Moving	454	.6	313	.2	161	.1	928	.2
Handlers, Equipment Cleaners, Helpers, and Laborers	1,102	1.5	2,048	1.1	2,129	1.4	5,279	1.3
Sub-Total	3,823	5.3	13,864	7.6	13,081	8.4	30,768	7.4
TOTAL	72,600	100.0	183,579	100.0	155,214	100.0	411,393	100.0

Source: United States, Bureau of the Census, *1990 Census of Population: Asians and Pacific Islanders in the United States* (Washington, D.C.: Bureau of the Census, 1993): 106, 115.

Filipino American men in 1990 were white collar—53.7 percent—as opposed to blue collar—46.3 percent. In this, Filipino-American men came close to the overall distribution of men in the national population—52.1 percent white collar and 47.9 percent blue collar. By contrast, more Filipino American women were white collar—71.2 percent—than were American women in general—63.9 percent.

It should be understood that many jobs within each category continue to be gender-defined. The differing male and female occupational patterns reflect the persistence of long-term, gendered trends in labor force participation. For example, clerical work and nursing have essentially been defined as women's work during the twentieth century, while the skilled trades remain a masculine preserve.

There are, however, interesting differences among men in the native-born and the pre-1980 and 1980–1990 immigrant cohorts. Among men, 48.3 percent of the native-born and 49.4 percent of the 1980s immigrants were white collar—fewer than American men in general, 52.1 percent of whom held such occupations. However, because 60.2 percent of pre-1980s immigrant males were white collar in 1990, the white-collar proportion among all Filipino Americans rose to 53.7 percent. As Table 7.1 also indicates, while 12.4 percent of pre-1980 immigrant men held service jobs in 1990, the percentage rose to 20.4 percent of immigrants arriving in the 1980s. Conversely, while 29.3 percent of pre-1980s immigrant men were in managerial and professional specialty occupations, only 17.4 percent of the 1980s immigrant men held such jobs.

The patterns differ for Filipino American women. All three cohorts—the native born and the pre-1980s and 1980s immigrants—exceed the proportion of women who are white collar in the nation as a whole. Nationally, 63.9 percent of all American women held white collar jobs, while 77.2 percent of native-born Filipino American women, 73.7 percent of the pre-1980s immigrants, and 71.2 percent of the 1980s immigrants did. However, this broad categorization masks important differences. Similar to the pattern among men, the proportion of female immigrants holding high-level occupations dropped from 35.1 percent of the pre-1980s Filipina immigrants to 26.1 percent of those arriving in the 1980s. Conversely, the percentage of immigrant women in service occupations rose from 14.4 percent for pre-1980s immigrants to 21.9 percent for women who arrived in the 1980s.

The differences between both the male and the female immigrant cohorts can likely be ascribed to three factors. First, changes in U.S. immigration policy after the mid-1970s made the migration of Filipino professional workers such as physicians more difficult in the 1980s. The drop was slightly less severe for women than men, in part because the demand for foreign nursing graduates remained strong. Second, it is likely that the 1980s immigrant stream, which included many who came via exemptions or family-based preferences, rather than occupational preferences, included men with a wider range of occupations. Finally, as the most recent arrivals, the 1980s immigrants might not have re-established themselves in their professions by 1990 because of difficulties in obtaining the licenses and credentials. "Making it" in American involves, of course, far more than the specific jobs that Filipino American immigrant adults hold. The income they earn and the standard of living they enjoy are "relatively higher in the U.S. [than in the Philippines], and often these economic gains are in absolute terms" (Pido 1985: 89). As noted in Chapter 6, in 1989, Filipino Americans had the third highest median household income—$43,780—among the nation's sixty ancestry groups, this statistic based largely on the earning power of pre-1980 immigrant-headed households whose median income was $49,051. For many of these Filipino American families, however, high household income rested on the pooled labor of multiple family members. Almost 30 percent of all Filipino American families, by contrast with 13.4 percent of all U.S. families, contained three or more workers in 1990. Thus, economic achievement comes with considerable effort, the repercussions of which can impact other aspects of the lives of Filipino Americans.

Domestic Discord, Divorce, and Child Abuse

Some commentators on American life—politicians, academics, columnists, and talk-show hosts alike—have decried an apparent breakdown in the nation's "values" in the late twentieth century. At their worst, these guardians of the nation's moral fabric ascribe problems such as domestic discord, divorce, and child abuse to a self-centered, frenetic pursuit of fulfillment which privileges an individual's personal or material goals over those of the family unit. More often than not, such criticism focuses on those preceived most clearly as "Americans," be they white or black. By contrast, comparable issues and problems confronted by the nation's immigrants evoke scant interest—unless seen as especially newsworthy or sensational.

Filipino American immigrants confront issues and problems of personal identity and interaction within their families, just as do native-born Americans, but they can sometimes face additional complications when understandings and practices brought from their homeland are challenged in an American setting. Like many in the nation, Filipino American families usually seek to keep their difficulties private, and, as has already been noted, their fear of shame (*hiya*) may make them especially reluctant to seek assistance from professionals defined as "outsiders." Still, troubles can become public when Filipino values and norms collide with those that are conventionally American.

At the outset, it is necessary to emphasize that the problems discussed below do *not* typically plague Filipino American families. But, as both scholarly and popular writing appears to indicate, some Filipino immigrants do find themselves caught between cultures over questions that might not even be asked in the Philippines. Infidelity and child abuse are the two concerns most often at issue.

Despite the strength of its colonial and post-colonial connections to the United States, the Philippines did not follow the lead of the United States with regard to the rising incidence of divorce in the twentieth century, undoubtedly because of the strength of its Roman Catholic heritage. Divorce in the Philippines, even on the eve of the twenty-first century, remains a legal impossibility. Only a church annulment or conversion to Islam can legally dissolve religious or civil vows. At the same time, both Filipino and American cultures have historically reflected a "double standard" regarding appropriate sexual behavior for men and women. Premarital sex and extramarital affairs define this gender divide—if practiced by men, tolerated; but if engaged in by women, abhorred. In Philippine culture, according to Danilo E. Ponce, masculinity "entails having 'power', and 'owning a lot of things.' " For a Filipino husband, having an extramarital relationship—with a *querida* or beloved who in practice becomes a second wife, or with a mistress for whom one has assumed financial support, or with a girlfriend who is more than a "one-night stand"—has less to do with experiencing either romantic or sexual love than with possessing a trophy. Knowing that her marriage cannot be dissolved legally, a Filipina wife, despite her emotional and psychological pain, typically suffers her husband's infidelities, even if another set of offspring results (Ponce 1986: 2–5).

Once outside the jurisdiction of Philippine law and custom, a Filipino immigrant couple confronts a new set of values and rules. The husband who continues Philippine behavior patterns regarding infidelity in the expectation that his wife will continue to acquiesce might now face the ire of a wife for whom divorce in the United States is an option. Similarly, a wife can no longer countenance her husband's transgressions by comforting herself with the knowledge that she can never be legally replaced. On the other hand, perhaps encountering less societal censure in the United States, an immigrant Filipina wife might "vent her anger at her husband by doing the unthinkable in the Philippines—hav[ing] an affair herself" (Ponce 1986: 6).

Along with changed mores, the exigencies of coping with life in a new setting may also unsettle Filipino American marriages. Couples accustomed to having hired help perform the mundane tasks of cooking, cleaning, and child care must now negotiate which partner will do what—while both are working to ensure the family's success. The presence in the household of aging parents and other kin who would not normally be sharing their home in the Philippines can also increase stress.

In 1990, nonetheless, separation and divorce were not as commonplace for Filipino American immigrants as among Americans in general. Among foreign-born Filipino American males 15 years of age and older, 4.8 percent were separated or divorced, in contrast with 9.2 percent of all American men; among females, 6.9 percent of the Filipina immigrants, in contrast with 11.9 percent of all American women.

Unless spousal abuse becomes obvious outside the walls of the family home, conflict between Filipino American husbands and wives rarely provokes official scrutiny. By contrast, suspected child abuse may generate prompt intervention. In such instances, social workers and psychologists sensitive to Philippine culture have begun to point to important differences between Filipino immigrant and mainstream American norms. Culturally sensitive clinicians believe that behavior deemed acceptable in the Philippines can sometimes be erroneously labeled child abuse—or, at least, inappropriate—in the United States. For example, if a Filipino immigrant father shares a bed with an eight-year-old daughter, the Filipino practice of "co-sleeping" can appear suspect rather than supportive. Similarly, the "constant teasing about genitals" that preadolescent boys endure in the Philippines is deemed improper by many Americans (Yap 1986: 131, 132).

Not all incidents reported as child abuse result, however, from cultural misunderstanding. In 1995, in their study of Filipino American depression and mental health issues, Aurora Tompar-Tiu and Juliana Sustento-Seneriches wrote: "Sexual abuse by parents, siblings, uncles, grandparents, stepparents, and stepsiblings has been increasingly reported among Filipinos in the United States, by comparison with those on sexual abuse in the Philippines" (Tompar-Tiu and Sustento-Seneriches 1995: 92).

Sometimes the line between cultural misunderstanding and actual assault is difficult to determine. In 1994, a Filipino immigrant couple living in the San Francisco Bay area lost custody of their five offspring over accusations of sexual abuse of the children by their paternal grandmother and an uncle. According to *The Philippine News*, "the grandmother may have spoken of the children's private parts in jest, and even touched them when she was giving them a bath, but the DSS [Department of Social Services] interpreted these as abuse." Told that regaining their custody required an admission that the abuse had indeed occurred, the thirty-two-year-old father, "a maintenance operator" at an area high school, faced a hard choice: " 'My wife is home everyday, but she has not seen anything wrong, . . . And if I do say that I believe the children, even if it were not true,' he added, 'What would happen to my mother? They will put her in jail' " (Manuel-Barros 1995: A15).

In sum, immigrant Filipinos can confront especially challenging situations involving professional qualifications, personal relationships, and cultural practices and values. New circumstances and altered situations can demand painful adjustments. Reconfigured identities rarely emerge without some tribulation.

FILIPINO AMERICAN ELDERS

Just as Filipino American youth and adults confront problems specific to their age and stage in life, so too do Filipino American elders. Older Filipino Americans, those 65 years of age and over, and numbering 100,995 in 1990, are overwhelmingly immigrants. In that year, native-born, elderly Filipino Americans numbered 5,408 (5.4 percent of this cohort). Born in the United States in 1925 or earlier, they likely share the worries of other older Americans with regard to health, family, and finances.

The 95,597 elderly immigrants have, no doubt, many of the same concerns. But, unique problems also confront those who arrive late in life to join adult immigrant offspring. During the 1980s, at least 9,185 Filipinos over the age of 65 in 1980 came to the United States. Some of the 25,343 Filipino who were between the ages of 55 and 64 when they migrated during the 1980s are now in the late 1990s over age 65, as well.

Many of these newcomers who immigrated for familial rather than occupational reasons enjoy the love and respect of their families and live lives centered in family togetherness. Those who reside in thriving Filipino American communities can also supplement kinship bonds with satisfying friendships and organizational memberships. But despite these positive aspects, being an elderly, immigrant Filipino growing old in the United States can be difficult, especially when financial insecurity proves traumatic.

Aging in a Different Culture

Following their adult children to the United States seems a natural choice for many elderly Filipino Americans. Given the high value accorded family ties in Philippine society, virtually permanent geographical separation from children and grandchildren appears, by contrast, untenable. And so they come to a milieu that, despite the presence of family, is nonetheless remarkably unlike the world from which they came. The 1990 U.S. Census revealed that 60.1 percent of elderly immigrants did "not speak English 'very well.' " Alice Bulos, appointed by President Clinton to the Federal Council on Aging in 1993, catalogs "their biggest problems . . . housing, transportation, health care cost, culture shock, loss of privacy and control over their lives, and the lack of political empowerment" (Serran and McBride 1994: 31).

While their children work long hours to establish careers and earn wages, *lola* and *lolo*—grandmother and grandfather—often become baby sitters, thereby substituting for the Philippines' poorly paid and virtually ubiquitous *yaya* or nanny. Living in Daly City, California, widowed grandmother Leonora Valmonte recounted her daily routine: " 'After breakfast I bathe Mika . . . , then I'll do some work in the garden before I fetch Maverick . . . from school. That's my exercise.' . . . She's home most of the time, baby-sitting, doing house chores or watching The Filipino Channel unless it's a weekend and then the whole family goes *pasyal* (on outings), or to church on Sundays" (Jocson 1996: 38). For some, the role can be satisfying.

But, at times, the differences between life in the Philippines and the United States can produce dismay and anger. Seventy-four-year-old Norberto V. Cleofas protested: "Back home, we say 'no sex.' Here they say, 'safe sex.' . . . Back home, four-letter words are spoken by the gutter kids and the uneducated. Here, 'F__,' 'S__,' and 'Kick your a__' are normal to high school kids. So, old people are under stress and tension when they have no means to control this obscene behavior" (Serran and McBride 1994: 32). Grandparents can clash with their adult children over the rearing of the youngest generation and ongoing estrangement can result. Such alienation in the elderly can also be exacerbated by their children's seeming indifference to their wishes and needs and by their children's control over most aspects of their lives—proper hierarchies turned upside down.

Affording Life in a Costly World

Family tension is not the only source of difficulty for many elderly immigrants. Financial woes—the struggle for a modest month-to-month maintenance—can also complicate their situation, especially when health problems and their attendant costs arise. Not having worked sufficient years in the United States, many are ineligible for Social Security, a private pension, or Medicare. Lifetime savings in Philippine pesos can become a very thin cushion in U.S. dollars. Private health insurance can be prohibitively expensive, and custodial care of the permanently impaired can stretch family resources to break-point. One Filipina physician practicing in the Midwest was forced to move her parents back to Manila because she could not afford the continuing care that her mother's stroke necessitated. Others have turned to government assistance, but, as we shall see in the next chapter, "reforms" proposing that programs such as Supplemental Security Income, Medicare, and food stamps be reserved for U.S. citizens may limit access by some Filipino immigrants in the future. According to the 1990 Census, 41,063 (43.0 percent) elderly Filipino immigrants did not yet qualify or had chosen not to apply for naturalization. Aged Filipino immigrant veterans have drawn particular concern since they began arriving in the United States in the 1990s to await naturalization. Their situation will receive extended discussion in the next chapter, as the discussion turns to the future of Filipino immigration.

8

The Future of Filipino Immigration

At the end of the twentieth century, the future of Filipino immigration remains an important issue for many Filipino Americans. At a personal level, policies affect families. Many post-1965 immigrants still hope to bring close kin to the United States. More broadly, as future immigration from the Philippines has become embedded in an ongoing, national debate over immigration policy in general, and has been linked to arguments over both affirmative action and social welfare policies, Filipino Americans have begun again to examine how they are perceived as a racially defined ethnic group. For many, the discussion remains private—in personal thoughts and in conversations with family and friends. But, other Filipino Americans have placed these issues and themselves squarely within the sphere of contemporary interest group politics and are struggling to raise awareness both within and outside Filipino America.

THE PHILIPPINE DIASPORA AND THE AMERICAN DREAM

The factors linking the Philippines to the United States have undergone profound change during the twentieth century. Philippine independence is now more than fifty years old. U.S. military bases, long an issue capable of plucking the chords of Philippine nationalism, were relinquished in 1991. From the 1970s on, increasing numbers of Filipino students have received substantial portions of primary, secondary, and even higher education in

Tagalog, now the national language called *Pilipino*, rather than in English. Although American "stars" are still visible, Philippine culture regularly establishes its own icons in that nation's popular consciousness; one such luminary, former actor Joseph "Erap" Estrada, won the Philippine presidency in 1998. And, the Philippine economy, for decades a proverbial step-child among the booming economies of other Southeast Asian nations, apparently "took off" during the mid-1990s—although the long-term impact of the economic downturn among Southeast Asian economies which began in mid-1997 remains to be seen.

Yet, even as all of these components have strengthened Philippine national identity, the attraction of the United States for Filipinos intent upon leaving their homeland remains. As Filipino Americans have grown more numerous since 1965, as they have produced an ethnic culture and identity receptive to the incorporation of newcomers from the Philippines, and as they have returned to visit and keep in contact with family and friends in the Philippines, Filipino Americans have themselves become part of the draw.

Although thousands of Filipinos reach the United States each year, and their number gives no sign of diminishing given current U.S. immigration policy, eventual immigration to the United States is not a realistic ambition for countless others. By default, they must choose other destinations around the globe. The result is a massive migration of Filipinos around the world, a phenomenon termed the "Philippine diaspora."

Brief examination of overseas Filipino migration to places other than the United States can help to clarify why the goal of reaching Filipino America remains so important. U.S. immigration law continues to stress the preservation of the nuclear family, at least to the extent that the spouse, minor children, and parents of newly naturalized citizens are exempt from the preference system and may enter immediately. As noted in Chapter 3, this exempt immigration has accounted for more than 50 percent of annual Filipino immigration in each year but one—1995—since 1979.

By contrast, Filipino migration to most other nations is temporary, rather than permanent. In 1994, for example, 719,602 Filipinos labored overseas as contract workers—565,226 (78.5 percent) on land, and 154,376 (21.5 percent) at sea. Among the top twenty-two receiving nations, the United States ranked twelfth, welcoming 7,035 workers. By contrast, Saudi Arabia, Hong Kong, and Japan ranked first, second, and third, admitting 215,361, 62,161, and 54,879 respectively (Battistella 1995: 594 and 596). These thousands of Filipinos have scant hope of permanent incorporation into their host society. They typically travel without their families, often for years at a time, returning only for periodic vacations before renewing their labor contracts to further advance the "fortunes" of their families.

Many are skilled professionals. Each year twenty-six Philippine medical schools graduate approximately 2,000 physicians, 68 percent of whom go abroad. During ten years spent overseas, Tony Salas earned enough as an accountant in Saudi Arabia to send his son to a private school, start a family business in Manila, and build and furnish a two-story home in the city's suburbs. " 'Everything you see here . . . is *katas ng Saudi*—a now-common term meaning fruits, or sweat, of Saudi,' " explained Tony's wife May for whom "the long years of sacrifice were worth it." But not all families survive these protracted absences unscathed. Filipino analysts record a litany of dire consequences—"marital break-ups, abandonment, drug and alcohol abuse and extended family life torn apart by quarrels over the precious dollars" (Cohen 1990: 32).

The worth of it all to individual families is, however, only one part of a cost-benefit analysis of overseas Filipino contract labor. Remittances funneled into the Philippines by the estimated 1.5 million Filipino workers laboring abroad have become a mainstay of the nation's economy. One analyst puts the value of remittances in 1996 at US$4.306 billion or approximately 5 percent of the Philippines GNP. Although much has been made of economic improvement in the Philippines in the mid-1990s, it is unlikely that the upswing has met the challenge of a 1990 population of 60.5 million, living in circumstances five times as dense as the world average. Hence, the Philippine diaspora will continue well into the twenty-first century. Among destinations, the United States will remain singularly attractive.

FILIPINO IMMIGRATION ENTERING THE TWENTY-FIRST CENTURY

Even as the number of Filipino Americans grows each year, key issues concerning the future of Filipino immigration and the fate of Filipino immigrants already in the United States persist as topics of concern and, on occasion, angry protest. Put most simply, the issues flow from two questions affecting not just Filipino Americans, but other immigrant groups as well: First, who can come, and stay? And, second, once here, to what are these "New Americans" entitled? As answers are sought, U.S. immigration and social welfare policies intersect and touch the lives of Filipinos here and in the Philippines.

This chapter examines the status of Filipinos arriving in the United States in 1995; the current operation of the preference system and the backlog of applications for immigrant visas; illegal immigrants, called TNTs (*tago-nang-tago*) by Filipino Americans; the impact of the Illegal Immigration Reform and Immigrant Responsibility Act of 1996 (IIRIRA); the debate over benefits for legal immigrants; and the campaign for veterans' benefits for Filipinos who fought in World War II. Finally, the potential impact of political action on future Filipino immigration and on the collective identity of Filipino Americans is assessed.

Filipino Immigrants and Nonimmigrants in 1995

During the time when this book was written, statistics on Filipino immigrants, temporary visitors, and temporary workers drawn from the *1995 Statistical Yearbook of the Immigration and Naturalization Service* (1997) were the most comprehensive then available. In 1995, 50,524 Filipinos qualified for family- and employment-based immigrant visas. During the five-year period from 1992 through 1996, the average yearly number stood at 55,165.

Immigrant visa holders are not, however, the only Filipinos admitted each year. During 1995, the 198,699 nonimmigrant Filipino admissions outnumbered the 50,524 immigrants from the Philippines by almost 4:1. Most were temporary visitors—101,197 admitted for pleasure and 26,118 for business purposes. Although the length of stay permitted these nonimmigrants might vary according to their purpose, a temporary visit extending beyond a year would be rare.

But other nonimmigrants expect to stay longer, and unlike temporary visitors, can become workers in the United States. In 1995, 14,587 temporary workers from the Philippines entered the United States. Most of these came as "skilled" temporary workers—5,306 registered nurses and 5,028 "workers with [other professional] 'specialty occupations.' " Other nonimmigrants in 1995 included 1,753 "temporary non-agricultural workers"; 1,280 exchange visitors; and 1,378 students who might, with permission, take employment while studying (U.S., Immigration and Naturalization Service, *Statistical Yearbook . . . , 1995*: 100, 110, 117, A.3–4, and A.3–11).

Thus, in a typical year in the 1990s, approximately one quarter of a million Filipinos enter the United States—for brief stays, for temporary work, or for permanent residence and eventual citizenship. Those who arrive on immigrant visas, as well as those who "overstay" the limits of their temporary admissions, thus replenish the "newcomers" among Filipino Americans, even as earlier arrivals become more settled in their identities as "New Americans."

The Preference System and the Immigrant
Visa Backlog

No other issue concerning the future of Filipino immigration is more deeply felt by so many Filipino Americans than the backlog in immigrant visa applications. Because the number of Filipinos seeking to join family members already in the United States consistently exceeds the annual limits, a massive backlog of immigrant visa applications has developed. In January 1990, for example, the number of Filipinos waiting for immigrant visas stood at 422,923—21,602 adult, unmarried children of a U.S. citizen; 77,156 adult, married children of a U.S. citizen; and 237,303 siblings of a U.S. citizen.

Family reunification for non-exempt kin is never rapid, and, over time, the wait experienced under several of the preferences has actually lengthened. Unmarried adult offspring who applied by September 1, 1985, waited just over eight and a half years for immigrant visas; before July 15, 1986, ten and a quarter years. Because the Immigration Act of 1990 lowered the total number of visas available worldwide each year under this preference, the wait will likely become still longer in the future.

For the married brothers and sisters of U.S. citizens, the prospects for immigration appear even more hopeless. By October 1996, their wait was nineteen years. Hypothetically, a thirty-three-year-old Filipino physician who migrated to the United States under an occupation-based preference in 1972 and then waited the mandatory five years before becoming a U.S. citizen in 1977 at the age of thirty-eight could, at that point, have filed a "petition" for an immigrant visa for his married, older sister, then forty-one years old. By 1996, when the U.S. embassy in Manila finally issued her that long-anticipated immigrant visa, he would have been fifty-seven; his sister, sixty.

Families on both sides of the Pacific now face difficult personal and financial considerations years after taking the initial step toward initiating a sibling's migration. The soon-to-be immigrant must wonder, "Is leaving so much in the Philippines, so late in life, really worth the sacrifice?" "For how long will my own immediate family now be separated by my move to the United States?" And, the sibling who signed the petition long ago may now ask: "Now, after all my years of hard work, when I am so much older, do I have the energy to help settle my sibling? Can I meet the more stringent financial obligations imposed by the affidavit of support, especially as I face retirement myself?" For many, like Tita Mendiola Brodt who lives in Berkeley, California, these hypothetical questions are irrelevant: "I have always wanted to bring my sister here. . . . I want to take care of her the way she took care of me when I was little" (Fernandez 1996: 26).

Because the same preferences and dates govern the processing of immigrant petitions from most other countries, not only Filipino Americans experience long years before family members awaiting immigrant visas can join them. Although Filipino and Chinese immigrants did unite at San Francisco's Union Square in August 1995 to protest proposed legislation eliminating immigration preferences for the adult children and siblings of immigrants, activist Filipino Americans have been unable to launch a viable campaign to speed the immigration process. Within a national climate which increasingly questions the ability of the United States to absorb all who arrive each year, expanding the numbers and diminishing the backlog appears highly unlikely.

TNTs—Illegal Immigrants

Because not all Filipinos have near relatives in the United States able to petition for their immigration, and because not all have been willing to wait the long years for legal entry, Filipinos have also become illegal or undocumented immigrants. Conceding that "estimating the size of a hidden population is inherently difficult," the Immigration and Naturalization Service placed the number of undocumented or illegal immigrants present in the United States at approximately five million in October 1996, among whom were 95,000 TNTs from the Philippines, which ranked sixth among sending nations, far behind Mexico's 2.7 million undocumented immigrants. Except for the Philippines and Poland, however, all of the top 15 countries were in the Western Hemisphere.

Rather than entering the United States without inspection by slipping across the border, Filipino TNTs typically overstay temporary visas—between 1985 and 1988, an estimated 10.7 to 14.5 percent of temporary visa holders (Warren 1990: 89). Arriving in the mid-1980s after their graduation from "an elite Manila university," John and Maria have " 'made it' here. He is employed as a manager at a major financial institution and owns a modest house in Los Angeles. . . . Together, they have built a quiet, comfortable and productive life" (Cavosora 1993: 43). Filipinos can also become illegal by violating the terms of their visas in other ways, for example, by working without authorization. Then in her late fifties, Anita came to New York City with a wealthy Filipino couple to be the nanny for their three children. Her employers promised her eventual legalization and a work permit. After five years in virtual slavery, she fled, found work with another Filipino family, and "has been able to send $600 a month to her eight children in the Philippines." Now sixty-five years old, Anita "hopes to one day petition for her children." Given U.S. immigration policies and visa backlogs, her alternative dream, retiring at home in Batangas, is probably more realistic (Cavosora 1993: 43).

Each day, John, Maria, and Anita risk detection, as did forty-three-year-old Gizella Thelma Laccay when she arrived from the Philippines at Seattle-Tacoma International Airport in October 1994, ostensibly on "a long-awaited family visit," but carrying a Social Security card and identification as a laboratory technician licensed in Florida—evidence of illegal employment on other "trips" to the United States. Arguing unsuccessfully that she had gotten the license "in hopes of getting permission to work . . . legally in the future," she chose to return to the Philippines rather than face deportation (Iritani 1994: A7).

Others have been luckier than Laccay. In 1995, for example, 15,693 (30.8 percent) Filipino immigrants were not new arrivals, but had instead adjusted their status. Whether these numbers will diminish in the late 1990s, given terms of the 1996 Illegal Immigration Reform and Immigrant Responsibility Act (IIRIRA), is being closely watched by those concerned with Filipino immigration.

The Illegal Immigration Reform and Immigrant Responsibility Act of 1996 (IIRIRA) and Its Impact on Filipino Americans

Issues relating to U.S. immigration policy took center stage once again in the early 1990s as part of a broader struggle over the future direction of the nation. In 1993, the forced withdrawal of two high-level Clinton nominees because of their hiring of undocumented immigrants as household workers called national attention to the persistence of illegal immigration as a problem. Simultaneously, critics of government-funded social welfare programs used the federal budget deficit to justify deep cuts in social services. Benefits provided to both legal and undocumented immigrants became an especially tempting target and critics again renewed the call for "immigration reform." The Illegal Immigration Reform and Immigrant Responsibility Act (IIRIRA) was signed by President Clinton in September 1996, after provisions considered extremely threatening to legal immigrants were eliminated.

As introduced in the House by Representative Lamar Smith, R-Texas, and in the Senate by Senator Alan Simpson, R-Wyoming, the proposed legislation originally recommended cutting the number of family reunification visas available each year by 30 to 40 percent and drew widespread criticism from all sides of the political spectrum, especially from those sensitive to family-related issues. Other provisions would have required that an immigrant's sponsor earn an income at least 200 percent of the poverty level and pay back the government for any emergency services provided under Medicaid. Such measures would have foreclosed family reunification for many Filipino American families of modest means.

The utilization of federal benefits and services by both legal and un-documented immigrants also came under attack in the proposed legislation. Immigrants who received a total of 12 months of assistance from a government-subsidized program during their first seven years of residence in the United States would have been deported, and undocumented children would have been forced out of the nation's public schools.

Ultimately, pressure from ethnic groups that would have been adversely affected and from the Clinton White House forced Congress to drop the proposed reduction in legal immigration. Congress refocused the final bill toward curbing illegal immigration and forcing legal immigrants and their sponsors to behave "responsibly"—meaning pay their own way.

The IIRIRA also made it more difficult for those already in the United States to adjust their status and enacted stringent new measures to discourage those tempted to enter without inspection or to overstay temporary visas for lengthy periods. Anyone caught attempting to enter the United States with fraudulent documents or without proper documents, as did Gizella, now faces "Summary Exclusion," immediate removal from the United States. If apprehended, such a person may no longer be permitted "Voluntary Depar-ture," a procedure which previously avoided official deportation and a lengthy bar against re-entry. Anyone who fraudulently claims U.S. citizenship on Form I-9, which is required of those seeking work, may be deported and barred from the United States for life. The dangers of the IIRIRA for John, Maria, and Anita, three of the estimated 95,000 undocumented TNTs from the Philippines, are obvious. Strengthening INS administrative authority over undocumented aliens and limiting their recourse to U.S courts is also trou-bling to those concerned about long-term trends toward administrative rather than judicial review of the law.

The IIRIRA also stressed "immigrant responsibility" through provisions designed to keep even legal immigrants from using social service benefits. The act required immigrant sponsors to earn an income of at least 125 percent of the U.S. poverty level, approximately $22,500. According to re-sults of an INS random survey conducted in 1994, one-fifth of Filipinos surveyed would not be able to meet the requirement. Signing an affidavit of support for a prospective immigrant now commits the sponsor to financial support for a minimum of five years—until the immigrant becomes a U.S. citizen or qualifies for Social Security with ten years of covered employment. Seeking "any form of 'welfare' within five years of getting . . . legal status, may result in deportation as a 'public charge' " (Danilov and Kay 1996: 1).

Through its provisions, the Illegal Immigration Reform and Immigrant Responsibility Act of 1996 clearly intends to expedite the exclusion of undocumented immigrants; implement penalties severe enough to deter others from becoming TNTs; and restrict immigration to those who can afford life in the United States without financial assistance from anyone but their own kin. One ought not conclude that this legislation represents simply the latest phase of "immigrant bashing." Rather, it must be understood as a part of the attempt to restructure the meaning of government and entitlement for all Americans, made patently clear in the Welfare Reform Act (WRA) of 1996 which will also have a considerable effect on Filipino Americans.

The Welfare Reform Act (WRA) of 1996 and the Debate over Benefits for Legal Immigrants

The Personal Responsibility Work Opportunity Act or "Welfare Reform" Act introduced in the Republican-controlled House of Representatives in July 1996, just four months before a presidential election, promised to severely reduce the nation's commitment to federal assistance for indigent Americans, a national commitment dating from the 1930s. Two of its main provisions targeted citizens: by restricting assistance to a lifetime maximum of five years, "welfare as we know it" would end. By requiring recipients to work after two years, the "free ride" would stop. Provisions directed at legal immigrants would refuse Supplemental Security Income (SSI) benefits to elderly and disabled non-citizens, deny non-citizens food stamps, and limit access by legal immigrants to health care benefits under Medicaid. More than 40 percent of the projected savings through welfare cuts, $23.7 billion of $54 billion over seven years, would come from eliminating assistance to legal immigrants (Gutierrez and Wellstone 1997: Sec. 1, 20).

After President Clinton signed the welfare reform bill in August 1996, immigrants and their advocates took steps to counteract its consequences. Seeking to avoid the provisions targeting non-citizens, immigrants of many nationalities poured into INS branch offices to file citizenship applications. Less than a month after the law's enactment, more immigrants were taking the oath of citizenship in California than at any other time in the state's history.

Simultaneously, many expressed concern about the impact of specific cut-

backs in states with large numbers of immigrant residents. Welfare cuts became an election issue, and local officials worried about the denial of prenatal
care to poor immigrant women and the exclusion of poor, elderly immigrants
from Medicaid-paid nursing home beds. As states prepared to refuse food
stamps to legal immigrants on September 23—400,000 in California alone—
the Clinton administration worked to stay the cuts in California and promised to "rethink some of the provisions on legal immigrants"—after the
November presidential election (Gunnison 1996: A1; Pear 1996: A21).

Three weeks after his re-election, President Clinton called upon Congress
to restore programs totalling approximately one-quarter of the welfare cuts
as part of a balanced-budget agreement to be negotiated in early 1997. By
spring 1997, bipartisan congressional support for the "reform" of "welfare
reform" emerged as governors and mayors of both parties realized the im-
pending impact of federal "welfare reform" on their own state and local
budgets.

The balanced budget agreed to by President Clinton and Republican congressional leaders in May 1997 restored SSI and disability benefits to elderly
and disabled legal immigrants already receiving such benefits and made those
legal immigrants already in the United States eligible to receive disability
benefits in the future. Future immigrants will be denied access to disability
benefits in the years ahead. In addition, to qualify for SSI cash assistance or
to receive food stamps, legal immigrants must now either become citizens or
have worked in the United States for at least ten years.

The impact of these changes on Filipino immigrants is impossible to assess
with precision. Filipino immigrants in need of social services are typically
literate and in better command of English than are their counterparts from
Mexico, Central America, and other Southeast Asian nations. Thus, legal
Filipino immigrants may qualify for naturalization more easily, and those
among them who are in need may thus benefit from the albeit now diminished support currently available to all U.S. citizens.

The Campaign for Benefits for Filipino Veterans of World War II

Although the Immigration Act of 1990 made approximately 50,000 Filipino World War II veterans who served in Philippine units eligible for U.S.
citizenship (see Chapter 3), major issues still plague a full resolution of their
situation. During the 1990s, their proponents satisfactorily resolved three
issues: first, the 1992 deadline for applications under the Act was extended
into 1995; second, the requirement mandating that applicants be interviewed

by the INS and take the oath of citizenship in the United States was altered to permit interviews and oaths in the Philippines—a change that enables Filipino veterans to file immigrant petitions for their adult families without having to come to the United States; and, third, the restriction of qualifying records to those found in the Central Records Depository in St. Louis was modified through court challenge to permit use of Philippine government military records.

Two remaining problems have proven more difficult. To enable the off-spring of Filipino veterans to join them in the United States without a lengthy wait, Representatives Nancy Pelosi of San Francisco and Norman Y. Mineta of San Jose included a provision in the Filipino Veterans Equity Act of 1992 to make the adult children and grandchildren of naturalized Filipino veterans immediately eligible for immigrant visas. Because the 1992 and subsequent versions of the Filipino Veterans Equity Act have failed, elderly veterans wonder if they will live long enough to bring their children to the United States. " 'Oh, no, I'm not going to make it,' [said] one elderly veteran sadly" (Pimentel 1994: A1, A24).

Finally, the continuing denial of full veterans' benefits to Filipino veterans of Philippine units—benefits including hospital and nursing home care, out-patient medical care, compensation for service-connected disabilities, pensions for low-income veterans with non–service-connected disabilities, burial benefits, dependents' educational benefits, life insurance, and home loan guarantees—has aroused vocal and visible protest during the 1990s. Some Filipino veterans arrived in the United States to claim citizenship believing that the "benefits" they would be granted were veterans' benefits. "They said it was benefits for veterans, but we did not know it was SSI," said Federico Juntalos, a seventy-five-year-old retired bus driver, who paid $400 more than the usual $600 price of a one-way ticket from Manila to Los Angeles for the services of a recruiter who advanced him the money for the trip (Berenstein 1995: 14). Nonetheless, SSI payments enabled Juntalos to pay the recruiter's charge on installment while awaiting naturalization in the 9-by-12 room he shared with another single veteran. Others have found that a monthly SSI check of approximately $600 allows them to send money home to their families in the Philippines where $100 or $200 can support a family of four for a month. Because entitlement to SSI cannot be taken back to the Philippines, naturalized Filipino veterans continue to endure harsh, lonely living conditions in America, conditions that would be alleviated by granting them full veterans' benefits.

In June 1997, hoping to gain publicity and generate support for their cause, a handful of California's estimated 12,000 frustrated Filipino veterans set up camp in a makeshift "Equity Village" in a Los Angeles park where twelve of their number chained themselves to a statue of General Douglas MacArthur. A month later approximately one hundred elderly veterans then took their fight for the Filipino Veterans Equity Act to Washington, D.C., timing their demonstration to coincide with the national convention of the Filipino Civil Rights Advocates (FilCRA). On July 26, fifteen veterans, along with Congressman Robert Filner (D-California), were arrested after chaining themselves to the White House fence. The protest resurfaced again in August, when about a hundred veterans, joined by 500 participants in the National Filipino American Empowerment Conference, marched to the White House, where police arrested fifteen who again chained themselves to the White House fence. Loida Nicolas Lewis (see Appendix II) paid the $50 fines for jailed protestors, in addition to donating $5,000 for the conference. Three months later, various organizations sponsored Veterans Day demonstrations. At Arlington National Cemetery, a dozen elderly Filipino veterans carried a black coffin draped with an American flag in protest as President Clinton, on his way to the official ceremony, waved as he rode past in his limousine.

Sponsored in the House by Representatives Filner and Benjamin Gilman (R-New York) and by Hawaii's Democratic Senators Daniel Inouye and Daniel Akaka, the Filipino Veterans Equity Act would grant pension, medical, and burial benefits to all of the approximately 70,000 Filipino World War II still living in the United States *or* in the Philippines, *irrespective* of citizenship. Prospects for passage of this bill are slim. The Congressional Budget Office has estimated its cost at $777 million, a sum which many in Congress find staggering.

If a veterans equity bill is ultimately approved, it will more likely be a version which restricts pension and medical benefits to the estimated 24,000 Filipino veterans naturalized under the Immigration Act of 1990—a version that is understandably opposed by the approximately 53,000 Philippine-based veterans who did not become U.S. citizens. This limited version of veterans' equity, costing an estimated $270 million, has gained the support of the Veterans of Foreign Wars and the American Legion.

Most recently, President Clinton's proposed 1999 budget targeted $25 million over five years for Filipino veterans, and, in March 1998, Representative Bob Stump (R-Arizona), Chair of the House Veteran's Affairs Committee, reversed his long standing refusal and agreed to hold hearings on the bill pending before his committee. Some Filipino veterans and their supporters appear willing to accept a lump sum payment of $20,000 (the same amount provided to Japanese Americans who were interned during World

War II and still living in the early 1990s) which would *not* require U.S. citizenship.

Political Action and Filipino Immigration at the Century's End

How might one summarize the challenges awaiting those who would be politically active in the cause of Filipino immigration at the end of the twentieth century? Quite clearly, the campaign for Filipino veterans has galvanized Filipino Americans as has no other. Revitalizing a long-dormant cause in the 1980s, activists succeeded in winning the right to U.S. citizenship for Filipino veterans in 1990. Among Filipino Americans, the goal of veterans' benefits arouses scant jealousy or ire. The granting of benefits to these men, at whatever level, will not diminish what others have, now or in the future.

A second goal, reunification of Filipino veterans with their adult children, is more problematic. Out of respect for the veterans' service and deference to their age, some would admit their children—and even their grandchildren—immediately. Whether other Filipino Americans who have spent years waiting for their loved ones will support this goal is by no means certain.

Would that we knew, with precision, just what proportion of Filipino American families expect to be joined in the United States by relatives still on preference-based waiting lists. With this information, we might have a clearer idea of just how important the issues of backlogs and overall numerical limitations will be in coming years. Of course, countless Filipino Americans whose family migration is complete nonetheless support immigration-related issues. Remembering their own past, they undoubtedly feel camaraderie with others still seeking closure.

Likewise, in the recent past, Filipino Americans have been remarkably unified in their determination to fight against proposals aimed at denying social service benefits to legal immigrants. Lillian Galedo, director of Filipinos for Affirmative Action, offered an explanation in 1994: "If we don't join immigrant rights efforts we may sadly find ourselves having to defend the rights of naturalized citizens in the near future" (Bacon 1994: 52). But immigration-related concerns are only part of the contemporary drama being scripted by Galedo and other activists who support a civil rights–based agenda. In an era encapsulated for many of these politically active Filipino Americans by passage of California's anti-affirmative action Proposition 209, the fate of Filipinos still in the Philippines does not, despite the rhetoric, fill the center stage.

9

Filipino American Identity as American Identity

Contemporary Filipino American identity is a complex issue imbedded in the complexity of the larger society. Where on a continuum between common bonds and multiple cultures will individuals, groups, and the nation itself choose to locate? Can broadly based civic loyalties be enhanced only at the expense of weakening more narrowly defined allegiances? Or, can attachments to a collective public and a particular segment be simultaneously strengthened? How, through their own agency and their interaction with others around them, will immigrants and ethnics, especially people of color, establish their identities and find their places in American life?

Although Filipino Americans share a common heritage, they are nonetheless diverse as a group—even if not generally recognized as such in the larger society. Despite being collectively labelled Filipino American, each individual thinking and acting within the context of self, family, and community defines a personal location. That location may shift with time and circumstance, and it may never be fully articulated. But it is encapsulated in how each individual constructs and responds to questions concerning national, ethnic, and racial identity. "Are you from the Philippines?" "Are you a Filipino—or, a Pilipino—or, a *kababayan*?" "Are you a Filipino American?" "Are you an Asian American?" "Are you a minority?" "Are you an American?" From the mental positionings of individuals, larger patterns emerge—and these are the topic of this chapter.

Whatever their age, these "New Americans" from the Philippines take pride in their ethnic heritage. Courtesy of the Ethnic Heritage Council, Seattle, Washington.

CONTINUING TIES TO THE PHILIPPINES

Given the extent of immigration from the Philippines during the last third of the twentieth century, the importance of continuing ties to the Philippines should come as no surprise. The census taken in the year 2000 will likely count more than two million persons of Filipino heritage, and some analysts expect that Filipino Americans will overtake Chinese Americans as the nation's largest Asian American group.

For the foreseeable future, Filipino Americans will continue to be an overwhelmingly immigrant population. Irrespective of substantial diversity among immigrants, the foreign-born will likely stress continuing ties to the Philippines, specifically to family members left behind, and more generally to the nation of their birth. These persistent bonds are reflected in various ways—through the remittance of dollars to family members, through personal communication by telephone, and through periodic visits to relatives and friends in the Philippines. Ironically, even acquisition of U.S. citizenship can reinforce rather than splinter transnational ties.

Remitting Dollars Home

For many foreign-born Filipinos, making it in America means sharing it with those left behind. Establishing oneself in the United States takes time and money, but most find ways to squeeze something—sometimes considerable sums by Philippine standards—out of a paycheck. These remittances reinforce pre-existing bonds while they enhance comfort and security—childrens' tuition, home furnishings, and consumer electronics—all become affordable with dollars sent from overseas.

Remittance companies advertise extensively in publications reaching Filipino immigrants. All proclaim their speed and reliability, and some stress the convenience of affiliation with a Philippine bank. In 1994, BPI Express tapped another sentiment—national loyalty: "YOUR REMITTANCE DOLLAR SUPPORTS MORE THAN JUST YOUR FAMILY. IT SUPPORTS A NATION. EVERY DOLLAR you send HOME . . . BUYS MORE than what your LOVED ONES need. Your REMITTANCE DOLLAR helps pay for essential imports VITAL to the PHILIPPINE ECONOMY" ("Your Remittance Dollar" 1994: 17).

For many Filipino immigrants in the United States, remitting money to family members in the Philippines is perceived as temporary, as a measure necessary only until their loved ones are themselves admitted into the United States as immigrants. Of course, some may continue to send remittances for many years, especially if aged parents return home or married offspring or siblings never make the journey.

Prospects are less certain for nonimmigrant Filipinos—the temporary workers and the TNTs. Their remittance pattern closely resembles that of over 4 million Filipino overseas contract workers (OCWs) laboring far from home, especially in the Middle East and in other Asian nations. Unless they are able to "adjust their status," permanent reunion on this side of the Pacific with their kin remains virtually impossible. Their remittances will continue to flow, as long as their strength as workers and their devotion to family persists.

"Reaching Out" by Telephone

Despite the satisfaction of sending dollars, and the joy of welcoming their arrival, the remittance transaction is far from personal—the check, the form, the clerk, the ATM, all intervene. Not so when one can "reach out" by telephone. And, that is just what AT&T and other telephone companies ask Filipino immigrants to do.

In January 1994, AT&T recognized the potential profit to be made from a systematized cultivation of Filipinos calling home when it launched its *AT&T Klub Pilipino*. "Regardless of the language they use, many Filipino Americans stay in touch with relatives back home." *Klub Pilipino* promised Filipinos making at least $25 a month in long distance calls to the Philippines tangible rewards for their loyalty to AT&T: "a subscription to *AT&T Klub Pilipino* with stories about Filipino American personalities and historical contributions; the documentary 'Filipino Americans: Discovering their Past for the Future,' [see Films and Videos] produced by the Filipino American National Historical Society with funding from AT&T; Birthday Regalo, a birthday card and gift; a Christmas card (*Pamaskong Handog*) and gift; and automatic entry in a sweepstakes to win a *balik bayan* ('homecoming') trip to the Philippines." In its first nine months, *Klub Pilipino* recruited 40,000 members (Cacas 1995: 15–16). Other companies, such as Primus Telecommunications, Inc. and Globe Telecom, an affiliate of the Ayala Corporation and Singapore Telecom, and Pacific Gateway Exchange, also sought Filipino American customers, with ads that mix English and Tagalog text.

Balikbayans and Their Boxes

In addition to sending money and telephoning, many Filipino immigrants also visit their homeland, at least periodically, if not regularly. Those returning to their homeland, as well as the American-born of Filipino heritage travelling in search of their families and their roots, are termed *balikbayans* (homecoming).

The frequency of "homecoming" likely depends on two crucial factors. "Going home" is not without cost. Visitors must not only pay for their transportation, if not also for their lodging and food, but by tradition must also bring *pasalubong* (gifts) to *all* whom they plan to see. "Going home" also requires close connections with family still in the Philippines. A trip can be occasioned by a crisis such as the illness of a parent. But, after chain migration that has reunited siblings in the United States, and after parents in the Philippines have died, cross-Pacific family ties necessarily diminish.

Even if a visit to the Philippines is a once- or twice-in-a-lifetime event, Filipino immigrants and their Filipino American offspring still relish that reconnection with the land of their birth or that brief contact with the land of their heritage. In his late twenties, New York–born illustrator Jordin Isip, who is three-quarters Filipino and one-quarter German, made a two-week visit to the Philippines. "Identity was something I never really questioned when I was 14 years old. I grew up with whites. . . . It's only now, when I started making money, that I've thought about it." As he continues work on this family tree, Isip notes: "I'm just trying to figure out our past and trying to see where it all began" (Sison-Paez "Art Courant" 1997: 36).

By contrast, other Filipinos continue to make the almost ritual return visits as *balikbayans*. The Philippine government under the martial law regime of Ferdinand Marcos initiated its official *balikbayan* program in 1973, in part to demonstrate the "changes made under martial law" to Filipinos living in the United States ("Balikbayan" 1973: 1). During the first six months of the program's operation, *balikbayans* brought 119 million pesos into the Philippines. The Philippine *Times Journal* reported with considerable amazement that one man arrived in La Union with $100,000.

The returnees' need to have *pasalubong* ready in large quantity for distribution upon arrival and the need to send "stuff," as well as dollars, home when a visit is impossible has generated a thriving business for shippers of *balikbayan* boxes. LBC Mabuhay U.S.A. Corporation suggests: "Join the Family Circle Club and save! Ship 6 balikbayan boxes and pay only for 5!" Another proclaims: "At Bayanihan, we make sure that your *balikbayan* boxes . . . reach their destination in the Philippines intact . . . [and that] an automobile gets to Cotabato instead of Timbuktu. . . . and if you can't go home to your folks, Bayanihan can send an Express 'Surprise' Regalo delivery of lechon, ice cream, cakes and flowers" ("LCB Mabuhay U.S.A. Corporation" 1996: 58; "The Shipping News" 1997: 62).

When they return to the Philippines, *balikbayans* with their "acquired habits" are easily identifiable as somehow different. Not aware of how much they have changed, *balikbayans* are humorously portrayed as doing the unthinkable by Philippine custom. They carry their own bags, clear their own dishes after family meals, buy everything made of mango that they can find, leave big tips in restaurants, and are courteous when waiting in lines. "If the balikbayan drives while in the Philippines, he or she will often be the one who stops for pedestrians and desists from trying to run them down. The balikbayan generally does not lean on his horn or try to squeeze his vehicle into the three feet remaining between himself and other cars stuck in the traffic" (Babst-Vokey 1996: 24). Perhaps, even more than the distance created by miles and years, altered perceptions and changed behaviors gradually set Filipino immigrants apart from the *kababayans* left behind.

Filipinos join immigrants from other nations in taking the oath of citizenship at the Flag Pavillion at Seattle Center in 1995. Courtesy of the Ethnic Heritage Council, Seattle, Washington.

Naturalization and Personal Loyalties

On the surface, the acquisition of U.S. citizenship by Filipino immigrants might be considered a severing of the ties binding them to their homeland. By pledging their allegiance to the United States, these Filipinos do renounce fealty to the country in which they were born. Obtaining citizenship can, however, be viewed from another perspective—as an act which reinforces personal loyalties to the members of one's family. Citizens and, to a lesser extent, permanent residents can bring spouses, minor children, and parents to join them in the United States with relatively little difficulty, at least if they meet current income requirements. In addition, though the wait is extremely long, citizens can ultimately be joined by their siblings. The process of family reunification is, consequently, a long one that can take well over twenty years to complete. Thus, even as an immigrant relinquishes political loyalty to the Philippines, attachments to family members are reinforced by naturalization.

As have most other Asians, post-1965 Filipino immigrants have sought U.S. citizenship relatively rapidly and in large numbers, by contrast with newcomers from Mexico. To illustrate, by 1993, 65.1 percent of immigrants who arrived from the Philippines between 1970 and 1979 had become citizens, while only 17.4 percent of immigrants from Mexico had naturalized (Portes and Rumbaut 1996: 120). The Filipinos' high propensity to naturalize can be explained by a combination of several factors: their conscious intent to use naturalization for family reunification purposes, their higher educational level, their greater distance from their native land, their pessimistic assessment of economic prospects in their homeland, and their negative perception of political conditions in the Philippines, at least during the Marcos years.

Because virtually all of these factors will likely persist, no substantial downturn in the proportion of Filipino immigrants who choose to become citizens appears imminent. Indeed, recent limitations on the ability of non-citizens to claim entitlements and benefits, despite their payment of taxes, may increase the proportion choosing to naturalize as rapidly as possible—although the current backlog of applicants awaiting naturalization may slow the process.

In 1990, Filipino Americans as a group were 70.3 percent citizens and 64.4 percent immigrants. Simultaneously, from the opposite perspective, 29.7 percent were not citizens, and 35.6 percent had been born in the United States. Native- or foreign-born, citizen or non-citizen, across and even within these broad categories, Filipino Americans claim multiple identities in the multicultural society that is today's nation.

MULTIPLE IDENTITIES IN A MULTICULTURAL SOCIETY

How does one respond to the question, "Where are you from?" Or, to the somewhat less tactful query, "What are you?" The recently arrived Filipino immigrant likely replies with a simple explanation: "From the Philippines." Or, "I am a Filipino." Ask the same questions of someone of Filipino or part-Filipino heritage who has been born, reared, and educated in the United States, and the response many be neither simple—nor gracious. "Where are you from?" "Chicago." "No, I mean where are you from originally?" "I was born and raised in Chicago." Puzzled silence followed by, "Well, what *are* you?" The response one chooses at this point clearly depends on who is asking and on just how good—or bad—the day has been. If the questioner seems well-meaning and genuinely curious, albeit clueless, one might answer in a straightforward way, even while bristling a bit inside: "My father came to the United States from the Philippines in 1926, and my mother is the daughter of Polish immigrants." By contrast, on a bad day, "Well, what *are* you?" can offer a challenge. Can one think up an answer that one has never used before? Can one smile while seething? "I'm from Venus; you must be from Mars."

How Filipino Americans perceive themselves, and how others perceive them, is complicated. Such perceptions emerge from personal circumstance and larger context. Will the Filipino immigrant who becomes a U.S. citizen now reply, "I am a Filipino American," rather than "I am a Filipino"? How will the immigrant's American-born children and grandchildren describe themselves? Obviously this choice, whether Filipino or Filipino American, is dependent upon heritage. Other descriptive identities flow from the broader milieu.

Filipino Americans as Non-white Americans

Whether foreign- or native-born, Filipino Americans have been defined as non-white in the United States, defined as "other" than the majority in a way that is generally pejorative and frequently racist. The Filipino American confrontation with racism has a direct, painful, and constricting history: called "monkeys" and "dogeaters," relegated to menial labor despite their qualifications, denied housing they could afford, refused professional credentials for which they qualified, forbidden to speak their language among themselves at work, and kept from enrolling in schools whose admissions requirements they met. To be sure, not all Filipino Americans have had these experiences. Some have functioned relatively unscathed, able to dismiss the occasional public insult as aberrant. Others have taken comfort in socially constructed racial hierarchies—although not "white," certainly not "black"—and in their ability to position themselves nearer the "white" than the "black."

Today, the polarization between white and black that characterized much of the discussion about race in the twentieth-century United States is giving way to the new reality of a nation confronting the many shades of color of the post-1965 immigration. During the years ahead, especially as their numbers grow, Filipino Americans will necessarily contend with shifting meanings for non-white. Where on the spectrum of race will Filipino Americans position themselves? Where on this kaleidoscope of color will they be placed by those they encounter?

Some Filipino American lives will be individual stories of success, personal confirmation of the contention that racial barriers do not exist or can be overcome by talent and persistence. But, other Filipino Americans will likely perceive their way blocked by race and think of themselves as trapped, along with other Americans of color, in dead-end jobs or under the proverbial "glass ceiling." Still other Filipino Americans, despite more comfortable economic circumstances than those enjoyed by Filipinos in earlier decades, may nonetheless find themselves targets of seemingly random racial violence.

On the night of April 14, 1996, fire, "believed to be a racially motivated arson," destroyed the South Everett, Washington home of forty-one-year-old social worker Norberto Bautista, who lived in the house, "a licensed-care facility for seniors," with his wife and "little girl," his sixty-four-year-old father-in-law, and four other older people. Neighbors pulled the residents from the burning structure, and one wrote to local newspapers: "We will not tolerate this form of cowardice and intimidation." Hospitalized for smoke inhalation, Salvador Ruiz, Bautista's father-in-law, died five days after the blaze (Kelley 1996: B-3).

A year later, on the night of April 11, 1997, Syracuse University senior Derrick Lizardo was beaten into unconsciousness when he and several of his friends—six Asians, including three Japanese foreign students, and one white—were attacked by a group of whites in the parking lot of a local Denny's restaurant where, according to Lizardo, they and a party of African and African American students had been denied service, "while Caucasians entering the restaurant were immediately seated." Lizardo credited the black students, who intervened, with saving his life (Ayuyang "Violence" 1997: 31).

Writing in the mid-1990s, the National Asian Pacific American Legal Consortium (NAPALC) ascribed increasing violence against native- and foreign-born Asian Americans to xenophobia and resentment against affirmative action. NAPALC noted that, despite cases which reach public notice, many incidents go unreported.

Despite the possibility of hidden violence, racial attacks on Filipino Americans remain relatively rare. When thinking about the harm that might befall themselves or their families, Filipino Americans likely worry, as do other Americans, more about random violence and crime, than about being targeted by race. Most probably think themselves more likely to be attacked or shot for being in the wrong place, at the wrong time, than for being nonwhite. Nonetheless, racial hate crimes such as those involving Norberto Bautista and Derrick Lizardo remind contemporary Filipino Americans of what the old-timers knew every day they lived in "the land of the free and the home of the brave." It can happen here—and it can happen to me.

Filipino Americans as Asian Americans

In 1980 and in 1990, the United States census grouped Filipinos among "Asians and Pacific Islanders" for purposes of analysis. Today, on college campuses across the nation, Filipino American students take part in month-long celebrations of their "Asian Pacific Heritage." Filipino American activists also participate with other Asian Americans in organizations that seek to advance common interests and realize common goals. To what extent do Filipino Americans really think of themselves as Asian Americans? Again, the answer depends on whom you ask.

American-born Emil Guillermo, the former host of National Public Radio's "All Things Considered" who is now an independent journalist and a columnist for *Filipinas* magazine, scathingly charged in 1995: "It's a bogus umbrella. . . . We use it as a protective mantle. It's supposed to bring people together, and we Filipinos play along because we need to. Because we can't go it alone" ([Ciria-Cruz] 1995: 40). The word "marginalized" regularly surfaces to describe Filipino Americans who participate in Asian American endeavors. Japanese Americans and Chinese Americans, and sometimes leaders from groups even newer to the polity, hold the power and drive the agenda.

Filipino American "marginalization" has been explained in several ways. Filipino immigrants, the overwhelming majority among Filipino Americans, emphasize Philippine- and immigrant-related matters. "Asian America is *terra incognita*, a distant, alien world" ([Ciria-Cruz] 1995: 40). By contrast, Asian America is much more comfortable turf for college-educated Japanese Americans and Chinese Americans whose immigrant experience is generations removed.

On college and university campuses, the American-reared children of Filipino immigrants are typically more concerned with career preparation than with forging Asian American alliances. When they do seek to find out who they are, they turn to Philippine culture and history for answers, a process that psychologist Leny Mendoza Strobel has called "the process of cultural identity formation," or, as one of her students termed it, "the 'born-again Filipino' experience" (Strobel 1996: 33). Scholars such as Strobel, Epifano San Juan, and Oscar Campomanes and writer N. V. M. Gonzalez stress reclaiming Philippine history and culture, destroying the sway of neocolonialism, and challenging the centrality of Japan and China as icons of Asian civilization as critical to strengthening the identity of Filipino Americans and furthering their ability to participate effectively in pan-Asian coalitions. Whether this becomes a quest pursued by the many or the few, and with what consequences, will only become apparent over time.

Operating within an Asian American political context has recently been perceived as increasingly necessary. Noting the congressional and media frenzy over Asian American campaign contributions during the 1996 election, Lillian Galedo, executive director of Filipinos for Affirmative Action, charged: "The scapegoating of Asians for what is wrong with campaign funding is typical of the anti-immigrant hysteria going on in this country" (Verzosa 1997: 28). Emil Guillermo further cautioned: "We may not like the strange phrase 'Asian Pacific American,' but we need it to bring us together. . . . There are roughly 7.3 million Asian Pacific Americans, three percent of the U.S. population. We barely show up as it is. . . . But combined, . . . suddenly, people take notice. . . . When politicians take Asian Americans to task over campaign contributions, believe me, Filipinos are lumped in. . . . Ethnically, yes, we're Filipino. And it's great to be proud. But Asian American is our political mask. If we don't put it on, no one knows we're at the party" (Guillermo 1997: 53).

Nonetheless, in the immediate future, utilizing an Asian American "umbrella" or "mask" will undoubtedly remain a difficult task for those who are more concerned with defining themselves in terms specific to how they function as Filipinos, as Filipino Americans, and as Americans of Philippine heritage.

Filipino Americans: Cohesion, Fragmentation, and Multiple Identities

As should be apparent by now, cohesion and fragmentation simultaneously characterize today's Filipino Americans. Being Philippine- or American-born, being an FOB (fresh off the boat) or an ARF (American-reared Filipino); being a pre-war, a post-war, a post-1965, or a very recent immigrant; being a child born in the United States to an old-timer, to a post-1965 professional, or to a TNT—all these factors of place, time, and circumstance can work, along with class, education, occupation, gender, sexual orientation, cultural awareness, political preference, and so many other factors, in simple and complex combinations, to forge bonds among some, while dividing them from others. Multiple identities among Filipino Americans are the result.

For some, place of birth—there or here—is most salient. "The divide between the immigrant and the U.S.-born cuts across the community like an ominous geological fault. . . . On the one hand, immigrants are always talking about what's happening in the Philippines; they're always hobnobbing with visiting bigwigs, and besides, their accent can be 'embarrassing.' On the other hand, the U.S.-born are no longer 'true Filipinos,' they have no concern for the homeland and are disrespectful of traditional values; they think they're better because they speak unaccented English" ([Ciria-Cruz] 1994: 44). If foreign-born activists stay "Philippine-focused," while American-born activists choose to be "Fil-Am-focused," will they split and in the process preclude realization of any common goals? Mark Pulido, who as a college student became the first Filipino American elected president of UCLA's student body, says simply, "Filipinos are Filipinos wherever we are, and issues and needs should transcend geography" (Pulido 1998: 24).

But do they? Even within families who enjoy unquestioned love and essential respect, cultural and generational differences can produce tension and disagreement. Divergent life experiences can also pull those who share Philippine heritage in different directions.

For some, the question of just how much and what kind of heritage really is sufficient also looms. Is Filipino American identity a question of blood? Must one be of Filipino heritage on both sides to qualify? Can one be half-Filipino—a *mestizo*—or a quarter-Filipino and still qualify? Must one look the part, or be of an acceptable color? Look more Filipino than not? Do the naturally blond *mestiza* and the noticeably part–African American *mestizo* both qualify?

Is Filipino American identity a question of knowledge? Must one speak the language, or at least understand it? Must one learn one's history—and if so, which one—Philippine or Filipino American, or both?

Is Filipino American identity a question of choice? Can one choose to marry someone who is not Filipino American, yet also choose to retain that identity and pass it on to one's children? In California, among U.S.-born Filipino Americans who married between 1982 and 1990, 56 percent of the women and 48.4 percent of the men chose spouses who were *not* Filipino American. What will the children of these Filipino American women—35.5 percent of whom married Asian American men of other groups and 20.5 percent of whom married Caucasian men—call themselves? What identity will be claimed by the offspring of these Filipino American men—27.4 percent of whom married Caucasian women and 21 percent of whom married Asian American women of other groups? If out-marriage is commonplace among Filipino American Californians who live in close proximity to others of their own ethnic group, one might expect the out-marriage rate to be even higher in locales where Filipino Americans are less likely to meet and therefore marry other Filpino Americans.

Who and what is the Filipino American today? Who and what will the Filipino American be in the future? No simple answers are adequate now, nor are they likely to serve in the decades to come.

Appendix I: Filipinos in the U.S. Census

Year	United States	Hawaii
1910	406	2,361
1920	5,603	21,031
1930	45,208	63,052
1940	45,876	52,569
1950	NA	NA
1960	181,614	
1970	336,731	
1980	774,640	
1990	1,419,711	
2000	2,100,000 (estimate)	

Source: Harry H. L. Kitano and Roger Daniels, *Asian Americans: Emerging Minorities,* 2nd ed. (Englewood Cliffs, NJ: Prentice-Hall, 1995): 87; United States, Bureau of the Census, *U.S. Census of Population: 1960—Subject Reports—Nonwhite Population by Race* (Washington, D.C.: U.S. Government Printing Office, 1963): 5; United States, Bureau of the Census, *1970 Census of Population—Subject Reports: Japanese, Chinese and Filipinos in the United States* (Washington, D.C.: U.S. Government Printing Office, 1973): 119; United States, Bureau of the Census, *1980 Census of Population—Race of the Population by States: 1980* (Washington, D.C.: U.S. Government Printing Office, 1981): 7; United States, Bureau of the Census, *1990 Census of Population, Asians and Pacific Islanders in the United States* (Washington, D.C.: U.S. Government Printing Office, 1993): 10.

Appendix II: Notable Filipino Americans

Carlos Bulosan (1911–1956), Author: Carlos Bulosan, novelist, autobiographer, and poet, is the best known Filipino American from the old-timers' generation—those who came to the United States before immigration restriction in 1935. Born to a peasant family in Pangasinan province in 1911, he attended high school in the Philippines before migrating to join an older brother in California at the beginning of the 1930s. Like many other young Filipino men in Depression-Era America, he found few opportunities for employment and substantial evidence of racial prejudice. In these years, Filipinos on the West Coast were largely restricted to work as dishwashers and busboys, cannery workers, and agricultural laborers. Sickly and eventually hospitalized for two years because of tuberculosis, Bulosan continued to educate himself and began publishing stories and poems about life in the Philippines. During World War II, a collection of pieces, some of them originally appearing in the *New Yorker, Harpers Bazaar,* and other well-known magazines, were published as *The Laughter of My Father* (1944). The book received critical acclaim and had successful sales.

Bulosan's lasting significance and his widespread popularity long after his death in Seattle in 1956 can be traced to his chronicle of the harshness of old-timer life in *America Is in the Heart* (1946). Described by one friend as "30% autobiography, 40% case history of Pinoy life in America, and 30% fiction" (Morantte 1984: 31), this book followed the young Filipino workers up and down the west coast from Alaska to the Southwest in an account replete with the violence of brawls, beatings, an attempted lynching, and the murder of a labor union leader. The narrator, partly based on Carlos himself, escapes from this world to dream of a better one. Since its reissue in paperback in 1973, *America Is in the Heart* has sold more than 25,000 copies and has been frequently featured in college courses on Asian American literature. In the early 1990s, Filipino American community theater groups performed Chris Millado's play, "America Is in the Heart," in San Francisco and Chicago, among other places. Though Bulosan was identified with the political left, by 1995 he had become sufficiently prominent to be praised publicly by Philippine President Fidel V. Ramos in a visit to Seattle.

Although Bulosan saw himself as a "writer in exile," in the words of Philippine author N. V. M. Gonzalez (Gonzalez 1984: 8), he wrote in English and largely for American readers, even when he drew his subject matter from his homeland. Bulosan's posthumously published novel about guerrilla warfare in the Philippines, *The Cry and the Dedication* (1995), includes explanatory material for those unfamiliar with the Islands. In recent years, his literary works have served not only to explain the Philippines and Filipino immigrants to Americans, but to explain the old-timers' generation to the U.S.-born children of the post-1965 generation of immigrants from the Philippines.

Benjamin J. Cayetano (1939–   ), Governor of Hawaii: Elected governor of Hawaii in November 1994, Democrat Benjamin J. Cayetano holds the highest elective office of any American of Filipino heritage. The son of a Filipino who left Pangasinan to labor on Hawaii's plantations and later worked as a waiter, Cayetano grew up in Honolulu's "tough," predominantly Filipino Kalihi neighborhood where he graduated from Farrington High School in 1958 and married at the age of eighteen. Soon a father, Cayetano took his family to Los Angeles in 1961 in search of a better life, later commenting about Hawaii in that era: "In those days, I never met a Caucasian who wasn't a boss" (Silva, "Straight Outta Kalihi" 1996: 33). "I remember going to places when I was a kid where no one would even speak to my father. . . . It was humiliating for him, but he would just take it. He didn't know any better. He'd been conditioned to think that was his station in life" (Arguelles 1992: 12). During the next decade, Cayetano worked his way through the University of California, Los Angeles, where he earned an undergraduate degree with a major in political science and a minor in American history, and Loyola University Law School, from which he graduated in 1971. Returning to Hawaii, he passed the state's bar examination in 1971.

After appointment to the Hawaii Housing Authority Commission, Cayetano won election to the Hawaii State House of Representatives in 1975. After two terms in the Hawaii State House, followed by two terms in the Hawaii State Senate and two terms as lieutenant governor of the state, Cayetano won Hawaii's 1994 gubernatorial race with 37 percent of the vote, defeating Republican Patricia Saiki and Honolulu Mayor Frank Fasi in a three-way race. Confronted by a gigantic state budget deficit during his first two years as governor, Cayetano enacted severe cuts in state employment and public spending. In explaining the political philosophy which led him to seven consecutive electoral victories in a multiracial state, Cayetano explains: "The only way to overcome the racial issue is to find common ground. . . . My campaigns have always been mixed—issue-oriented and performance-based." "My advice to candidates is to run a broad-based campaign for all the people. I've seen Filipino candidates run for office spending time only in the Filipino community and the result is predictable—defeat" (Arguelles 1992: 12; Silva, "Straight Outta Kalihi" 1996: 57). Cayetano won reelection in 1998.

Victoria Manolo Draves (1924–   ), Olympic Gold Medalist: In 1948, at the first Olympic competition held after World War II, Victoria Manolo Draves became the first woman in Olympic history to win two gold medals in diving by beating her rivals in the three-meter springboard and ten-meter platform events. Her journey to the top of her sport was not easy.

Born in 1924 in San Francisco to Theodore Manolo and his English immigrant wife Gertrude Taylor, Victoria Manolo Draves "was raised in the low-income South of Market neighborhood" (Ayuyang, "Diving Star" 1996: 28). When her parents could not afford dancing lessons, Manolo Draves turned to diving which she could practice at a public pool. Her "discovery" by the coach for the Fairmont Hotel Swimming and Diving Club furthered her training, but also confirmed the racism of the era. Forced to compete under her mother's maiden name as Victoria Taylor because of hostility against Filipinos, Manolo Draves later remarked: "I ran into a considerable amount of prejudice" (Ayuyang, "Diving Star" 1996: 29). In the absence of a sponsor, juggling full-time work as a secretary with diving practice continued to limit her progress, until Lyle Draves, a coach from Iowa then living in Oakland, agreed to work with her in 1943. They married in 1946.

Manolo Draves trained hard for the Olympics, practicing six hours and doing 105 dives each day. After garnering Olympic gold and retiring from competitive diving, she was honored in Manila by President Elpidio Quirino and visited Orani, Bataan, the hometown of her father who had died in 1945. Saying "I didn't start out being an actress, . . . and I wasn't about to make a fool of myself," Manolo Draves turned down B-movie "native girl" roles, but did spend a few years touring in the United States and Europe with several water shows (Ayuyang, "Diving Star" 1996: 30). She left performing in 1953 to begin raising four sons and, in the mid-1990s, lived in retirement with Lyle, her husband of more than fifty years. She has been inducted into the International Swimming Hall of Fame in Fort Lauderdale, Florida.

Roman Gabriel (1940–), Professional Football Player: Professional football player Roman Gabriel is a second-generation Filipino American whose father came to the United States in 1925, worked as an attendant for the Pullman Company in Chicago, and married an Anglo-American woman, moving with her to North Carolina. Born in Wilmington, North Carolina, in 1940, Gabriel graduated from North Carolina State University, where he was an all-American quarterback, a scholastic all-American, an all-conference baseball player, and the first-round draft choice of the Los Angeles Rams, for whom he played from 1962 to 1972. As a Ram, Gabriel broke team records for passing, yardage, and touchdowns, and led the team to two division championships and a 57–22–5 record between 1966 and 1971. He was voted the National Football League's Most Valuable Player in 1969 (Doroska 1974: 152–157).

Gabriel was noted for his determination and extra effort. At six-foot-three and 225 pounds, he was hard to tackle. A team leader, he rallied fellow players behind Rams coach, George Allen, when Allen was threatened with firing by the team's owner over a "personality dispute." Off the field, Gabriel pursued business interests with fellow Ram Merlin Olsen and played a Cherokee Indian in "The Undefeated," a Hollywood film starring John Wayne and Rock Hudson. Proud of his heritage, he told interviewers, "I like to say there's only one Filipino in the NFL and that's me" (Chesley 1969: 24–28). After his decade with the Rams, Gabriel played three seasons with the Philadelphia Eagles. In his NFL career, Gabriel completed more than 200 touchdown passes. He was later associated with the World Football League and with Long Beach State University as a coach and, back in North Carolina, with the minor league baseball Charlotte Knights as its president.

Jessica Hagedorn (1949–), Novelist: Author Jessica Hagedorn has attracted more attention than any other contemporary Filipino American literary figure. Her first novel, *Dogeaters* (1990), received front page notice in the *New York Times Book Review*, along with a photograph of the author in a zipped-up leather jacket, with long dangling earrings and close-cropped hair. A few months later *Dogeaters* was a finalist for the National Book Award.

Born in the Philippines in 1949, Hagedorn moved with her mother and two brothers to San Francisco in the early 1960s. An early protege of writer Kenneth Rexroth, she soon joined a multicultural community of Bay Area creative artists, and has written poems and screenplays in addition to *Dog-eaters* and her second novel, *The Gangster of Love* (1996). Hagedorn has also edited an anthology of 48 Asian American writers, *Charlie Chan is Dead* (1993).

Unlike earlier Filipino American writers as Carlos Bulosan, Bienvenido Santos, and Jose Garcia Villa whose subjects were peasant life in the Philippines or the hard times of the single male immigrants to the United States in the old-timers' generation, Hagedorn's novels emphasize contemporary, urban and familial themes. *Dogeaters*, mostly set in the Philippines, contrasts Hollywood images in the minds of middle-class children with the lurid realities of Manila in the Marcos years. In *The Gangster of Love*, Hagedorn concentrated more directly on the lives of post-1965 immigrants and their children in the United States. Once again, the deceptive quality of American popular culture renders Filipino life more complex, in this case in the relations between a young woman, Rocky Rivera, her mother in San Francisco, and the members of her rock band, from which the book takes its title, in New York City.

Hagedorn's career has not been without controversy. Some Filipino Americans were angered by the title of *Dogeaters*, seeing only the ethnic slur of an epithet used by whites against Filipinos. In a move that put off some American readers, Hagedorn interspersed Tagalog words and phrases in an English narrative, much as many post-1965 Filipino Americans do. One reviewer, while praising the book, saw its "exoticisms" as "tiresome," "more a nervous tic than a desire to make connections across the gulf of culture" (d'Alpuget 1990: 38). A National Book Award jurist questioned the artistic merit of the book (Cohen "Book Awards" 1990: B1). But, Hagedorn remains a writer to be reckoned with, bringing the experience of Filipino Americans into an emerging multicultural mainstream of contemporary American literature.

Venancio C. Igarta (1911–), Artist: Born in Sinait, Ilocos Sur, and orphaned at the age of one, Venancio C. Igarta arrived in the United States at the age of 18, his passage paid by older siblings who could neither read nor write, but mortgaged family land so that he might acquire an American education. Too poor to attend school, Igarta picked fruit in California and then travelled to New York City by bus, where his talent was discovered by chance while he worked as "an all-around man in a psychiatric clinic for rich patrons along Park Avenue" (Sison-Paez "Igarta Unbound" 1997: 47).

During the 1930s, he studied through a scholarship at the National Academy of Design and at the Art Students' League. In 1940, his painting, "Northern Philippines," was shown at the Metropolitan Museum of Art, and he subsequently won praise from art critics in the *World Telegram* and *The New York Times*. Revealed as a "Filipino artist" by *Fortune* magazine, which published his work, he also won accolades from Filipino literary giant Jose Garcia Villa who called him "the only Filipino artist worth meeting in New York" and became his life-long friend (Sison-Paez "Igarta Unbound" 1997: 48; "Venancio C. Igarta: Master Painter" 1998: 42).

During a long fallow period following a bitter divorce in the 1950s, Igarta destroyed many of his paintings and worked to support himself by "mixing colors" for "a manufacturer of silk-screened art paper" (Sison-Paez "Igarta Unbound" 1997: 48). After retiring, he turned once again to his painting, utilizing what he had learned on the job to perfect his techniques as a colorist. His paintings capture his origins and his life in their depiction of the back-breaking labor of the *manongs*, in portraits of those he has met, and in self-portraits frequently set against a "*sawali* (split-bamboo wall) . . . a reminder . . . of his working-class origins" (Sison-Parez "Igarta Unbound" 1997: 50).

In 1992, still a citizen of the Philippines, he returned to Manila for a retrospective of his work, "*Ang Pagbabalik ni Igarta*" (The Return of Igarta), at the Metropolitan Museum of Manila. In 1997, suffering from kidney failure and undergoing dialysis three times a week, he continued to reside in the studio apartment in New York City into which he had moved in 1954 in a neighborhood primarily Italian and now Chinese. Pondering his life, Igarta mused: "I have no regrets. I never dreamed that a farmer like me could reach this far" ("Venancio C. Igarta: Master Painter" 1998: 42).

Loida Nicolas Lewis (1942–   ), Corporate Executive: Although an immigration lawyer by profession, in 1994, one year after the death of her fifty-year-old husband, Reginald F. Lewis, Loida Nicolas Lewis became the chair and CEO of the company he had acquired in 1986, TLC Beatrice, an international food conglomerate with extensive operations in Europe. In 1996, TLC Beatrice was simultaneously the largest African American–owned company and the 68th largest privately held company in the United States. At his death, Reginald F. Lewis was the United States' richest African American and had an estimated wealth of $400 million.

Educated in the Philippines and a member of the Philippine bar, Loida Nicolas Lewis met and married her husband, a Harvard Law School graduate, in New York City in the late 1960s. "It never occurred to me that I fell in love with a person of color. I fell in love with him because of what he was. . . . As persons of color, our relationship was that of a man and a woman adjusting to each other's character. Racial differences were never a factor in our relationship. Cultural differences, yes" (Silva, "On Her Own" 1996: 32). After she became, in 1974, the first Asian woman who had attended law school outside the United States to pass the New York State bar exam, she practiced immigration law and authored two books, *How the Filipino Veteran of World War II Can Become a U.S. Citizen* (1991) and *101 Legal Ways to Stay in the USA (Or: How to Get a Green Card According to the Immigration Act of 1990* (1992). When TLC Beatrice began to falter during the year after Reginald Lewis' death from brain cancer, Loida Lewis took the helm of the company which she and her two daughters had inherited and, in the following two years, became "Wall Street's darling" by virtue of her "unexpected success" in making the company profitable by implementing various "draconian moves." Despite her shift into the corporate world, Lewis remains a proponent of affirmative action—"I just call it leveling the playing field" and an opponent of xenophobia—"immigrants are being made the scapegoats. The real problem is the changing global situation. The world is getting very competitive. [W]ith the economy getting better, the xenophobia will end" (Silva, "On Her Own," 1996: 30–33; see also, Alejandro, "Loida: Portrait of A Writer" 1992: 8–9; "The Glass Ceiling" 1995: 59).

Philip Vera Cruz (1904–1994), Labor Leader: The life of labor leader Philip Villamin Vera Cruz, who died in June 1994 in his ninetieth year, spanned the century and several waves of Philippine immigration. Like his younger compatriot, Carlos Bulosan, Vera Cruz came to the United States in the 1920s in search of an American education and in hopes of bettering the condition of his family in the impoverished Ilocos region of northern Luzon. To some extent, he achieved both goals, but not in the way he intended. Through work in orchards, a box factory, hotels and restaurants in Spokane, Minneapolis, and Chicago, he put his brother through law school in the Philippines and contributed to the support of his mother, while achieving an American high school diploma and the equivalent of two years of college over a ten-year period. Returning to California from Chicago during World War II, he became a farm worker and participated in sporadic, unsuccessful attempts to unionize agricultural labor from the 1940s onward. When a thousand Filipinos went on strike in Delano in September 1965, Vera Cruz, over sixty, became a leader of what soon became the United Farm Workers of America, AFL-CIO.

A thoughtful, independent-minded radical, Vera Cruz supported a range of causes during his years as Second Vice President of the United Farm Workers of America. He worked hard to establish the Paolo Agbayani Retirement Village, sponsored by the union and built by volunteer help, to house the aging members of the "old-timer" generation of agricultural workers. Though often dissatisfied with the internal politics of the union and with the subordination of the Filipino minority to the Mexican American majority he stayed on because, "I knew that in the UFW I had a voice, if only a limited one, which I wouldn't have had if I was outside the union. I was able to speak to workers of all races and to people from all over this country and the world" (Scharlin and Villanueva 1992: 75). In 1977, he resigned his union office in protest against what he saw as United Farm Workers of America President Cesar Chavez's partiality toward the regime of Ferdinand Marcos in the Philippines. He continued to speak out and in the last years of his life, was an honored *manong* hero to Filipino American college students of the post-1965 immigrant generation. He returned to the Philippines in 1988, for the first time in more than sixty years, to receive an award from President Corazon Aquino.

Glossary

abaca	Manila hemp, a plant used for its fiber
abuloy	alms for the dead
adobo	pork, chicken, and/or seafood stew cooked in vinegar, soy sauce, garlic and pepper
alaskeros	pre-1935 Filipino immigrants who worked in Alaska's canneries
amor propio	self-respect
ampalaya	bittermelon (also *amargoso*)
arnis	Philippine martial art performed with empty hands, sticks, or bladed weapons
Ati-Atihan	festival held annually in Kalibo, Aklan, which combines commemoration of a legendary meeting in the year 1213 between aboriginal Atis and Bornean emigres with the Feast of the Holy Child, celebrated on the second Sunday in January
bagoong	fermented shrimp paste
báho	four-stringed bass, played in the *rondalla*
bakla	gay man
balikbayan	homecoming; term used to describe a Filipino returning to the Philippines for a visit

baluga	black
banduria	stringed instrument having six pairs of double strings; the lead instrument in the *rondalla*, a stringed band
barangay	pre-Spanish kinship unit composed of families; under the Spanish, a village
barcada (also *barkada*)	a Philippine peer group or social clique; in the United States, more commonly, a gang
baro	blouse
barong tagalog	the traditional, embroidered, pocketless, collared shirt worn by Filipino men
bibingka	sweet, sticky rice cake made with coconut milk and topped with a broiled layer of thick coconut cream and brown sugar
bienvenida party	party given to welcome a traveller
carabao	Philippine water buffalo, used as a draft animal
comadre	female co-parent; also *kumadre* and *kumare*
compadrazgo	co-parenthood, a horizontal relationship among adults created through sponsorship on important occasions, an aspect of *compadrinazgo*
compadre	male co-parent; also *kumpadre* and *kumpare*
compadrinazgo	the system of ritual kinship created through sponsorship at important events such as baptism, confirmation, and marriage
damo	marijuana
delicadeza	tact
despedida party	party given to bid farewell to a traveller
dinuguan	stew made with pork meat and blood and flavored with hot peppers
eskrima (also *escrima*)	a Philippine martial art
Filipino/a	today, a person born in the Philippines or a person whose ethnic heritage is rooted in the Philippines; during the Spanish colonial period, a person of Spanish heritage born in the Philippines

Flores de Mayo	month-long celebration during May which is dedicated to the Blessed Virgin
gitara	Philippine adaptation of the Spanish guitar, played in the *rondalla*
guisado	in cooking, the technique of sautéing tomatoes, garlic and onions in oil
halo-halo	sundae made with sweetened garbanzo and kidney beans, sweetened fruit such as jackfruit and *macapuno*, crushed ice, vanilla or mocha ice cream, and evaporated milk
hiya	shame
ilustrado	member of the late nineteenth- and early twentieth-century Filipino elite, typically European-educated
indio	during the Spanish colonial period, a native of the Philippines
jusi	cloth woven from the inner fibers of the *abaca* plant
kababayan	countryman
kalderetta	goat meat stew
kali	a Philippine martial art
kare-kare	oxtails stewed in peanut sauce
kola	train on a woman's *saya* or skirt
kulintang	an orally transmitted form of traditional music from Mindanao and the Sulu Archipelago that is played on gongs and drums
laud	stringed instrument, lower in pitch than the *banduria*, played in the *rondalla*
leche flan	a Spanish, egg custard dessert topped with caramel
lechon	whole, roasted pig
lola	grandmother
lolo	grandfather
longganisa	Filipino-style sausage
loob	inner self

lumpia	Filipino egg roll
lumpia Shanghai	fried Filipino egg roll
lumpia ubod	Filipino egg roll made with hearts of palm
macapuno	sweetened, preserved strips of coconut
mahinhin	coy
mano po	in greeting an elder, the phrase used in combination with the bringing of the elder's hand to the forehead of the younger person to show respect
manong	older brother; the plural, *manongs*, has been applied by younger Filipino Americans to now elderly Filipinos who arrived in the United States before 1935
merienda	snack, usually eaten in mid-afternoon
mestizo/a	person of mixed racial ancestry
Misa de Gallo	midnight mass on Christmas Eve; also the final mass of *Misas de Aguinaldo*
Misas de Aguinaldo	series of pre-dawn, Christmas season masses, beginning on December 16 and ending at midnight on Christmas Eve
nanang	godmother
nanay	mother; also *inay*
nangka	strips of sweetened, preserved coconut in syrup
ninong	godfather
Noche Buena	supper held after the *Misa de Gallo*, the Christmas Eve midnight mass
octavina	small, guitar-shaped stringed instrument, played in the *rondalla*
padrinazgo	godparenthood, a vertical relationship established at baptism; an aspect of *compadrinazgo*
paella Valenciana	festive Spanish dish of meats and seafood
pakikisama	getting along with others
pancit	noodle dish typically made with *sotanghon*, transparent bean noodles

pandanggo sa ilaw	the dance of lights, a traditional Philippine dance
pañuelo	scarf-like piece of fabric which is draped around the neck and shoulders over a *baro*, blouse
pasalubong	gifts brought by travellers to relatives and friends
pasyal	an outing
patis	thin, salty shrimp or fish sauce
peninsulare	during the Spanish colonial period, a Spanish-born person living in the Philippines
pensionado	Filipino student sent to study in the United States on a government scholarship in the early twentieth century
Pilipino	replacing "F," which does not exist in Tagalog, with "P," this politically derived spelling of Filipino originated in the United States in the late 1960s as a nationalistic rejection of the Philippines' American colonial past
piña	cloth woven from pineapple leaf fibers
pinakbet	boiled stew of vegetables, greens, and pork
Pinay	slang term for a Filipina
Pinoy	slang term for a male Filipino, originally applied to those who migrated to the United States before World War II
po	an interjection used when speaking to elders to show respect; also *ho*
querida	beloved; a mistress with whom a married Filipino man has established a long-term relationship, sometimes resulting in the birth of children
rellenong manok	baked chicken stuffed with ground meat, raisins, bread crumbs, onion, sweet relish, whole hard-boiled eggs and pieces of hot sausage
rondalla	form of Filipino music played on stringed instruments
sakada	agricultural contract laborer recruited by Hawaiian planters in the early twentieth century
Salubong	an Easter Sunday ceremony during which statues of the Blessed Virgin, wearing a black shroud of mourning, and of the Risen Christ are carried in a procession

Santa Cruzan	the rite commemorating the discovery of the true cross which is re-enacted during May as a religious procession with beauty queens dressed as biblical characters
sari-sari	Philippine variety store
saya	skirt
sinamay	traditional, wide, often transparent sleeves on a *baro* or blouse which slope over the shoulders and are stiffened to highlight their width
singkil	Muslim Filipino court dance
sotanghon	transparent bean noodles
tago-nang-tago (TNT)	meaning "hiding and hiding"; an illegal immigrant
tapiz	piece of fabric tied around the waist and worn over the *saya* or skirt, thus leaving only the bottom of the skirt visible
tatay	father; also *itay*
terno	gown combining the separate elements of early twentieth-century Filipina dress
tikling	bird whose movements are reflected in the *tinikling* dance
tinikling	the bamboo or bird dance, a traditional Philippine dance popular in the United States
tita	aunt
tito	uncle
tocino	cured pork
ube	purple yam
ubod	hearts of palm
utang na loob	debt of gratitude
walang hiya	slang for "without shame"
yaya	nanny

Bibliography

FILMS AND VIDEOS

Bontoc Eulogy. 56 minutes, video, 1995. The story of over 1,100 Filipinos "exhibited" at the 1904 World's Fair in St. Louis. NAATA/CrossCurrent Media funded.

A Dollar a Day, Ten Cents a Dance. 29 minutes, video and 16mm film, 1984. A history of the Filipino men who migrated to the United States prior to 1935 as told through interviews and archival footage. NAATA/CrossCurrent Media.

Dreaming Filipinos. 52 minutes, video and 16mm film, 1990. A negative satire examining what it means to be Filipino and Filipino American. NAATA/CrossCurrent Media.

East of Occidental. 29 minutes, video and 16mm film, 1986. A documentary history of Seattle's International District, and the Filipino, Chinese, and Japanese immigrant workers who settled there. NAATA/CrossCurrent Media.

The Fall of the I-Hotel. 58 minutes, video and 16mm film, 1993 revised (1983). Recounts the battle over the 1977 destruction of the International Hotel in San Francisco, and addresses the history and the plight of the evicted, many of them elderly Filipinos unable to find low-cost replacement housing. NAATA/CrossCurrent Media.

Fated To Be Queer. 25 minutes, video and 16mm film, 1992. Four Filipinos living in San Francisco discuss their issues and concerns as gay men of color living in San Francisco. NAATA/CrossCurrent Media.

Filipino Americans: Discovering their Past for the Future. 54 minutes, video, 1994. An in-depth look at the 400-year history of Filipino Americans, based on interviews with historians, archival photos and documents. NAATA/CrossCurrent Media.

The Great Pinoy Boxing Era. 30 minutes, video, 1994. The story of prize-winning boxers of the 1920s, 1930s, and 1940s, men who were heroes among Filipinos of the era. NAATA/CrossCurrent Media.

Green Pastures: Filipinos in the Heartland. 58 minutes, video, 1997. Tells the story of post-1965 Filipino immigration through the lives of three families living in Kansas. Alamo Productions.

In No One's Shadow: Filipinos in America. 28 minutes, video and 16mm film, 1988. An overview of the Filipino American experience from 1900 to the late 1980s. NAATA/CrossCurrent Media.

My America . . . or Honk if You Love Buddha. 87 minutes, video, 1996. Explores the history and future of Asian Americans as part of contemporary multicultural America. Sai Communications.

Savage Acts: Wars, Fairs, and Empire. 30 minutes, color video, 1995. Examines the interplay between American expansion at the turn of the twentieth century and changes in American culture as expressed in world's fairs between 1893 and 1904. American Social History Project, City University of New York.

Silencio. 9 minutes, video, 1996. Explores the adjustment of a young Filipino American to his predominantly Caucasian workplace in San Francisco in 1951, and explores the impact of racism as his brother "passes" as Italian-American. NAATA/CrossCurrent Media.

White Christmas. 24 minutes, video and 16mm film, 1993. The producer looks at the Philippines after living in the United States for five years. NAATA/CrossCurrent Media.

Yo-Yo Man. 12 minutes, video and 16mm film, 1978. The yo-yo, a Philippine toy popular in the United States, is demonstrated by 77-year-old Filipino Nemo Concepcion, who demonstrated for the Duncan Yo-yo Company and became a champion, winning contests throughout the United States. Documentary Educational Resources.

DISTRIBUTORS

Alamo Productions. P.O. Box 1940, Lawrence, KS 66044; 785–841–4143.

American Social History Project. Center for Media and Learning, City University of New York, 33 West 42nd Street, New York, NY 10036–8099; 212–966–4248, ext. 201.

Documentary Educational Resources. 5 Bridge St., Watertown, MA 02172; 617–926–0491.

NAATA/CrossCurrent Media. (National Asian Telecommunications Association). 346 9th St., San Francisco, CA 94103; 415–863–0814. http://www.lib.berkeley.edu/MRC/NAATACAT.html

Sai Communications. 22D Hollywood Ave., Ho-Ho-Kus, NJ 07423; 800–343–5540.

BOOKS AND ARTICLES

"About Rebay." *Bigayan* (Summer 1992): 3, 7.

Acierto, Maria Guillen. "The Filipino World War II G.I. Brides in Chicago, Illinois—1946 to Today." *Filipino American National Historical Society Journal* 3 (1994): 69–70.

"Across Oceans of Dreams: Songs of the Manongs." *Filipinas* (January 1993): 31.

Acuzar, Luis Reyes. (Interview [SC81-Fil-0021a], November 16, 1981). Filipino American National Historical Society Archives. Seattle, WA.

Agsalud, Joshua, and Karen Motosue. "Kapuripuri: 75 Years of Filipino Labor." *The Filipinos in Hawaii: The First 75 Years.* Juan C. Dionisio, ed. Honolulu: Hawaii Filipino News Specialty Publications, 1981: 79–83.

The Aklan Newsette. 3:1 (June 1991).

Alba, Victoria. "Kulintang: Ancient Music of Mindanao Brought to the Modern World." *Filipinas* (September 1992): 25–28.

Alcantara, Ruben. "1906: The First Sakada." *The Filipinos in Hawaii: The First 75 Years.* Honolulu: Hawaii Filipino News Specialty Publications, 1981(a): 27–50.

———. *Sakada: Filipino Adaptation In Hawaii.* Washington, D.C.: University Press of America, 1981(b).

Alegado, Dean T. "The Filipino Community in Hawaii: Development and Change." *Social Process in Hawai'i: A Reader.* Peter Manicas, ed. New York: McGraw-Hill, 33 (1991): 92–118.

———. "Filipino Entrepreneurship in Hawaii." *Heritage* (Winter 1996): 12–14.

Alejandro, Reynaldo. *The Philippine Cookbook.* New York: Perigee Books, 1985.

———. "Loida: Portrait of A Writer." *Heritage* (March 1992): 8–9.

———. "Noche Buena." *Filipinas* (December 1992): 60–61.

Alfafara, C. T. "The Caballeros de Dimas-Alang All These Years." Caballeros de Dimas-Alang, Inc., *Fifteenth Triennial Grand Convention* (January 18 to 26, 1958). Filipino American National Historical Society Archive. Seattle, WA.

Allen, James P. "Recent Immigration from the Philippines and Filipino Communities in the United States." *Geographical Review* 67 (April 1977): 195–208.

Almendrala, Laarni C. "Frozen Assets." *Filipinas* (July 1997): 43–44.

———. "Oh, Brother!" *Filipinas* (December 1995): 23–24.

———. "The Pulitzer Two." *Filipinas* (June 1997): 26–28.

———. "The Sound of Silence." *Filipinas* (March 1997): 24–26.

———. "What's Luck Got To Do With It?" *Filipinas* (August 1993): 17, 46.

Almirol, Edwin B. "Rights and Obligations in Filipino American Families." *Journal of Comparative Family Studies* 13:3 (Fall 1982): 291–306.

Alo, Celan, and Joselito Uy, eds. *CIPAS Silver Anniversary, 1970–1995.* Springfield, IL: privately printed, 1995.

Alsaybar, Bangele "Nonoy." "Lost in L.A.: Gangs, Pinoy Style." *Filipinas* (June 1993): 10–11, 67.

Alzona, Encarnicion. *A History of Education in the Philippines, 1565–1930*. Manila: University of the Philippines Press, 1932.

"The APPA and APPA Auxiliary In Focus 1995 Calendar." n.p.: APPA Auxiliary, 1994.

"Aquino Honors Cecile Licad." *Philippine News* (October 2–8, 1991): 14.

Aranda, Cris. "Immigrant Journal." *The Philippine Review* (May 1994): 8.

Arguelles, J. R. Lagumbay. "Ben Cayetano: Breaking Stereotypes." *Filipinas* (October 1992): 11–13.

Arkipelago. (http://www.columbia.edu/~eth6,arki.html).

Ayuyang, Rachelle Q. "Angelo in America." *Filipinas* (January 1996): 39–41.

———. "Capital Gains." *Filipinas* (October 1996): 31–33, 60.

———. "Catch a Diving Star." *Filipinas* (July 1996): 28–30.

———. "On Pains and Needles." *Filipinas* (August 1996): 51–52.

———. "Violence on the Menu." *Filipinas* (October 1997): 31–32.

———. "You Gotta Love Him." *Filipinas* (February 1997): 30–32, 34, 50.

Babst-Vokey, Arlene. "Spot the Balikbayan." *Filipinas* (April 1996): 24.

Bacdayan, Albert. "Remembering Philip Vera Cruz." *Heritage* (September 1994): 9.

Bacho, Peter. *Cebu*. Seattle, WA: University of Washington Press, 1991.

"Back on the Road: A Survey of the Philippines." *Economist* (May 11, 1996): 1–17.

Bacon, David. "An Ill Wind Blows." *Filipinas* (August 1994): 18–19, 52.

———. "Living the Legacy of Unionism." *Filipinas* (January 1997): 18–21.

"Balikbayan: First Batch of 130 Overseas Filipinos from Hawaii Here." *Bulletin Today* (September 22, 1973): 1.

Barkan, Elliott Robert. *Asian and Pacific Islander Migration to the United States: A Model of New Global Patterns*. Westport, CT: Greenwood Press, 1992.

———. "Whom Shall We Integrate?: A Comparative Analysis of the Immigration and Naturalization Trends of Asians Before and After the 1965 Immigration Act (1951–1978)." *Journal of American Ethnic History* (Fall 1983): 29–57.

Barrios, Mary Angela, S. P. C., Emma S. Castillo, Rosita G. Galang, Paulina C. Santos, Norma G. Tiangco, Elvira C. Vergara, and Esperanza P. Villamor. "The Greater Manila Speech Community: Bilingual or Diglossic?" *The Filipino Bilingual: Studies on Philippine Bilingualism and Bilingual Education*. Emy M. Pacasio, ed. Quezon City: The Ateneo de Manila University Press, 1977: 83–90.

Battistella, Graziano. "Data on International Migration from the Philippines." *Asian and Pacific Migration Journal* 4:4 (1995): 589–599.

Bautista, Lourdes, Gloria Chan-Yap, Araceli Hidalgo, Ma. Isabelita Riego de Dios, R.V.M., and Adelaida Paterno. "The Filipino Bilingual's Language Orientation." *The Filipino Bilingual: Studies on Philippine Bilingualism and Bilingual Education*. Emy M. Pacasio, ed. Quezon City: The Ateneo de Manila University Press, 1977: 72–82.

Bayanihan Philippine Dance Company. New York: Dunetz & Lovett, 1977.

Bello, Madge, and Vincent Reyes. "Filipino Americans and the Marcos Overthrow: The Transformation of Political Consciousness." *Amerasia* 13:1 (1986–87): 73–83.

"Benjamin J. Cayetano: Governor of Hawaii." *Heritage* (Spring 1996): 15–16.

Berenstein, Leslie. "A Debt Unpaid." *Los Angeles Times* (May 28, 1995): "City Times," 1, 12–14.

Berganio, Jacqueline T. Jamero, Leonardo A. Tacata, Jr., and Peter M. Jamero. "The Prevalence and Impact of Alcohol, Tobacco, and Other Drugs on Filipino American Communities." In *Filipino Americans: Transformation and Identity.* Maria P. P. Root, ed. Thousand Oaks, CA: Sage Publications, Inc., 1997: 272–286.

Bernardo, Rudolfo S. "Building Character Schoolwide: The Allen Experience." n.d.

"Bid to Restore SSI." *Filipinas* (April 1997): 52.

"Bienvenido Santos, Filipino Author, 84." *The New York Times* (January 12, 1996): A25.

"Bienvenido N. Santos, 1911–1996." *Filipinas* (February 1996): 12.

"Bob Medina." *Fil-Am Image* (September 1996): 16, 61.

Brands, H. W. *Bound to Empire: The United States and the Philippines.* New York: Oxford University Press, 1992.

Brozan, Nadine. "From Minority Activist to Feminist Leader." *The New York Times* (July 6, 1985).

Brush, Barbara L. " 'Exchangees' or Employees? The Exchange Visitor Program and Foreign Nurse Immigration to the United States, 1945–1990." *Nursing History Review* 1 (1993): 171–180.

———. "The Rockefeller Agenda for American/Philippines Nursing Relations." *Western Journal of Nursing Research* 17:5 (1995): 540–555.

Buchholdt, Thelma Garcia. *Filipinos in Alaska: 1788–1958.* Anchorage, AK: Aboriginal Press, 1996.

Bulosan, Carlos. *America Is in the Heart.* New York: Harcourt Brace and Company, 1946.

———. *The Cry and the Dedication.* Philadelphia: Temple University Press, 1995.

Cacas, Samuel R. "Marketing the Mainline to Manila." *American Demographics* (July 1995): 15–16.

Callos, Tom. "Don't Mess with Diana." *Filipinas* (March 1996): 49–50.

Campbell, R. M. "Duo Weds Best of Both Worlds." *Seattle Post-Intelligencer* (February 14, 1990): C12.

Campomanes, Oscar V. "The Institutional Invisibility of American Imperialism, the Philippines, and Filipino Americans." *maganda six* (1993): 7–9, 60–62.

Caoili, Bert. "The Filipino Community Center, our legacy." *Filipino American Herald* (August 1997): 14.

Carino, Benjamin V., James T. Fawcett, Robert W. Gardner, and Fred Arnold. *The*

New Filipino Immigrants to the United States: Increasing Diversity and Change. Honolulu: East-West Center, Papers of the East-West Population Institute, Number 115, May 1990.

Cavosora, Richard J. P. "Behold, the Backlash." *Filipinas* (November 1993): 42–43, 45–46.

Chan, Sucheng. *Asian Americans: An Interpretive History.* Boston: Twayne Publishers, 1991.

"Charles Uy: Visualize More Awards." *Filipinas* (November 1996): 57.

Chesley, Frank. "The Many Worlds of Ram Quarterback Roman Gabriel." *On View* (April 1969): 24–28.

Chew, Connie. "He's the Cat's Meow." *Filipinas* (August 1993): 21, 60.

"Chicago Boys Active." *The Filipino Students' Magazine* (December 1906): 21.

Chin, Steven A., and Dexter Waugh. "Despite successes, Filipino teens have highest Asian dropout rate." *San Francisco Examiner* (September 18, 1989): A1, A10.

Chun, Ki-Taek. "The Myth of Asian American Success and Its Educational Ramifications." *The Asian American Educational Experience: A Source Book for Teachers and Students.* Don T. Nakanishi and Tina Yamano Nishida, eds. New York: Routledge, 1995: 95–112.

Cinco, Maria Cristina M. "Who Takes Care of the Care Giver?" *Filipinas* (September 1994): 16–18.

[Ciria-Cruz, Rene P.] "Honor Our History—Vote." *Filipinas* (October 1996): 4.

———. "How Far Have We Come?" *Filipinas* (October 1994): 40–44.

———. "Looking for Asian America." *Filipinas* (May 1995): 39–40, 74.

———. "It's the Values, Stupid." *Filipinas* (November 1996): 16–19, 28.

———. "Meek Is Weak." *Filipinas* (July 1997): 4.

———. "Ready to Rumble." *Filipinas* (October 1997): 35, 52.

Claverán, Virginia González. "Un Documento Colonial Sobre Esclavos Asiáticos." *Historia Mexicana* 38:3 (January–March 1989): 523–532.

Cohen, Margot. "Divorce Filipino-style." *Far Eastern Economic Review* (October 1989): 49, 52.

———. "Labour Pains." *Far Eastern Economic Review* (March 8, 1990): 32–33.

Cohen, Roger. "Charles Johnson and Ron Chernow Win Book Awards." *New York Times* (November 28, 1990), B1.

"Community Groups Seek Solution to Youth 'Wars.'" *Filipino American Bulletin* [Seattle, WA] (May 1992): 1, 8.

Conner, Elcee Cagas. "PEACE Helps Victims of Mt. Pinatubo Eruption." *Heritage* (March 1992), 24–26.

"Conversations with Cecile." *Seattle Times* (February 16, 1992).

Cordova, Fred. "Wanted: A 'Damned Good Pinoy Publication.'" *USA Filipino* (August 1987): 5, 12.

———. *Filipinos: Forgotten Asian Americans—1763—Circa 1963.* Dubuque, IA: Kendall Hunt Publishing, 1983.

Cravotta, Dave. "Byte the Bulletin." *Filipinas* (July 1993): 47, 52.

Crouchett, Lorraine Jacobs. *Filipinos in California: From the Days of the Galleons to the Present.* El Cerrito, CA: Downey Place Publishing House, 1982.

Cullather, Nick. *Illusions of Influence: The Political Economy of United States–Philippine Relations, 1942–1960.* Stanford, CA: Stanford University Press, 1994.

d'Alpuget, Blanche. "Review of *Dogeaters.*" *New York Times Book Review* (March 25, 1990): 38.

Daniels, Roger. "Asian Americans: The Transformation of a Pariah Minority," *Amerikastudien* 40 (1995): 469–483.

Danilov, Dan P., and Allen E. Kay. "Key Features of the Illegal Immigration and Immigrant Responsibility Act of 1996," *United States Immigration News* (November 1, 1996): 1–4.

Daspin, Eileen. "French Quarters." *In Style* (July 1997): 146–151.

De Bevoise, Ken. *Agents of Apocalypse: Epidemic Disease in the Colonial Philippines.* Princeton, NJ: Princeton University Press, 1995.

DeBrosse, Jim. "At School, Word Is 'Values.'" *Dayton Daily News* (August 15, 1994): 1–2B.

Dimalanta, Purita A. "The Mrs. Filipino Community Pageant." *Pamana: Half-A-Century of Filipino Community Life in the Emerald City.* Seattle: n.p., [1986]: 159–163.

Dionisio, Juan C., ed. *The Filipinos in Hawaii—The First 75 Years.* Honolulu: Hawaii Filipino News Specialty Publications, [1981].

Domingo, Benjamin B. *The Philippines and Hawaii.* Manila: Foreign Service Institute, 1983.

Donato, Marilyn Ranada. *Philippine Cooking in America.* Kansas City: Circulation Service, 1972, rev. ed., 1977.

Doroska, Lud, ed. *Great Pro Quarterbacks.* New York: Grosset and Dunlap, 1974.

Dowdy, Zachary R. "Culture Class." *Filipinas* (June 1993): 12–13.

Dugger, Celia W. "New Alliances and Attitudes on Aid." *The New York Times* (August 1, 1997): A23.

Edwards, Randall. "Character Education: Popular, But Effective?" *Monitor: American Psychological Association* (March 1995): 42.

Egan, Timothy. "Mail-Order Marriage, Immigrant Dreams and Death." *The New York Times* (May 26, 1996): 12.

Enriquez, Nestor Palugod. "My Coming to America." *Heritage* (Spring 1997): 13–14.

Espina, Marina E. *Filipinos In Louisiana.* New Orleans: A. F. Laborde and Sons, 1988.

Espiritu, Yen Le. *Asian American Panethnicity: Bridging Institutions and Identities.* Philadelphia: Temple University Press, 1992.

———. *Filipino American Lives.* Philadelphia: Temple University Press, 1995.

Esteban, F. M. "Fifty years of the Legionarios del Trabajo." *Philippine News* (May 16–22, 1974): 14.

Evangelista, Oscar, and Susan Evangelista. "Continuity and Change Among the Second-Generation Filipino-Americans in Seattle, Washington." *Philippine Historical Association Historical Bulletin* 27:1–4 (1982): 164–177.

Fabros, Alex. "The Boogie Woogie Boys." *Filipinas* (September 1993): 38–43.

"Facts About LEAP." Los Angeles: Leadership Education for Asian Pacifics, Inc., 1996.

Fallows, James. "A Damaged Culture." *Atlantic Monthly* (November 1987): 49–58.
"Family-Unfriendly." *Filipinas* (May 1997): 51.
Fawcett, James T., and Robert W. Gardner. "Asian Immigrant Entrepreneurs and Non-Entrepreneurs: A Comparative Study of Recent Korean and Filipino Immigrants." *Population and Environment: A Journal of Interdisciplinary Studies* 15:3 (January 1994): 211–238.
Faypon, Eliodore. "History of the Chicago Knights of Rizal." In "Order of the Knights of Rizal and its Auxiliary North America and Canada Chapters Regional Meeting, June 17–18, 1989, Chicago, Illinois, Dr. Jose Rizal Memorial Center, 1332 W. Irving Park Road, Chicago, Illinois." Chicago: n.p., [1989].
"FCC Holds Coronation of Mrs. Philippines USA." *Heritage* (December 1992): 18.
Feria, Dolores S., ed. *Goodbye to Winter: The Autobiography of Sophie Schmidt-Rodolfo*. Quezon City, Philippines: New Day Publishers, 1987.
Fernandez, Modesto. "Who Will Feel Their Pain?" *Filipinas* (October 1996): 24–26.
"Fifth International Assembly, Knights of Rizal, July 15, 16, 17, 1994." *Tambuli USA* (Summer 1994): 23.
"The Fighting Filipinos." *Filipinas* (October 1995): 1–2.
Filipinas: A Magazine for All Filipinos (May 1992–Present).
"The Filipino American Community in Southern California." LEAP Forum Registration Form. September 29, 1990.
"Filipino Civil Rights Advocates—A New National Civil Rights Group." *Bigayan* (Spring 1995): 1, 8.
Filipino Students' Magazine (1905–1906).
"Filipino Task Force's Youth Survey on Alcohol, Drugs, Sex, Gangs & Family." Vallejo, CA: Fighting Back Partnership, [1993].
"Filipino Veterans and Naturalization." *The Asian American Encyclopedia*. Vol. 2. Franklin Ng, ed. New York: Marshall Cavendish, 1995: 468–469.
"Filipino World War II Veterans To Get A Hearing." National Federation of Filipino American Associations press release. March 19, 1998.
"Filipino WWII Veterans' Day: Getting Clinton's Attention." *Heritage* (Winter 1997): 8.
"Filipino WWII Vets Can Become US Citizens." *Bigayan* (Fall 1991): 3.
"Filipino Youth Activities." *Seattle Post-Intelligencer* (May 24, 1994): A7.
"Filipinos in the Military." *The Filipinos in Hawaii—The First 75 Years*. Juan C. Dionisio, ed. Honolulu: Hawaii Filipino News Specialty Publications, [1981]: 115–117.
"Filipinos Press Claims for U.S. Aid as Veterans." *The New York Times* (August 24, 1997): A23.
"The First Pensionados." *Graphic* (August 17, 1932): 8–9, 56, 63.
"First 'Pista sa Nayon' Set Aug. 4." *Filipino American Bulletin* 1:6 (April 21–May 21, 1990): 1, 19.
Flores-Meiser, Enya P. "Filipino Values." *The Asian American Encyclopedia, Vol.*

2: Chinese in railroad construction—Hmong Religion, Franklin Ng, ed. New York: Marshall Cavendish, 1995: 467–468.

"41 US solons sponsor Veterans' Equity Act." *Philippine News* (August 19–25, 1992): 1, 5.

Francisco, Mariel Nepomuceno, and Fe Maria C. Arriola. *The History of the Burgis.* Quezon City, Philippines: GCF Books, 1987.

Freedberg, Louis. "Immigrants rushing to citizenship." *San Francisco Chronicle* (September 17, 1996): A1.

———. "Sign of Relief Over Return of Immigrants' SSI." *San Francisco Chronicle* (June 27, 1997), A3.

Friday, Chris. *Organizing Asian American Labor: The Pacific Coast Canned-Salmon Industry, 1870–1942.* Philadelphia: Temple University Press, 1994.

"From the Editor." *Filipinas* (July 1997): 4.

"Fulgado New Prexy of UP Alumni Assn." *Heritage* (Spring 1996): 6.

Gabriela. ⟨http://www.gabnet.org⟩.

Galang-Macaraeg, Gigi. "Waiting to Exile." *Filipinas* (April 1997): 25–26.

Galedo, Lillian. "A Message to Filipino Graduates." *Bigayan* (Summer 1996): 2, 4.

———. "We Won't Go Back." *Perspectives on Affirmative Action . . . and Its Impact on Asian Americans.* Los Angeles: Asian Pacific American Public Policy Institute, 1996.

Garza, Melita Marie. "Filipinos Forge New Identity." *Chicago Tribune* (September 14, 1992): Section 2, 7.

———. "Welfare Bill Threatens Immigrants." *Chicago Tribune* (July 22, 1996): 2C, 2.

Gerona-Adkins, Rita M. "Filipino veterans plan move with Congress." *Philippine News* (March 5–11, 1997): A1, A10–A11.

"A Glance at Welfare Reform and Legal Immigration." *Atlanta Constitution* (August 15, 1996): D2.

"The Glass Ceiling." *The Economist,* 336:7929 (August 26, 1995): 59.

"Goldilocks Goes Mass-Market." *Filipinas* (June 1996): 72.

Gonzalez, N. V. M. "Introduction." In P. C. Morantte, *Remembering Carlos Bulosan.* Quezon City, Philippines: New Day, 1984.

———. "Introduction." In Bienvenido N. Santos, *You Lovely People.* Quezon City, Philippines: New Day Publishers, 1955.

Gordon, Linda. *Pitied But Not Entitled: Single Mothers and the History of Welfare, 1890–1935.* Cambridge, MA: Harvard University Press, 1994.

Guerrero, Milagros C. "The Provincial and Muncipal Elites of Luzon During the Revolution, 1898–1902." *Philippine Social History: Global Trade and Local Transformations.* Alfred W. McCoy and Ed. C. de Jesus, eds. Manila: Ateneo de Manila Press, 1982: 155–190.

Guillermo, Emil. "After Us, the Deluge." *Filipinas* (January 1998): 36, 39, 41.

———. "Label of the Month." *Filipinas* (May 1997): 53.

———. "Win Manong." *Filipinas* (November 1996): 25.

Gunnison, Robert B., and Greg Lucas. "Showdown over Food Stamps." *San Francisco Chronicle* (September 20, 1996): A1.

Gutierrez, Luis, and Paul Wellstone. "Restore Fairness to Legal Immigrants." *Chicago Tribune* (May 2, 1997): Sec. 1, 20.

Guyotte, Roland L., and Barbara M. Posadas. "Celebrating Rizal Day: The Emergence of a Filipino Tradition in Twentieth-Century Chicago." *Feasts and Celebrations in North American Ethnic Communities.* Ramon A. Gutierrez and Genevieve Fabre, eds. Albuquerque, NM: University of New Mexico Press, 1995: 111–127.

Hacker, Andrew. *Money: Who Has How Much and Why.* New York: Scribner, 1997.

Hagedorn, Jessica. *Dogeaters.* New York: HarperCollins, 1990.

———. "Tribute [to Bienvenido N. Santos]." *Filipinas* (March 1996): 47.

Harrod, Frederick S. *Manning the New Navy: The Development of a Modern Naval Enlisted Force, 1899–1940.* Westport, CT: Greenwood Press, 1978.

Hart, Donn V. *Compadrinazgo: Ritual Kinship in the Philippines.* DeKalb: Northern Illinois University Press, 1977.

"Hate at Denny's." *Filipinas* (July 1997): 33.

Haynes, V. Dion. "California seeks alternatives for college affirmative action." *Chicago Tribune* (July 14, 1997): 3.

Hearn, Lafcadio. "Saint Malo: A Lacustrine Village in Louisiana." *Harper's Weekly* XXVII:1371 (March 31, 1883): 196–199.

Henry, Jim. "Victoria Manolo Draves." *Notable Asian Americans.* Helen Zia and Susan B. Gall, eds. New York: Gale Research Inc., 1995: 71–72.

Heritage: Magazine of Filipino Culture, Arts and Letters (Quarterly, June 1987–Present).

Herszenhorn, David M. "Punitive Actions Are Advised in Discrimination at Denny's." *New York Times* (August 15, 1997): B–4.

"In Imelda Marcos's Shoes: Cecile Licad." *Elle* (March 1987): 46.

Inouye, Daniel K. "Filipino Veterans." *Heritage* (December 1992): 5.

"Institutionalized Bias." *Boston Globe* (April 25, 1997): A22.

Ira, Luning Bonifacio, and Isagani R. Medina. "What Will They Think of Next?" *Turn of the Century.* Gilda Cordero-Fernando and Nik Ricio, eds. Quezon City, Philippines: GCF Books, 1978: 207–225.

Iritani, Evelyn. "Coming to America." *Seattle Post-Intelligencer* (December 21, 1994): A7.

Iyer, Pico. *Video Night in Katmandu: And Other Reports from the Not-So-Far East.* New York: Vintage Books, 1988.

Jackson, Richard. "Over the Seas or to the Hills: Population Growth and Impact in the Philippines." *Geography* 79:342 (January 1994): 78–83.

Joaquin, Nick. *A Question of Heroes.* Manila: Filipinas Foundation, 1977.

Jocson, Korina M. "Autumn of the Matriarchs." *Filipinas* (March 1996): 38–39.

Jones, Arthur. "The Marcos Goon Squad Comes Calling." *The Progressive* (August 1983): 16.

"Jose Rizal and Leonor Rivera." In "Order of the Knights of Rizal, Chicago Chapter And Its Auxiliary, In commemoration of the 92nd death anniversary of Dr. Jose P. Rizal, Rizal Day 1988, Installation of Officers, Literary & Musical Program, Friday, December 30, 1988, 7:00 p.m., Dr. Jose Rizal Memorial Center, 1332 W. Irving Park Road, Chicago, Illinois." Chicago: n.p., [1988].

"Judge Halts California Cutoff of Prenatal Care to Illegal Aliens," *The New York Times* (November 28, 1996): A27.

"Judge Rules in Dimas-Alang Case." *Philippine Press USA* (July 1989): 4.

Jundis, Orvy. "Getting A Kick Out of Filipino Martial Arts." *Filipinas* (August 1993): 56–57, 66.

Jung, Carolyn. "Filipino fund-raising celebration comes up short." *The Philippine Review* (May 1994): 3.

Karnow, Stanley. *In Our Image: America's Empire in the Philippines.* New York: Ballantine, 1989.

Kaut, Charles. "Utang Na Loob: A System of Contractual Obligation Among Tagalogs." *Southwestern Journal of Anthropology*, 17:3 (1961): 256–272.

Kelley, Tina. "Neighbors Rally Against Arson, for Everett Family." *The Seattle Times* (April 25, 1996): B-3.

Kerkvliet, Benedict J. *The Huk Rebellion: A Study of Peasant Revolt in the Philippines.* Berkeley and Los Angeles, CA: University of California Press, 1977.

Kiester, Sally Valente. "Bold Fusion." *Filipinas* (May 1996): 39–41.

Kitano, Harry H. L., and Roger Daniels. *Asian Americans: Emerging Minorities.* 2nd ed. Englewood Cliffs, NJ: Prentice-Hall, 1995.

Kobylarz, Xenia P. "A Hard Look in the Mirror." *Filipinas* (November 1997): 20–24.

Kolker, Claudia. "Tide turns in U.S. for Filipino nurses." *Houston Chronicle* (July 8, 1996): 1A, 6A.

Kramer, Gene. "Filipino Vets Seek American WWII Benefits." *The Arizona Republic* (July 27, 1997): A3.

Lacson, Lolita L. "Filipinos in the Affluent Society." *Philippine Panorama* (September 22, 1974): 6–7.

Laguitan, Raul N. "Two Bahala Na Gang Moms Cry Justice For Jailed Sons." *The Philippine Review* [Sacramento, CA] (May 1992): 5.

Laquian, Eleanor R., and Irene D. Sobreviña. *Filipino Cooking Here and Abroad.* Manila: National Book Store, 1977.

Lawler, Jennifer. *The Martial Arts Encyclopedia.* Indianapolis: Masters Press, 1966.

Lawsin, Emily Porcincula. "Beyond 'Hanggang Pier Only': Filipino American War Brides of Seattle, 1945–1965." *Filipino American National Historical Society Journal* 4 (1996): 50–50G.

"LCB Mabuhay U.S.A. Corporation." *Filipinas* (August 1996): 58.

"Legal Immigrants Would Benefit Under New Budget Agreement." *The New York Times* (July 30, 1997): A13.

"Legionarios celebrate 60th ann'y." *Philippine News* (March 14–20, 1984): 1–2.

"Legiyonarios del Trabajo set confab Nov. 6–10." *Philippine News* (October 30–November 5, 1991): 30.

Levy, Art. "The Bride's Garden." *Sarasota Herald-Tribune* (August 31, 1996): 1–2E.

Lewis, Loida Nicholas. *101 Legal Ways to Stay in the USA (Or: How to Get a Green Card According to the Immigration Act of 1990)*. Berkeley, CA: Nolo Press, 1992 (2nd ed. 1996).

Lipat, Christine T., Trinity A. Ordona, Cianna Pamintuan Stewart, and Mary Ann Ubaldo. "Tomboy, Dyke, Lezzie, and Bi: Filipina Lesbian and Bisexual Women Speak Out." *Filipino Americans: Transformation and Identity*. Maria P. P. Root, ed. Thousand Oaks, CA: Sage Publications, 1997: 230–246.

Liu, John M. "The Contours of Asian Professional, Technical and Kindred Work Immigration, 1965–1988." *Sociological Perspectives* 35:4 (1992): 673–704.

Liu, John M., Paul M. Ong, and Carolyn Rosenstein. "Dual Chain Migration: Post-1965 Filipino Immigration to the United States," *International Migration Review* 25:3 (Fall 1991): 487–513.

Llorente, Elizabeth. "Green Card Blues—Nurse, 26, Facing Deportation to Philippines." *The Record, Northern New Jersey* (April 24, 1997): L1.

Magner, Denise K. "College Faulted for Not Considering Differences in Asian-American Groups." *Chronicle of Higher Education* (February 10, 1993): A32, A34.

Manalansan, Martin F., IV. "Searching for Community: Filipino Gay Men in New York City." *Amerasia Journal* 20:1 (1994): 59–73.

Manuel-Barros, Astrid. "Couple Cries Foul over Raps of Child Abuse," *Philippine News* (September 27–October 3, 1995): A1, A15.

"Marcos on Trial." *The Nation* (April 12, 1986): 509.

"Maria Luisa Mabilangan Haley Named to President-Elect Bill Clinton's Transition Team." *Heritage* (December 1992): 9.

Matthee, Imbert. "Politicizing Asian Americans." *Seattle Post-Intelligencer* (March 15, 1996): A1, A4.

"Maximo Fabella: Maximum Resource." *Filipinas* (January 1997): 48.

May, Glenn Anthony. *Battle for Batangas: A Philippine Province at War*. New Haven, CT: Yale University Press, 1980.

McCoy, Alfred W. "A Queen Dies Slowly: The Rise and Decline of Iloilo City." *Philippine Social History: Global Trade and Local Transformations*. Alfred W. McCoy and Ed. C. de Jesus, eds. Manila: Ateneo de Manila Press, 1982: 297–358.

———. "Quezon's Commonwealth: The Emergence of Philippine Authoritarianism." *Philippine Colonial Democracy*. Ruby R. Paredes, ed. Yale Southeast Asia Studies Monograph Series, #32. New Haven, CT: Yale University Press, 1988: 114–160.

McCoy, Alfred W., and Ed. C. de Jesus, eds. *Philippine Social History: Global Trade and Local Transformations*. Manila: Ateneo de Manila Press, 1982.

McDonnell, Patrick J. "Immigrant Welfare Use Varies Widely." *Los Angeles Times* (July 30, 1997): B1.

McLennan, Marshall S. "Changing Human Ecology on the Central Luzon Plains: Nueva Ecija, 1705–1939." *Philippine Social History: Global Trade and Local Transformations.* Alfred W. McCoy and Ed. C. de Jesus, eds. Manila: Ateneo de Manila Press, 1982: 57–90.

Melegrito, John. "Irene's Agenda." *Filipinas* (May 1993): 6–8, 61.

Melendy, H. Brett. *Asians in America: Filipinos, Koreans, and East Asians.* Boston: Twayne Publishers, 1977.

Memories: 75th Filipino Immigration (Maui Filipino Anniversary Commemoration, 1906–1981). Wailuku, Maui, HI: Maui Committee to Celebrate the 75th Anniversary of the Filipino Immigration to Hawaii, 1981.

Mendez, Paz Policarpio, and F. Landa Jocano. *The Filipino Family in Its Rural and Urban Orientation: Two Case Studies in Culture and Education.* Manila: Centro Escolar University Research and Development Center, 1974.

Montreal, Lani T. "Their World's A Stage." *Filipinas* (February 1998): 16–17, 50.

Morantte, P. C. "Remembering Bienvenido N. Santos." *Heritage* (Spring 1996): 35–37.

———. *Remembering Carlos Bulosan.* Quezon City, Philippines: New Day, 1984.

Morente, Precy. "Sounds Like Home." *Filipinas* (July 1997): 21–22.

Mydans, Seth. "Pressure for English-Only Job Rules Stirring a Sharp Debate Across the U.S." *The New York Times* (August 8, 1990): A10.

"National Membership Meeting" Schedule, FilCRA, July 25–27, 1997.

Natividad, Larry D. "The Launching of a Filipino Student Literary Magazine, *Maganda.*" *Heritage* (June 1991): 22–23.

"Newly Elected President of Filipino Ford Club." *The Philippine Republic* (May 1929): 15.

"1994 Annual Grand Lodge Convention and Banquet and Ball [of the Gran Oriente Filipino]," September 21 to September 24, 1994. Filipino American National Historical Society Archive. Seattle, WA.

Nolan, James L., Karla C. Shippey, Molly E. Thurmond, Alexandria Woznick, and Edward G. Hinkelman. *Philippines Business: The Portable Encyclopedia for Doing Business with the Philippines.* San Rafael, CA: World Trade Press, 1996.

"Not So Model Minority." *Filipinas* (June 1997): 68.

"The #1 Asian Station in the San Francisco Bay Area." *Filipinas* (August 1996): 53.

O'Boyle, Lily Gamboa, and Reynaldo G. Alejandro. *Philippine Hospitality: A Gracious Tradition of the East.* New York: Acacia Corporation, 1988.

Ochoa, Dante. "Vets Chain Selves, Vow Hunger Strike until Equity Bill Passes." *Philippine News* (June 25–July 1, 1997): A1, A10.

"OCW Remittances." Melanie Milo <mmilo@pidsnet.pids.gov.ph> to philippinestujdies–1@nepean.uws.edu.au, September 12, 1997.

Okamura, Jonathan Y. "Filipino Organizations: A History." *The Filipinos in Ha-

waii—The First 75 Years. Juan C. Dionisio, ed. Honolulu: Hawaii Filipino News Specialty Publications, [1981]: 73–77.

———. "Filipino Hometown Associations in Hawaii." *Ethnology.* 22:4 (1983): 341–353.

Okamura, Jonathan Y., and Amefil R. Agbayani. "Pamantasan: Filipino American Higher Education." *Filipino Americans: Transformation and Identity.* Maria P. P. Root, ed. Thousand Oaks, CA: Sage Publications, 1997: 183–197.

Olandria, Willie, and Ruth Olandria. "Oregon War Brides." *Filipino American National Historical Society Journal* 3 (1994): 67–68.

Ong, Paul, and Tania Azores. "The Migration and Incorporation of Filipino Nurses." *The New Asian Immigration in Los Angeles and Global Restructuring.* Paul Ong, Edna Bonacich, and Lucie Cheng, eds. Philadelphia: Temple University Press, 1994: 164–195.

Ong, Paul, and John M. Liu. "U.S. Immigration Policies and Asian Migration." *The New Asian Immigration in Los Angeles and Global Restructuring.* Paul Ong, Edna Bonacich, and Lucie Cheng, eds. Philadelphia: Temple University Press, 1994: 45–73.

"Order of the Knights of Rizal Foreign Area Council." *Tambuli USA* (Summer 1994): 6.

Orquiola, Ray. "Bakery Restaurant: The Filipino Never Leaves Home Without It." *Filipinas* (July 1992): 31–35.

Paredes, Ruby R. "Introduction: The Paradox of Philippine Colonial Democracy." *Philippine Colonial Democracy.* Ruby R. Paredes, ed. Yale Southeast Asia Studies Monograph Series, #32. New Haven, CT: Yale University Press, 1988: 1–12.

———, ed. *Philippine Colonial Democracy.* Yale Southeast Asia Studies Monograph Series, #32. New Haven, CT: Yale University Press, 1988.

Pear, Robert. "For Legal Immigrants, a Welfare Reprieve." *The New York Times* (October 3, 1996): A21.

Pet, Catherine Ceniza. "Re-Locating Home: Filipino Nurses and Community Formation in Postindustrial America," unpublished paper, Organization of American Historians Annual Meeting, Chicago, March 28, 1996.

Peters, Jens. *Philippines.* 6th ed. Hawthorne, Victoria, Australia: Lonely Planet Publications, 1997.

Peterson, Jonathan. "Filipinos—A Search for Community." *Los Angeles Times* (May 24, 1989): 1, 14, 15.

"Phase I Balikbayan Program." *Times Journal* (March 6, 1974): 1.

Pianin, Eric, and John F. Harris. "President, GOP Agree on Balanced Budget Plan; Last-Minute Disputes Swept Away By $225 Billion Revenue Windfall." *Washington Post* (May 3, 1997): A1.

Picache, Beverly. "Filipino World War II Veterans: Fulfilling a 50-year-old Promise." *Filipinas* (November 1992): 24–29.

"Pictorial." *Bulletin of the Filipino American Historical Society.* IV:5 (December 20, 1991), 50.

Pido, Antonio J. A. *The Pilipinos in America: Macro/Micro Dimensions of Immigration and Integration.* New York: Center for Migration Studies, 1985.

Pilapil, Virgilio R., M.D. "A Brief History of FilAmHisSo and Its Graduate Recognition Program." *Heritage* (June 1991): 19–20.

———. "Filipinos of Central and Southern Illinois," unpublished paper, Illinois State Historical Society Annual Meeting, April 22, 1995.

———. "The First Filipino Settlement in the United States." *Bulletin of the Filipino American Historical Society* 9:4 (November 1, 1996): 43–46.

———. "The Midwest Connection." *Heritage* (March 1992): 20–23.

———. "The Midwest Connection." *Heritage* (Winter 1997): 32–34.

Pimentel, Benjamin. "Filipino Vets Face Troubled Lives in U.S." *San Francisco Chronicle* (March 16, 1994): A1, A19, A24.

———. "Immigration rights bill prompts protest in S.F." *San Francisco Chronicle* (August 28, 1995): A12.

"Pinoy Profile," *Heritage* (Spring 1997): 15.

"PinTouch Telecom." *Filipinas* (June 1998): 60–61.

"Pistahang Filipino." *Filipinas* (April 1998): 27.

"Plan for CDA Unification." *Philippine Press USA* (October 1990): 1, 10.

"Pols Progress." *Filipinas* (January 1997): 15.

Ponce, Danilo E. "Extramarital Affairs: Meaning and Impact on the Filipino Immigrant Family." *Pilipinas* (Fall 1986): 1–10.

Poole, Fred, and Max Vanzi. "Marcos's Secret War in America." *The Nation* (May 12, 1984): 577–579.

Portes, Alejandro, and Rubén G. Rumbaut. *Immigrant America: A Portrait.* 2nd ed. Berkeley, CA: University of California Press, 1996.

Portes, Alejandro, and Min Zhou. "The New Second Generation: Segmented Assimilation and Its Variants among Post-1965 Immigrant Youth." *Annals of the American Academy of Political and Social Science* (1993): 74–98.

Posadas, Barbara M. "Crossed Boundaries in Interracial Chicago: Pilipino American Families Since 1925." *Amerasia Journal,* 8 (Fall 1981): 31–52.

———. "The Hierarchy of Color and Psychological Adjustment in an Industrial Environment: Filipinos, the Pullman Company and the Brotherhood of Sleeping Car Porters." *Labor History* (Summer 1982): 349–373.

Posadas, Barbara M., and Roland L. Guyotte. "Aspiration and Reality: Occupational and Educational Choice among Filipino Migrants to Chicago, 1900–1935." *Illinois Historical Journal* 85:2 (Summer 1992): 89–104.

———. "Unintentional Immigrants: Chicago's Filipino Foreign Students Become Settlers." *Journal of American Ethnic History* 9:2 (Spring 1990): 26–48.

"Primus Telecommunications, Inc." *Filipinas* (June 1998): 81.

"A Prudent Act of Restoration." *Chicago Tribune* (May 17, 1997): Sec. 1, 22.

Pulido, Mark Emmanuel. "Washington Manifesto." *Filipinas* (May 1998): 24.

———. "Youth Gangs and the Filipino Community." *PN* [*Philippine News*] *Magazine* (April 10–16, 1991): 12.

Quimpo, Susan F. "Mothers and Daughters: Pains of Endearment." *Heritage* (May 1994): 50–51.

Rafael, Vicente. *Contracting Colonialism: Translation and Christian Conversion in Tagalog Society Under Early Spanish Rule.* Ithaca, NY: Cornell University Press, 1988.

"Ramos Emphasizes the U.S.-Philippine Connection." *Seattle Post-Intelligencer* (November 22, 1993): A4.

Reimers, David M. *Still the Golden Door: The Third World Comes to America.* 2nd ed. New York: Columbia University Press, 1991.

Republic of the Philippines. Department of Education. Bureau of Public Schools. "Report of Wm. Alex. Sutherland, Superintendent of Filipino Students in the United States, for the Year Ending June 30, 1905." *Annual School Reports. 1901–1905.* Reprinted. Manila: Bureau of Printing, 1954.

"Richard S. Bustillo: Filipino Martial Arts Gurò." *Heritage* (June 1991): 7–9.

Rigor, Conrado N., ed. *PAMANA: Half-A-Century of Filipino Community Life in the Emerald City.* Seattle, WA: Filipino Community of Seattle, 1987.

Roces, Alfredo, and Grace Roces. *Culture Shock! Philippines: A Guide to Customs and Etiquette.* 3rd ed. Portland, OR: Graphic Arts Center Publishing Company, 1992.

Rodis, Rodel. "Immigration limit bills stalled." *Philippine News* (January 22–28, 1997): A4.

"Rodolfo 'Rudy' S. Bernardo." *Fil-Am Image* (September 1996): 50.

Rumbaut, Rubén G. "Passages to America: Perspectives on the New Immigration." *America at Century's End.* Alan Wolfe, ed. Berkeley, CA: University of California Press, 1991.

Rydell, Robert W. *All the World's a Fair: Visions of Empire at American International Expositions, 1876–1916.* Chicago: University of California Press, 1984.

Salamanca, Bonifacio S. *The Filipino Reaction to American Rule, 1901–1913.* N.P.: Shoe String Press, 1968.

Salanga, Alfrredo Navarro. *The Children of Lam-ang: The Folk Culture of the Ilocos Region.* Manila: The Educators Press, 1984.

Salopek, Paul. "Deadly clash of cultures on the streets: Cambodian, Filipino gang wars in Chicago." *Chicago Tribune* (March 3, 1996), 1.

Santa Maria, Nathaniel. "Making Work Respectable: Filipina Room Cleaners in San Francisco's Hotel Industry." Filipino American National Historical Society, Fifth National Conference, San Mateo, California, August 4–6, 1994.

Santos, Bienvenido N. "The Fighting Filipinos." *Filipinas* (October 1995): 19–20.

———. "Pilipino Old Timers: Fact and Fiction." *Amerasia* 9:2 (1982): 89–98.

———. *You Lovely People.* Quezon City, Philippines: New Day Publishers, 1955.

Santos, Hector. "Old Soldiers Never Die." *Filipinas* (September 1997), 16–17, 20.

Salyer, Lucy E. *Laws Harsh As Tigers: Chinese Immigrants and the Shaping of Modern Immigration Law.* Chapel Hill, NC: University of North Carolina Press, 1995.

Scharlin, Craig, and Lilia V. Villanueva, eds. *Philip Vera Cruz: A Personal History of Filipino Immigrants and the Farmworkers Movement.* Los Angeles: UCLA Labor Center, 1992.

"Search to Involve Pilipino Americans, Inc. (SIPA)." *Heritage* (June 1991): 24.

Serran, Tony N., and Melen McBride. "Growing Old in America: No Place Like 'Back Home.'" *Filipinas* (November 1994): 30–33.

"75th Diamond Jubilee [of the Gran Oriente Filipino]," August 17–19, 1995. Filipino American National Historical Society Archive. Seattle, WA.

Sharma, Miriam. "Labor Migration and Class Formation Among the Filipinos in Hawaii, 1906–1946." *Labor Immigration Under Capitalism: Asian Workers in the United States before World War II.* Lucie Cheng and Edna Bonacich, eds. Berkeley, CA: University of California Press, 1984(a): 579–611.

———. "The Philippines: A Case of Migration to Hawaii, 1906 to 1946." *Labor Immigration Under Capitalism: Asian Workers in the United States before World War II.* Lucie Cheng and Edna Bonacich, eds. Berkeley, CA: University of California Press, 1984(b): 337–358.

Shatzkin, Kate. "Seattle's *barcadas.*" *The Seattle Times* (July 7, 1992): A1, A2.

Shinagawa, Larry Hajime, and Gin Yong Pang. "Asian American Panethnicity and Intermarriage." *Amerasia Journal* 22:2 (1996): 127–152.

"The Shipping News." *Filipinas* (June 1997): 62.

Silva, John L. "Activist Jaime Geaga: Life Without Fear." *Filipinas* (June 1995): 47–48.

———. "On Her Own." *Filipinas* (February 1996): 30–33.

———. "The Filipino Channel: Will It Click?" *Filipinas* (August 1994): 36.

———. "Straight Outta Kalihi." *Filipinas* (May 1996): 32–34, 57.

Sison-Paez, Marites. "Art Courant." *Filipinas* (January 1997): 34–36.

———. "Igarta Unbound." *Filipinas* (October 1997): 46–48, 50.

Smith, Mary. "Veterans' Benefits for Filipino Veterans." The Library of Congress, Congressional Research Service, CRS Report for Congress, updated February 8, 1993.

"Social Adjustment." *Mabuhay International Monitor* 1:6 (June 1992): 3.

Solis, Melchizedek Maraon. "Barangay in America." *Philippines Press USA* (August 1987): 7.

———. "Heirs of Rizal: Historical Update on the Caballeros de Dimas-Alang, Inc." Caballeros de Dimas-Alang, Inc., *1989 Grand Inaugural Banquet and Ball* (Janaury 7, 1989). Filipino American National Historical Society Archive. Seattle, WA.

"SSI—A Two-Edged Sword." *Filipinas* (August 1994), 20.

Spickard, Paul R. *Mixed Blood: Intermarriage and Ethnic Identity in Twentieth-Century America.* Madison, WI: The University of Wisconsin Press, 1989.

Sreenivasan, Sreenath. "Newscasts in Tagalog and Songs in Gaelic." *The New York Times* (September 8, 1997): D-11.

Stamets, John. "The Manila Connection." *The Progressive* (January 1983): 20–21.

Strobel, Leny Mendoza. " 'Born-Again Filipino': Filipino American Identity and Asian Panethnicity." *Amerasia Journal* 22:2 (1996): 31–53.

Sturtevant, David R. *Popular Uprisings in the Philippines, 1840–1940.* Ithaca, NY: Cornell University Press, 1976.

Sutherland, William Alexander. *Not By Might: The Epic of the Philippines.* Las Cruces, NM: Southwest Publishing Company, 1953.

"Symposium—Overcoming Teen Tribulations." *Chapter One: Newsletter* [Filipino American National Historical Society, Oregon Chapter] (October 1, 1996): 3–4.

Tatak Pilipino: Original Pilipino Classics (Summer 1997).

Tatak Pilipino: Musika ng Laki (Original Pilipino Music) (Summer 1998): 1–73.

" 'Tender Trap' Awaits Pinoys from the U.S." *Bulletin Today* (December 10, 1973): 1, 7.

"TFC: The Filipino Channel." *Filipinas* (October 1995): 32–33.

Thomson, James C., Jr., Peter W. Stanley, and John Curtis Perry. *Sentimental Imperialists: The American Experience in East Asia.* New York: Harper and Row, 1981.

Thurman, Skip. "Social Safety Net for Immigrants Safe—For Now Benefits Restored for Legal Immigrants, but Future Help Doubtful." *Christian Science Monitor* (May 21, 1997): 4.

Tiongson, Antonio T., Jr. "Throwing the Baby Out With the Bath Water: Situating Young Filipino Mothers and Fathers Beyond the Dominant Discourse on Adolescent Pregnancy." *Filipino Americans: Transformation and Identity.* Maria P. P. Root, ed. Thousand Oaks, CA: Sage Publications, 1997: 257–271.

Tiongson, Nicanor G. "The Dressing Tradition." *Turn of the Century.* Gilda Cordero-Fernando and Nik Ricio, eds. Quezon City, Philippines: GCF Books, 1978: 112–133.

Tompar-Tiu, Aurora, and Juliana Sustento-Seneriches. *Depression and Other Mental Health Issues: The Filipino American Experience.* San Francisco, CA: Jossey-Bass Publishers, 1995.

Toomey, Sheila. "Homegrown TV Strives for Filipino Unity." *Anchorage Daily News* (November 12, 1997): A-1, A-8.

Torres, Vic. "Duel in Daly City." *Filipinas* (August 1993): 12–16.

"Turn to KTSF Channel 26 for the Best in Filipino and Fil-Am Programming." *Filipinas* (January 1997): 46.

"Union Maid." *Filipinas* (March 1996): 10.

United States. Department of Commerce. Bureau of the Census. *U.S. Census of Population: 1960. Subject Reports: Nonwhite Population by Race: Social and Economic Statistics for Negroes, Indians, Japanese, Chinese, and Filipinos.* Washington, D.C.: U.S. Government Printing Office, 1963.

———. *1970 Census of Population—Subject Reports: Japanese, Chinese and Filipinos in the United States.* Washington D.C.: U.S. Government Printing Office, 1973.

———. *1980 Census of Population. Race of the Population by States: 1980.* Washington, D.C.: U.S. Government Printing Office, 1981.

————. *1990 Census of Population: Asians and Pacific Islanders in the United States—1990 CP-3-5.* Washington, D.C.: Bureau of the Census, 1993.

United States. Immigration and Naturalization Service. *Statistical Yearbook of the Immigration and Naturalization Service, 1986–1995.* Washington, D.C.: U.S. Government Printing Office, 1987–1997.

————. "Immigration to the United States in Fiscal Year 1995–1996." (http://www.ins.usdoj.gov/public/stats/132.html and 999.html).

United States. National Archives. Bureau of Insular Affairs (cited as BIA Records). Record Group 350. Washington, D.C.

United States. War Department. Bureau of Insular Affairs. *Fifth Annual Report of the Philippine Commission, 1904.* Part 3. "Report of the Superintendent [Wm. Alex Sutherland] of Filipino Students in the United States Covering the Filipino Student Movement, from Its Inception to June 30, 1904." Washington, D.C.: Government Printing Office, 1905.

"Update." *The Filipino Guardian Immigrant Journal* (March 6–19, 1992): 11–12.

Valeros, Florentino B., and Estrellita V. Gruenberg. *Filipino Writers in English.* Quezon City, Philippines: New Day Publishers, 1987.

Valladares, Ed. "Becoming a Citizen." *Bigayan* (Spring 1998): 1, 7.

Vallangca, Caridad Concepcion. *The Second Wave: Pinay & Pinoy (1945–1960).* San Francisco, CA: Strawberry Hill Press, 1987.

Vallangca, Roberto V. *Pinoy: The First Wave.* San Francisco, CA: Strawberry Hill Press, 1977.

"Veloria Applauds Regulations on Mail Order Bride Industry." *Northwest Asian Weekly* (February 15–21, 1997): 4.

"Venancio C. Igarta: Master Painter." *Filipinas* (June 1998): 42.

Veneracion, Jaime B. "Mexican Footprints." *Filipinas* (July 1997): 20–22.

Ventura, Sylvia Mendez. "The Filipino As Americans or Filipino Americans in San Francisco: Walking the Thin Line Inbetween." *Mr. & Ms.* (Manila) (March 27, 1979): 14–16.

Verzosa, Veronica. "What Does John Huang Have To Do With Me?" *Filipinas* (May 1997): 27–28, 30.

"Veterans Demand Benefits." *Austin American-Statesman* (July 27, 1997): A12.

"Victory for Vets." *Filipinas* (March 1998): 16.

Villaseran, Abby. "Hot Gifts for the Holidays." *Filipinas* (November 1996): 72.

Vinluan, Ermena, and Ding Pajaron. "Bittersweet Aloha." *Filipinas* (May 1996): 36–37.

Virata, Rufy. "My younger boy . . ." *Filipinas* (May 1993): 72.

Walch, Richard E., Jr. "America's Philippine Policy in the Quirino Years (1948–1953): A Study in Patron Client Diplomacy." *Reappraising an Empire: New Perspectives on Philippine-American History.* Peter W. Stanley, ed. Cambridge, MA: Harvard University Press, 1984: 285–306.

Waltz, Lynn. "Filipino Gangs' Unlikely Turf: Suburbia." *The Virginian-Pilot/The Ledger-Star* (July 28, 1991): B1, B4.

Warren, Robert. "Annual Estimates of Nonimmigrant Overstays in the United States: 1985 to 1988." *Undocumented Migration to the United States: IRCA and the Experience of the 1980s.* Frank D. Bean, Barry Edmonston, and Jeffrey S. Passel, eds. Santa Monica, CA: Rand Corporation, 1990: 77–110.

Wei, William. *The Asian American Movement.* Philadelphia, PA: Temple University Press, 1993.

Weinberger, Caspar W. "One Way to Fix Our Schools." *Forbes* (May 6, 1996): 33.

"Welfare Crumbs." *Washington Post* (June 6, 1997): A26.

"Welfare Fraud." *Washington Post* (April 28, 1997): A18.

"Welfare Reformed." *Filipinas* (October 1997), 83.

Wiley, Mark V. *Filipino Martial Arts: Cabales, Serada, Escrima.* Rutland, VT: Charles E. Tuttle Company, 1994.

Wilson, Duff, and Susan Byrnes. "Ad in Magazine Led to Marriage." *The Seattle Times* (March 3, 1995): 1,16,17.

Wolf, Diane L. "Family Secrets: Transnational Struggles Among Children of Filipino Immigrants." *Sociological Perspectives.* 40:3 (1997): 457–482.

Women's Feature Service. "Fly-by-Nightingales?" *Filipinas* (April 1994): 16, 66.

"The Writings of Bienvenido N. Santos." *Heritage* (Spring 1996): 37.

Yap, Joselyn Geaga. "Philippine Ethnoculture and Human Sexuality." *Journal of Social Work and Human Sexuality.* 4:3 (Spring 1986): 121–134.

"Your Remittance Dollar." *Filipinas* (October 1994): 17.

Zhou, Min. "Segmented Assimilation: Issues, Controversies, and Recent Research on the New Second Generation." *International Migration Review.* 31:4 (Winter 1997): 975–1008.

Index

About the Author

BARBARA M. POSADAS is Professor of History and Director of the M.A. Concentration in Historical Administration at Northern Illinois University, DeKalb. She is a member of the editorial boards of *Amerasia,* the *Journal of American Ethnic History,* and the *Journal of Women's History* and is the Director of the Filipino American National Historical Society.